1 MONTH OF
FREE
READING

at
www.ForgottenBooks.com

By purchasing this book you are eligible for one month membership to ForgottenBooks.com, giving you unlimited access to our entire collection of over 700,000 titles via our web site and mobile apps.

To claim your free month visit:
www.forgottenbooks.com/free714808

ISBN 978-0-484-61949-3
PIBN 10714808

EVIDENCES

AGAINST

CHRISTIANITY.

By JOHN S. HITTELL.

5586.

PUBLISHED BY THE AUTHOR.

San Francisco.
1856.

PREFACE.

I. Christianity, directly or indirectly, comes home to, and has a strong influence upon, every educated thinking man of this age. It is a subject which the great majority of thinking men are compelled to study more or less, and which for the convenience of students should be set forth as clearly and completely as possible, within a reasonable space. The religious doctrine which deserves consideration at all, should be considered on both sides, and the tenets of the Christian can urge no good claim to be exempt from the general rule. The "Evidences of [for] Christianity" have been written and published by nearly, if not quite, a hundred authors, many of them men of recognized literary ability; but the Evidences *against* Christianity had, previous to the composition of this work, never been written in a connected shape, and the arguments of skeptics were never fairly represented by orthodox writers. So far are the rigidly righteous from desiring to give a fair hearing to the other side, that it is well understood among the book writing advocates of Christianity, and has been openly expressed by the North British Review, * a high authority among them, that it is a great evil of books written in defense of the Bible, one-sided as they all are, that "they repeat and give currency to the *fallacious* arguments which they wish to expose!" Every person of education learns that Hobbes, Tindal, Toland, Shaftesbury, Bolingbroke, Hume, Gibbon, Paine, Burns, Byron, Shelley, Tennyson, Lyell, Gliddon, Carlyle, Emerson, Franklin, Jefferson, Madison, Bentham, Brougham, Romilly, Bowring, Greg, Parker, Hennell, Montaigne, Bayle, Voltaire, Rousseau, Diderot, D'Alembert, La Place, Arago, Mirabeau, Napoleon, D'Holbach, Volney, Buffon, Beranger, Cousin, Comte, Lessing, Wieland, Goethe, Zschokke, Frederick the Great, Humboldt, Agassiz, Fichte, Schelling, Hegel, De Wette, and Strauss,† are or were more or less inclined to doubt, and to express their doubts, of the truth of Christianity. These are great names, and the religious opinions of such men are surely worthy of notice. But it is no slight task to learn those opinions, scattered as they are through hundreds

---

* May, 1854.   † See Appendix, note 1.

of volumes, many of which are with difficulty to be found, and require a great expense of time and money for their examination. Besides, the writings of some of these authors are not easily to be understood, even by the thorough-bred student, and are quite unintelligible to the masses, who depend for their support upon their physical labor. From the skeptical writings of these and kindred men, I have tried to compile a book for the million,—to give within a small space, a clear view of the principal evidences against Christianity. A few of the ideas advanced will perhaps be recognized as original, but it is not necessary that they should be specially designated here. The work is now published and herewith offered to the public. A large class of my countrymen—a very respectable class—a class to whose opinions I am in no wise insensible, will consider the composition and publication of this work as conclusive proof that the writer is a very unwise, even a bad man, and an enemy to God, to religion, and to society: but I cannot in these matters follow the dictation of others. He who wishes to do credit to humanity, must seek for his rule of action within and not without. The book is published in the belief that it will do good, and in the strongest confidence that it can do no evil. It is written carefully and conscientiously, and does not, to the author's knowledge, contain one untrue statement or unfair argument, or objection to Christianity, which can be satisfactorily controverted. It is true that little is said on the affirmative side of the question, but it was useless in such a work to repeat the substance of those able, clear and complete essays, on the Evidences of Christianity, which are to be had of every bookseller. I seek to rob no man of his faith ; if anybody desire to shut his eyes to the light, I shall not tear them open by force. But, on the other hand, if any one should wish to learn what may be said against Christianity, I will endeavor to teach within a few hours, what he could not elsewhere learn without months of study. If the attempt to save labor in the acquisition of such knowledge,—if the diffusion of such knowledge be wrong, let the sin be on my own head.

Before undertaking the labor, I satisfied myself that if the Bible be the word of God, no attack which I could make upon it by an appeal to reason, would do the least injury or discredit to it. But rather I may hope, that if my book should find readers, it may aid to dispel various crude, superstitious and debasing notions prevalent among Christians and taught by the Church. Such are the belief in the miracles of the ancient and modern priests, in ghosts, in the possession of the human body by devils, in an anthropomorphic God, in special providences, in the duty of the people to submit unresistingly to their rulers, in the virtue of persecuting heretics, in the sinfulness of unbelief and many other kindred tenets. The skeptical writings of the last century had a great influence to purify the Christian faith on these and similar points of doctrine, and I know no reason why good should not be done in the same way now. But my expectations and incentives were not to purify Christianity, but to aid in breaking it down entirely. I have satisfied myself by an examination, neither hasty nor superficial, of the whole subject, that the letter of Christianity and its spirit—in so far as that differs from natural religion and morality—are false and productive of evil; that they form the first and greatest barrier now obstructing the social, political, and moral progress of the human race; that they cannot exist much longer in general acceptation among civilized nations; and that the sooner they be stricken down, the better it will be for all. I do not offend the moral sense of a large portion of my fellow citizens and friends without a feeling of sadness, but believing as I do in regard to the influence of the Bible—believing with all the sincerity of which I am capable—I would be untrue to my conceptions of the dignity of human nature, if I should be deterred from giving expression to these opinions by the disapproval of others. Full of faith in the intelligence and morality of the mass of the American people, and satisfied that for them, at least, light on both sides of such a question as Christianity, cannot be evil; and fearing (except for the ill-performance of my task) no literal or figurative cross or stake, * which have been threatened from time immemorial against all religious teachers, who should proclaim the esoteric doctrines long taught to the initiated only, I shall not stop short at the exoteric, but will freely speak the whole truth, as I understand it, and as it may be applicable in this place. " I persuade† myself that the life and faculties of man, at the best but short and limited, cannot be employed more rationally or laudably than in the search of knowledge, and especially of that sort which relates to our duty and to our happiness. In these inquiries, therefore, wherever I perceive any glimmering of truth before me, I readily pursue and endeavor to trace it to its source, without any reserve or caution of pushing the discovery too far, or opening too great a glare of it to the public. I look upon the discovery of anything which is true as a valuable acquisition to society, which cannot possibly hurt or obstruct the good effect of any other truth whatsoever."

This book, as now presented to the public, has been prepared for publication in California, and is quite different from what it might have been, if prepared to be issued in New York; where the expenses of publication are much less, and where the persons, disposed to read a book upon a religious subject, are more numerous. Many portions of the argument will no doubt be found very unsatisfactory on account of brevity, but it was not possible to make the book larger, with any hope of escaping pecuniary loss in the publication.

---

* See Appendix, note 2.   † The Rev. Dr. Middleton's Free Inquiry. Preface.

INTRODUCTION.

II.   It is probable that every one, into whose hands this book will fall, knows and will recall to mind the denunciations pronounced by the Christian Church against all persons who doubt the truth of the Bible, against all who express such doubts, and against all who read books intended to question or overthrow the Christian faith. *   The reader may say, " I have been taught to believe that all persons who do not accept the Bible will be punished with infinite pains in everlasting Hell; this book is written to lead me to reject the Bible : is it right for me to read such a work ?   And if I do read it, shall I give a fair hearing to what the author has to say—shall I begin by considering the question at issue (the truth and immediate divine origin of the Bible,) to be open and undecided— shall I doubt, and question, and investigate both sides and every unclear point, and demand conclusive evidence previous to settling into firm belief, as I would in questions of science or of political philosophy ?"   The Church replies, "Do not read the book; listen to nothing that may imperil your eternal salvation; and if you do read, keep before your mind the fact that the Bible is the word of God, and is necessarily of higher authority than your reason; remember that the Bible contains the teachings of divine and infinite wisdom; remember that your mind is finite and fallible, and cannot comprehend the infinite; and remember that the truths beyond reason appear contrary to it.   Let these facts be fully impressed upon your mind, and listen to the words of the Holy Scripture as a little child would listen—with implicit faith and obedience—to the words of a wise and good parent."   The reader asks, " How do you know that the Bible is the word of God ?"

Yes, that is the question : How do we know that the Bible is the word of God ? In reply to the demands of the Church I shall make four points :

1. The prohibition of free inquiry bears fraud upon its face.
2. The only proper test for truth in religion is reason.

* See Appendix, note 3.

3. It is the right and duty of every man to examine both sides of religion before believing.

4. Belief in untruth after free inquiry is better than the adherence to truth without free inquiry.

The prohibition of free inquiry bears fraud upon its face. It is just such a trick as might reasonably be resorted to, to protect a false religion. What a glorious plan—to bring up a whole nation in an undoubting faith in, and a boundless fear of, a confederated set of priests, whom it supports in luxury and power, and whose authority dare never be questioned! The prohibition of free inquiry has been used to protect many fraudulent creeds. Every nation of men has its priests, who live by their creed, live well by it, are supported in luxury and high consideration by it, and who consequently are highly interested in its support. Their profession gives them a peculiar influence over the people, and in many States they have been almost omnipotent, politically. Their words were received with superstitious awe, and they could entertain a hope of success that a prohibition of free inquiry would be successful. There were such bodies of professional priests in ancient Egypt, in Babylon, in Persia, in Gaul, in Phœnicia, in Judea, in Etruria, and in Greece. There are such priests now in Japan, in Hindostan, in Thibet, in Arabia, in Russia, in France, in England, and in Utah, and also among many other civilized and barbarous nations. The priests in no two of the lands specially mentioned above, taught or teach the same creed. There have been at least two hundred different religious creeds taught and extensively received among men, different from, and inconsistent with, each other, and all necessarily false, except one. These creeds were not only false, but their priests knew them to be false. Cicero said he did not know how two Roman augurs (priests) could meet without laughing at each other. Many of the Buddhist priests in China have confessed to Protestant missionaries that their creed was false, but they could not say so publicly, for if they did they would lose their means of support. The Catholic priests in Spain laughed at Blanco White, when he confessed to them with great seriousness that he doubted the inspiration of the Bible. *They* had got beyond that long before. A large number of the Catholic clergy in France publicly declared during the great Revolution that their creed was a fraud. It is no secret that there is much skepticism among the Protestant clergy of the United States. And yet all these separate sets of priests make the same claim, that *their* creed is the word of God, and is exempt from examination by reason. They not only declare doubt to be a heinous sin, but wherever they have sufficient influence they make it a crime, punishable severely by the civil law. Moses said the man who would not follow the Levites should die: in Egypt, death was the penalty for rebellion against the priests, or for the killing—even if accidental—

of one of the sacred animals, such as a cat or an ibis: in Greece, Socrates had to die because he was suspected of encouraging doubt of the prevalent creed; and Anaxagoras—the teacher and friend of Pericles—had to fly from Athens because he said that rain was caused not by the immediate will of God—the orthodox doctrine—but by the condensation of vapor in the air according to general laws. The same prohibition of doubt and free inquiry prevails now among the Bramins, the Buddhists, and the Mohammedans; and that prohibition which is thus made to serve as a protection for the four principal creeds on the earth, each accepted by more than a hundred millions of men, and each inconsistent with all the others—that prohibition bears fraud upon its face. Truth wears no defensive armor, shuns no enemy, and fears no fight: her only and constant prayer is for light and for a chance at the foe.

The only proper test for truth in religion is reason. Reason is the word of God, given to man for his guidance. Without it he has no guide, and the revelation which does not appeal to his reason and agree to its demands is no revelation. That reason is the only proper test for truth in matters of science, or political, moral and social philosophy, has never been denied; and there is no good reason why a distinction should be made in this regard between those branches and religious philosophy. If the Bible was first adopted without reason, then it should be examined by reason now, to prevent the continuance of error; if it was investigated by reason in the beginning, then we should have the same privilege which our forefathers had. There is no probability that truth will lose ground by free discussion; and he who expresses fears that it will, betrays at once his belief that his cause is bad.

It is not only the right but it is the duty of every man to examine the evidences on both sides of a question before adopting a firm belief on either side. On any other principle there will never be any progress in arriving at truth. Doubt is the beginning of philosophy—its mother and constant companion. He who believes what is told him on the mere say-so of others is always reckoned a fool. It may be very well for a child, entirely lacking in judgment, to receive as true everything told to it, but something different is expected from men of mature years. They should not only accept no doctrines without investigation, and reject all proved to be untrue, but they should also reject all not proved to be true. But in matters of religion it is peculiarly the duty of every man of intelligence to investigate, and demand conclusive evidence before believing. The subject is every day before him; it is frequently under public discussion; information upon it may be obtained with comparative ease; and the matter may be said to be within the comprehension of every one—at least, every one must form some opinion upon it. The decision is one of high importance; for upon it may depend much of a man's mode of thought, theory of duty, and course of life. We know that religious opinions at this day render a large majority of the human race subject to debasing superstitions, to illiberal prejudices, and to mental darkness generally. It is not only so to-day, but it always has been so. It was so in ancient Egypt, Babylon, and Gaul; it is so in modern Hindostan, in Ceylon, in Spain, in Turkey, and in many other countries which it is not necessary to name. A large proportion of the wars, the despotic governments, the illiberal laws, the inquisitory persecutions of good and wise men, and the opposition to beneficent reforms is chargeable to the self-styled ministers of God. We not only know that the creeds have been false, and that they have been productive of almost unparalleled evils, but we know that they were conceived in fraud, and are still maintained by the grossest deception over a large portion of the earth's surface. We not only know the fraud, but we comprehend the entire baseness of the motives at the bottom of it. This knowledge should be a warning to every man to avoid the pit into which so many others have fallen. Every manly feeling, every sentiment of honor, the devotion to truth, the love of fair play, the hatred of superstition and tyranny, indignation at ecclesiastical deceptions, opposition to intolerance, love of peace and good-will to man—all combine to determine every man to use every reasonable exertion to avoid being duped into slavery to a false creed, with all its concurrent errors—all combine to induce him to distrust tradition as a guide to religious truth—all combine to induce him to place the fullest confidence in his reason as the only reliable guide in the search for truth—all combine to induce him to examine both sides before believing either. It does not follow because most creeds are false that all are; it does not follow because the great majority of priests are deliberate deceivers, that all are. Let not the Christian faith and the Christian priests be condemned beforehand; give them a fair hearing. The sins of priests in general have been here particularly referred to, not to prejudice the mind of the reader against the Christian clergy, but to awaken him to the importance of making a particular investigation.

Belief in untruth after free inquiry is better than adherence to truth without free inquiry. Human reason is fallible, and liable to error. No man can have any satisfactory assurance of possessing the perfect truth: many men have felt confident of such possession, but have been in error, as we know of a certainty; and knowing the mistakes of other men in this matter we should be careful not to imitate them. That which we accept as truth, but which will in all probability be proved within fifty years to be untrue, cannot be of any great value in itself. But even if we could attain to pure truth, and make ourselves certain of the attainment, it would be of no value if it were not appreciated as valuable and sacred. An idiot may believe sincerely that Jesus was the son of God, but surely that mere belief is no merit. A child may believe that the earth moves round the sun, but the mere repetition of such an opinion brings little blessing to his mind. It is the how and why which does the good. The highest end of all philosophy is not the possession of truth, but rather the purifying and elevating influences of the devotion to truth, and the mental light,—the correct habits of thought attained in its search. He who is trying to get hold of religious truth merely for the purpose of buying sugar candy with it, in this world or another, does not deserve the name of a philosopher, and does no honor to that of a man.

THE BIBLE THE WORD OF GOD.

III. The fundamental dogma of Christianity, as the latter presents itself in this age, is that the Bible is the word of God—a divinely inspired revelation of the nature of man's moral and religious duties, and of the realities ot the spiritual world. With that dogma the Christian religion must stand or fall. The Bible asserts that all men are descended from one human father, that he transgressed the divine command, and thereby caused all his posterity to be born in sin, subject to the divine wrath; that the Almighty chose Abraham and his offspring to be a favorite nation: and that God is one, but composed of three persons, of whom one, Jesus Christ, came down to earth, lived thirty years on earth in the human form and was crucified, thus atoning for the sin of Adam. I propose to consider the truth of Christianity, by examining whether its foundation (the Bible) be true. In the course of this examination it will be necessary to consider the contents of the book, and the principal points of doctrine therein taught. These points must stand or fall with the alleged book—revelation.

In examining whether the Bible be the word of God, it is proper that we should consider some preliminary questions, such as whether there is an antecedent probability that a book-revelation would be given to man,—what that book-revelation, if given, might be expected to contain, and whether there are any peculiar difficulties in the examination of the subject? Such questions are perfectly proper. "We * must suppose that if the Creator would communicate truth to his creatures, he gave them minds originally capable of sympathizing with it. In a word, the first revelation of God to man must have been an inward revelation." "When this revelation† [of philosophic reason] is clear and certain by intuition or necessary induction, no subsequent revelation supported by prophecies or miracles can supersede it." If a book-revelation should appeal to reason, and correspond to it, then we may properly ask the preliminary questions above referred to.

Paley contends that there "is an antecedent probability that God would grant a direct revelation to teach man his duties and the moral nature of the universe, which are not clear by the light of natural religion; and that it is consistent with the nature of a good deity that he should give some sanction to truth and justice among men, further than that discoverable to the unassisted human reason." There is undoubtedly such a probability to the man who believes with Paley in a personal God, who formed man the chief object in creation, and who sees the great majority of the human race living in accordance with the teachings and impulses of their natural minds, in the deepest ignorance, superstition, brutishness and misery. Perhaps it would be better to say, that a man with Paley's views of the divine government of the universe, should believe that there *ought* to be a revelation, but whether external, in a book, or internal, by increasing man's intelligence, might admit of a doubt. But to the man who does not accept the Christian conception of the deity, the probability might be just on the other side.

But admitting the antecedent probability that a book-revelation of the will of God has been given to man, is there an antecedent probability that the Bible is that book-revelation? No: there the probabilities are not in favor of the Bible. There have been, at least, fifteen or twenty different books inconsistent with each other, and each said by its friends to be *the* word of God, and the only word of God. The chances antecedent to the examination are then, at least, fourteen to one against any particular book. The Jews have their Mosaic Law, the Christians have their New Testament, the Mohammedans have their Koran, the Mormons have the "The Book of Mormon," the Hindoos have their Vedas, the Parsees have their Zend-Avesta, the ancient Egyptians had their books of Thoth, the Romans the Sibylline books, and the Buddhists have their gospels. By no possibility can all these books be divine revelations.

Are there any peculiar reasons why we should look with distrust upon all these books, represented to be divine revelations? Yes, there are—all these books, except one, must necessarily be fraudulent; and by these fraudulent

---

* Morell—Philosophy of Religion.

† John Adams's Letter to Thomas Jefferson, Dec. 25, 1813.

revelations a very large proportion, if not a very large majority, of the human race, for three or four thousand years past—back, indeed, as far as history extends, have been deluded. The knowledge of these great delusions should make us peculiarly careful, that we may not be deceived in the same manner; and we can exercise our care the more willingly since we may be sure that the more thorough our examination of a subject, the more likely it is that the exact truth will be attained. We not only know that such frauds were committed, but we also understand the motives to which they owed their origin. History tells us that in ancient times the people were very ignorant and superstitious, and easily imposed upon: the priests were numerous, and so influential that they could induce the people to believe or do almost anything. It was the common belief among the political rulers that government could not be firmly established, or morality preserved without the aid of superstition, the terror of the gods, and an implicit faith that the laws were of divine origin. Strabo expresses a common opinion among Greek and Roman magistrates when he says: "It is impossible to conduct women and the gross multitude, and to render them holy, pious, and upright by the precepts of reason and philosophy: superstition, or the fear of the gods must be called in aid, the influence of which is founded on fictions and prodigies. For the thunder of Jupiter, the ægis of Minerva, the trident of Neptune, the torches and snakes of the furies, the ivy-adorned spears of the gods, and the whole ancient mythology, are all fables, which the lawgivers who formed the political constitutions of States, employed as bugbears to overawe the credulous and simple." Robertson, after quoting the above in his history of India, adds—"These ideas of the philosophers of Europe were precisely the same which the Bramins had adopted in India, and according to which they regulated their conduct with respect to the great body of the people. As their order had an exclusive right to read the sacred books, to cultivate and teach science, they could more effectually prevent all who were not members of it, from acquiring any portion of information beyond what they were pleased to impart." Neither did such views expire with ancient times. They are still common even in the most enlightened countries, and men are to be met on all sides, who assert positively that whenever their respective forms of faith shall die, there will no longer be any security for peace, order, morality and human happiness.

What should be the characteristics of the antecedently probable book-revelation, judging from other antecedent probabilities? Alexander, in his "Evidences of [for] Christianity" gives notice that if any such question is to be asked and answered in advance, he will confess judgment at once. "If reason be permitted proudly to assume the seat of judgment, and to decide what a revelation ought to contain in particular; in what manner and with what degree of light it should be communicated: whether it should be made perfectly at once, or gradually unfolded; and whether from the beginning it should be universal; no doubt the result of our examination of the contents of the Bible, conducted on such principles, will prove unsatisfactory, and insuperable objections will occur at every step of the progress." Mr. Alexander appears to acknowledge that reason is against him: but we know nothing of his "insuperable objections;" we are here to find the truth; and whatever the result of our examination, provided that it be conclusive, it cannot be unsatisfactory.

Reason, "proudly assuming the seat of judgment," would probably demand that a book-revelation, before being accepted by man and made the guide of his conduct, should be proved to be of divine origin by conclusive affirmative evidence on each of the following points:

1. That the revelation was written by an author known to us by name and character.

2. That the book was published by its author.

3. That it was then received and extensively circulated as a divine revelation.

4. That it has been preserved in purity as written.

5. That the doctrines taught were original.

6. That the doctrines are true.

7. That they were undiscoverable by human reason.

8. That the doctrines are more powerful for good than any mere human teaching.

9. That the revelation is written with superhuman ability, and contains all the information in regard to religion and morality, undiscoverable by human reason and proper for man to know.

Various able and celebrated advocates of Christianity have commented at length on all these points, as connected with the Bible, and in each have pretended to find strong evidence of the truth of their faith; and therefore it can hardly be considered unfair to consider them here as essential points. It has been said that conclusive evidence on each of these points should be necessary to prove that the Bible is a divine revelation. The burden of proof rests properly upon Christianity: for it is a dictate of the plainest common sense that in religion, as in science and intellectual philosophy, every system should depend on the strength of the evidences in its favor rather than upon the weakness of the testimony against it. The fact that the Bible is in common acceptation, and that its enemies are and have long been the assailants, does not give its advocates the right to shift the burden of proof upon the other side; for Christianity, though it may be the established form of faith as regards society in general, is not established in reference to the man who is about to examine whether it be true or not; and such is the position of every man who takes up this book, with intent to give it a fair hearing. However, these remarks about the burden of proof are only intended to fasten the attention of the reader more closely upon the nature of the question. I claim to be able to furnish conclusive proof that Christianity is not of superhuman origin, and to obtain strong if not unanswerable evidence for the negative upon each of the cited points.

AUTHENTICITY.

IV. Do we know the human authors of the several books of the Bible, and were the books published while their authors were living, and then received as inspired? An affirmative reply to this question or to these questions is necessary to support the claim of Christianity to a divine origin. The theory in regard to all the alleged divine book revelations, is that they were written by men, acting under the influence of direct divine inspiration. Now, it is not probable that an omnipotent deity would choose to reveal his will for the guidance of all future generations of men, through men of no character or reputation, who should be forgotten so soon as life should leave their bodies. Much less is it probable that a blood-thirsty tyrant, a hypocrite, a coward, or a professioual thief, would be chosen as the medium of communicating truth to man from heaven. It is not enough to be ignorant whether the medium was bad; we wish to know that he was good; and a strong cloud must remain upon a book claiming to be a divine revelation, until all doubt upon that subject be removed.

The books of the Bible in regard to the authenticity of which there is the most dispute, are the Pentateuch, Joshua, Isaiah, Jeremiah, Daniel, Matthew, Mark, Second Peter, and Second and Third John. The authors of Judges, Ruth, Samuel, Kings, Chronicles, and Esther, are not mentioned in these books or in any authoritative tradition.

V. The Pentateuch, as the first five books of the Bible are called, claims Moses for its author, (Deut. XXXI. 9, 24,) and was repeatedly accredited by Jesus. It is argued by Christian writers that the Pentateuch must have been authentic because it contained a complete and minute code of laws, and it is absolutely incredible that the Jews should have received such laws from a man whom they did not know, or that they should have accepted such a code with the assurance that it had long been in use in their nation; the books of Moses describe the manner in which a number of the peculiar observances of the Hebrews began, such as the Sabbath, the feast of the passover, circumcision, &c.; and there is always a natural and strong probability that the person reputed among his own nation to be the author of a book, did really write it. Now the Pentateuch, as the constitution and almost the only written law of Judea, must necessarily have always been before the eyes of the people, and in all ages Moses was held to be its author.

The arguments to prove that Moses was not the author, or at least was not the sole author of the Pentateuch, are numerous. The presumption in favor of the authenticity of the book, because of its acceptation among the Jews, is very weak. That people was frequently conquered and subjected to the bitterest captivity—and once even removed to a distant land—after the ostensible era of Moses. During their captivities it is not probable they could preserve their few manuscripts. Soon after the Babylonish captivity, in the year 624 B. C., the Pentateuch, then an unknown book among the Jews, was found by Hilkiah, a priest, which fact is certified by two books of the Bible, (2 K., XXII. 8—2 Ch., XXXIV. 14). When the King of Judea heard of the discovery of the ancient manuscript, of its claims to be a divine revelation, and of its inconsistency with the state of affairs in Judea at that time, "he rent his clothes," "saying, go and inquire of the Lord for me and for them that are left in Israel and in Judah, concerning the words of the book that is found." This fact of Hilkiah's discovery, stated by an authority which cannot be denied by Christians, completely destroys the presumptious in favor of the authenticity of the Pentateuch drawn from the supposed publication of the laws during the lifetime of the author, the description of the manner in which certain ancient customs originated, and the common belief among the Jews that Moses was the author of the Pentateuch.

There is also much evidence to show that the book was not written till after the time of Moses.

In Deut. XXIX. 28, the writer, speaking nominally as a prophet, and foretelling what Jehovah will do to Israel if the latter shall not obey the law and the priests, says that "then men shall say" "the Lord rooted them out of their land in anger, and in wrath, and in great indignation, and cast them into another land, *as it is at this day.*" This is evidently a prophecy written after the Babylonish captivity, with the addition of a clause which betrays the fraud. Again in Deut. XXXIV. 6, the writer says, "And he [the Lord] buried him [Moses] in a valley in the land of Moab, over against Bethpeor; but no man knoweth of his sepulchre *unto this day.*" So the writer of that portion of the Pentateuch, and of how much more is not known, lived so long after the death of Moses that even the site of the tomb of the great prophet and lawgiver was forgotten. That same phrase "*unto this day,*" used in similar manner, and furnishing equally strong evidence against the theory that Moses was the author of the Pentateuch, may be found in the following verses: Deut. III. 14, X. 8, XXIX. 4.

In several passages there are evidently explanations written after the time of Moses; as in Ex. XVI. 36, Deut. III. 5, XI. 30, XXXII. 48, 49, Num. XXI. 16. A book entitled "The Wars of the Lord" is spoken of, (Num. XXI. 14,) whereas there could scarcely have been such a book written during the life of Moses, or, if written, he would never have referred to it.

The writer of the Pentateuch evidently did not dwell upon the same side of the Jordan with Moses. See Gen. I. 10, Num. XXII. 1, XXXV. 14, Deut. I. 1, 5, III. 8, 20, 25, IV. 41, XI. 30.

The commandments are mentioned, (Ex. XVI. 28, Gen. XXVI. 5,) whereas they were not given till afterwards, (Ex. XX. 9). Priests are spoken of in Gen. XIV. 18, 20, and Ex. XXI. 22, whereas priests were not chosen by Jehovah till later, (Ex. XXIII., XXIX). The tabernacle is referred to in Ex. XXXIV. 34, 35, and was not built until afterwards, (Ex. XXXVI., XL). In Lev. XXV. 32, 34, the Levites are supposed to possess landed estates, which they did not acquire till long afterwards, (Num. XXXV. 1-5). Unclean beasts are spoken of when Noah was going into his ark, though the distinction between the clean and unclean was not made till many hundred years later, after the Israelites left Egypt. Tithes are mentioned (Gen. XXVIII. 22,) long before the giving of the law. The Gentiles are spoken of (Gen. X. 5,) before the promise to Abraham made a distinction between Jew and Gentile. The writer of Genesis (XII. 6, XIII. 7,) says, "the Canaanite was then in the land," a remark which would not be made till after they were out; and they were expelled after the time of Joshua. In Lev. XVIII. 28, the expression is used "that the land do not vomit you out as it did the nations before you," but the nations remained in the land during the life of Moses. The names of "the kings that reigned in the land of Edom, before there reigned any king over the children of Israel," are given in Gen. XXXVI. 31, but there were no kings in Israel till 450 years after the death of Moses. The author of Exodus (XVI. 34,) represents the Jews as eating manna till they arrived at the land of Canaan; but Moses did not live to get there. The Pentateuch mentions a number of places not known to Moses; such as Hebron, (compare Gen. XIII. 18, with Josh. XIV. 15, XV. 13,) Dan, (Gen. XIV. 14, Deut. XXXIV. 1, Jud. XVIII. 29,) Haroth-jair, (Num. XXXII. 41, Deut. III. 14, Jud. X. 34,) and Ophir, (Gen. X. 29, 1 K. IX. 28). In these verses there are numerous anachronisms of which a writer in the alleged position of Moses could not possibly have been guilty, but which were very natural in a later writer, who ante-dated his book. The early Hebrew prophets never mention Moses or refer to the ten commandments; and in the books of Judges and Samuel the writers betray an ignorance of the Mosaic code which can only be explained on the supposition that it was unknown or not received as the supreme law of the land.

These passages cited, and numerous similar passages which it is not worth while to cite particularly, show beyond a reasonable doubt that Moses did not write the Pentateuch in its present shape. But there is also proof that a large portion of the book could not possibly have been written by him. Genesis appears, on close examination, to be a compilation from two older documents, containing similar accounts of the creation, the deluge, the generations of men, and the history of the Jews. This fact is admitted by most of the great biblical and philological scholars who have written at any length upon the books of Moses within the last twenty-five years. These two ancient documents are styled the "Jehovistic" and "Elohistic," from the different names of "Jehovah" and "Elohim," which they respectively apply to the Deity. The "Elohim" of the original Hebrew is translated "God" in the English version, and "Jehovah" is rendered as "the Lord." The Elohistic story begins with the first verse of Genesis and continues to the fourth verse of the second chapter; in which thirty-four verses the Deity is mentioned thirty-three times, and invariably as "God" in English, and "Elohim" in Hebrew. These verses give a complete history of the creation of the universe, with the works of each of the six days, and the rest of Elohim upon the seventh "from all his works which he had made." On the fifth day the water at the divine command produced all fish and fowls; and on the sixth day land animals were called into life—man and women being the last, and created together. At the fourth verse of the second chapter the Jehovistic document begins, and relates another story of creation—a story complete in itself, and having no reference whatever to the Elohistic narrative. The creation is represented as having been completed in one day. The fowls were formed out of the ground. Adam was made before the beasts, and Eve last of all. These two narratives cannot by any possibility be made to harmonize. The two documents can be traced throughout the Pentateuch, and cause much confusion, and many contradictions, repetitions and inconsistencies. Both documents were evidently compilations of old Jewish traditions, but the authors had not received the traditions in the same shape. Thus, the Jehovistic tradition (Gen. IV., 16-24) says, that the decendants of Cain, Adam's eldest son, were Enoch, Irad, Mehujael, Methusael and Lamech; while, the Elohistic compiler, speaking as though he had never heard that Adam had such a son as Cain, says (Gen. V., 3-26) that Seth's descendants were Enos, Cainaan, Mahaladel, Jared, Enoch, Methusaleh and Lamech. It is evident that the same traditional persons were referred to, but credited to different sons of Adam. Noah is directed by Elohim to take two of every species of animal into the ark (Gen. VI., 19, 20); but Jehovah directs him to take pairs of unclean beasts and sevens of clean beasts (Gen. VIII., 2). The story of the deluge is twice told. One of the most remarkable repetitions is in regard to the appropriation of the wife of one of the patriarchs by a foreign monarch. When Abram was seventy-five years old (Gen. XII., 4), and Sarai his wife was sixty-five, (Gen. XVII., 17), they were about to enter Egypt; and the father of the faithful seeing that his spouse, notwithstanding her years, was yet a very beautiful woman, and knowing the amorous nature of the Pharaohs, bethought him that it would be well to pretend that Sarai was his sister. They entered the valley of the Nile, and Pharaoh fell in love with the old lady and took her into his harem without opposition; but "the Lord plagued Pharaoh and his house with great plagues," till that monarch discovered that he was trespassing upon Abram's preserves, (Gen. XII., 10-19). Twenty-five years later, when Sarah, then only ninety years old, was apparently still beautiful, though "it had ceased to be with her after the manner of women," (Gen. XVIII., 11), Abimelech siezed her at Gerar, after Abraham had told the same story as in Egypt about her being his sister. Twenty or thirty years later still, another similar event happened to Rebekah among the uncircumcised Philistines, who took her on Isaac's representation that she was only his sister, (Gen. XXVI). There is a contradiction about Abimelich's interview with Abraham and Isaac, between Genesis XXI., 22-34, and Genesis XXVI., 26-33, and there was evidently only one interview. The manner in which Esau disposed of his birth-right is differently represented in Genesis XXV., 27–35—XXVII., 1–40.

The following columns give the most important divisions of the Elohistic and Jehovistic papers; and upon comparison of the passages many contradictions and awkward repetitions will be found, to which we have not space here to call attention in detail:

	ELOHISTIC.	JEHOVISTIC.
Creation...........Genesis	L, 1—II., 3............	Genesis IL, 4; III., 24
Genealogies........ "	V., 1–32............	"　　IV., 1–26
Deluge............ "	VI., 9–22............	"　VI., 1–8; VII., 1–5
Deluge............ "	VII., 11–16............	"　　VII., 17, 23
Rainbow........... ' "	IX., 1–17............	"　　VIII., 20–22
Noah.............. ·· '	IX., 28　	" ·　IX., 20–27
Genealogies........ "	XL, 10–26............	··　　X.
Abraham's Covenant. "	XVII.　	··　　XV.
Sodom............ "	XIX., 29　	"　XIX., 1–28, 30–38
Siezure of wife..... ··	XX.　	" XII.10-19,XXVI. 1-11
Isaac and Ishmael.. "	XXL, 1–21............	"　　XVI.
Abimelech........ "	XXL, 22–34............	"　　XXVI., 26–33
Abraham tempted.. "	XXII., 1–13............	"　　XXII., 14–18
Abraham tempted.. "	XXIII.	
Abraham tempted.. "	XXV., 1–18	
Isaac's marriage.... "	XXV., 19–21, 24–26.......	"　　XXIV., XV., 22, 23
Esau.............. "	XXV., 27–35............	"　　XXVII., 1–40
Esau.............. "	XXVII., 46; XXVIII., 9..	"　　XXVII., 41–45
Quails............Exodus	XVI.　　............	Exodus XI.
Commandments.... "	XX., 1–13	Deut. V., 6–21
Lord and Moses.... "	VI., 30; VII. 12.........	Exodus IV., 10–16
Horeb ....Num.	XX., 1–13　	"　　XVII., 1–7

Leviticus is principally Elohistic: the fragmentary character of Numbers may be easily discovered; and Deuteronomy is mostly Jehovistic. De Wette and many other very able biblical critics think that the Elohistic document was written about 1000 B. C., and the Jehovistic paper somewhat later.

The evidence that the editor of the Pentateuch made his book by patching together two old documents, is so strong that no author of reputation has made a serious attempt to refute it. Most of the advocates of the divine origin of Christianity dodge the question entirely, as Bishop Watson did in his reply to Paine's Age of Reason. Among the great scholars who have recognized the patchwork, are Eichhorn, Bauer, Astruc, Moeller, Illgen, Vater, Gramburg, Stachelin, Hartman, Ewald, Von Bohlen, Tuch, Kenrick, Palfrey and De Wette.

Archbishop Whately* confesses that the account given in Genesis of the Creation and of some other of the earliest events, is probably a tradition of an "ancient revelation, [reported to have been given before the time of Moses, but ignored by him,] and was very likely committed to writing long before the time of Moses."

Palfrey, one of the most learned, able, candid and upright of the Christian authors, acknowledges that Genesis is formed by the union of fragments; but he contends that Moses was the editor, and intended Genesis merely as an introduction to the four inspired books of the law. In giving this law to the Hebrews, Moses thought it proper to explain the history of Abraham, Isaac and Jacob, "what communications they had received from the Deity," what title they had to Canaan, from which they were about to expel other nations, and to show the origin of the religious observances of the Jewish patriarchs. All the information necessary on these points he found in old traditions, which he accepted and published as he found them. Palfrey says: "If we assume Moses to have been divinely instructed in what he recorded in Genesis, we do it altogether without authority from him. Communications received from the Deity, and recorded in the later books of the Pentateuch, he announces as such, saying repeatedly, 'The Lord spake unto Moses,' and 'The Lord said unto me.' But neither this language, nor any equivalent, anywhere occurs in Genesis. The reasons of the case would not justify the supposition. The introduction of a pure religious system into an idolatrous world is proper matter for direct revelation, nor without such revelation could Moses or any other man become possessed of it. Not so with historical materials. On the one hand, the need of them is not so urgent; and on the other, it is the common course of things for them to be collected and handed down in a more or less pure and trustworthy state. Each age instructs its successor; nor is it to be doubted that notices, such as they were, of earlier times existed in the time of Moses, as in every other period since there was anything to record or report. The actual existence of such notices before Moses' time, is referred to on the face of the record. Different parts of the composition are marked by varieties of style and language, effectually distinguishing them from one another, and indicating that they had several sources. The contents of such parts are sometimes of a nature to show that they not only had not a common origin, but that they were not elaborated by Moses, when they had come into his hands, so as to make one consecutive and consistent narrative. I think we shall have occasion to own that different portions, distinguished by diversities of style referred to, sometimes repeat, and sometimes—which is of yet more consequence—contradict one another." Morell

* "The Rise, Progress and Corruptions of Christianity."

makes an equally candid confession. Let it be remarked in regard to Palfrey's theory, that—

1. It is the only standing point left at all for educated men pretending to believe in the divine inspiration of the Bible.

2. The theory was not advanced till it became impossible to defend the assertion that Moses was the sole author of Genesis.

3. It convicts Moses of having incorporated falsehood in the Holy Scriptures, and of having done his task as editor badly.

4. It reduces the accounts of the creation, the fall of man, the great age of the antediluvians, the marriage of the sons of God with the daughters of men, the deluge, the confusion of tongues, the destruction of Sodom, the choice of Abraham and the institution of circumcision, to mere fables.

5. The truth of Genesis and its inspired authorship is frequently asserted in other portions of the Bible.

6. If the fall of man be a fable, there is no foundation for the scheme of redemption, which is the corner-stone of Christian doctrine.

Critics say that the style of the Pentateuch is too polished for so rude an age as that of Moses, and bears a close resemblance to works written in the time of David. De Wette observes: " The opinion that Moses composed these books is not only opposed by all the signs of a later date, which occur in the book itself, but also by the entire analogy of the history of Hebrew literature and language. But even admitting it was probable, on account of the influence the Pentateuch had on the language of the Hebrews, and on account of the analogy of the Syriac and Arabic languages, that during a period of nearly a thousand years the Hebrew language had changed as little as it would appear on this hypothesis, from the slight difference between the style of the Pentateuch and other books of the Old Testament, even the latest of them—still, even then it would be absurd to suppose that one man could have created beforehand the epico-historical, the rhetorical and poetic styles in all their extent and compass, and have perfected these three departments of Hebrew literature, both in form and substance, so far that all subsequent writers found nothing left for them but to follow in his steps."

Thus much for the question whether Moses wrote the Pentateuch ; and even if the proof were conclusive that he did write it, there is yet no evidence that the book was published and received as inspired during the lifetime of the author, as it ought to have been, if of divine origin.

JOSHUA.

VI. The book known as the book of Joshua claims to have been written by that chieftian (XXIV, 26), but the claim is not sustained by any satisfactory evidence, while there is a large amount of testimony to show that Joshua could not have been the author. The book remarks (VI. 27,) that Joshua's fame was noised throughout all the country: a mode of expression in regard to self in very bad taste for a mere human writer, but much worse if it pretended to have been written by divine inspiration. In XVI, 2, Luz is mentioned, but Luz was not built till after the death of Joshua; (Jud. I, 26). The children of Dan are said to have taken Leshem (XIX, 47), but that place (Laish), is said in Jud. XVIII, 27, 29, to have been taken long after. Joshua is, on two different occasions, reported to have taken Hebron and destroyed the place with its people (X, 36, 37, XI, 21), and yet the place appears afterwards (XIV, 12, 13) as not conquered after all. Debir was twice conquered and destroyed, according to Joshua (X, 38, 39, and XV, 17): and, much later, it was again subjected to the same operation, (Jud. I, 11, 13). Theodore Parker thinks that the author of Joshua had access to the documents at present contained in the book of Judges.

Compare   Joshua XV, I, 10   with   Judges I, 20.
"   " XVIII, 12   with   "   I, 27.
"   " XIX, 47   with   "   XVII.
"   " XXIV, 28, 31 with   "   II, 6, 9.

The Jebusites and children of Judah are represented in Joshua XV, 63, as dwelling together in Jerusalem to *this day*, whereas it is a well known fact that Jerusalem was not conquered till the time of David, (2. S. V. 5. 1. Ch. XI. 4.). We are not informed that the children of Judah dwelt any considerable time in Jerusalem before the conquest; and they could not possibly have dwelt there in the time of Joshua, as the phrase "to this day" would lead us to believe. A similar anachronism appears in Jud. l, 7, 51. The book of Jasher is mentioned (Josh. X, 31) as authority for the miraculous arrest of the Sun, but according to 2. S. I. 18, the book of Jasher could not have been written till after the time of David.

JUDGES.

VII. The book of Judges bears the mark of having been written by different persons, but the date of its composition is not clear. Chapters XVII, XIX, XX, and XXI refer to a time earlier by twenty-eight years than XVI, two hundred and sixty-six years earlier than XV, two hundred and forty-five years earlier than XIII, one hundred and ninety-five years earlier than IX, ninety years earlier than IV, and fifteen years earlier theean chapter I. The following passages bear the appearance of having been written after the alleged date of the book—I. 7, 21. VI, 24. X. 4. XV. 19. XVII. 16. XVIII 30. XXI, 25.

SAMUEL.

VIII. The books of Samuel, originally but one book, sometimes called the "First and Second Book of Kings," do not profess, and are not claimed to have been written by the prophet Samuel, but appear to be named after him, because the record is mainly occupied with his acts, and the history of the Jews during his life. The numerous contradictions appear to show that the book is a compilation or collection of old papers. Compare

Saul's knowledge of David, 1. S. XVI, 14, 23. XVII, 31, 40. XVII, 55. XVIII, 5.

Direction of Hachilah, 1. S. XXIII, 19. XXVI, 1.

Where David spared Saul, 1. S. XXIV, 10. XXVI, 5.

Saul chosen King, 1. S. IX, 1. VIII. X, 16. X, 17, 27.

Saul's Death, 1. S. XXXI, 2-6, 8-13.   2. S. 1, 2-12.

A number, 1. S. XVIII, 27.   2. S. III, 14.

Anointment of David, 1. S. XVI, 1-13.   2. S. V, 1-3.

Samuel's seeing Saul, 1. S. XV, 35.   1. S. XIX, 24.

Archæological expressions going to show that the book was revamped, if not, written after the date of the events recorded are found in 1. S. IX, 18. XIII. 18. XXVII, 6. XXX, 25. 2. S. IV, 3. VI, 8. The book comes down ostensibly to 1015 B. C., when David died; but in I. S. XXVIII, 6, the phrase is used that " Ziklag pertaineth unto the kings of Judah *unto this day:*" an expression which could hardly have been written till long after the separation of Judah and Israel, and that separation did not occur till after the death of David. The mistake in representing David as bringing the head of Goliah to Jerusalem, (1. S. XVII, 54,) as if that city had then belonged to the Jews, and been their national capital, while it was really in the hands of the Jebusites, could not possibly have been made till long after the time of David. It is not known, even by tradition, who was the author of the books of Samuel.

KINGS.

IX. The books of Kings, sometimes called the "Third and Fourth books of Kings," were originally one. They contain the history of the Jews from the accession of Solomon, 1015, B. C., until the revolt of Jeroboam and the ten tribes in 975, B. C., and the history of Judah from that time till 624, B. C. There is likewise a partial history of the rebel kingdom of Israel for 241 years from Jeroboam to Hosea. The phrase "*unto this day,*" used frequently, shows that the narrative was written long after the occurrence of the events: See— 1. K. VIII, 8. IX, 13, 21. X, 12. XIII, 19. 2. K. VIII, 22, X, 27. XIV, 7. XVI, 6. XVII, 23, 34, 41. It is supposed that the same author wrote or compiled Samuel and Kings.

CHRONICLES.

X. The Chronicles are but one book in the Hebrew, and are styled "The Annals." They begin by giving the genealogy of David from Adam downward, and then commencing with David's elevation to power, they give the history of the Jews and the kingdom of Judah till the return from the Babylonish captivity in 535, B. C. The writer of the Chronicles sought to glorify the kingdom and throne of Judah, and David particularly. He does not mention David's concubines, or his cruelty to the Moabites and to the men of Rabbah, or his murder of Uriah for the purpose of getting exclusive and indisputed possession of Uriah's wife, or his murder of Saul's seven sons, or the penalty threatened for the idolatry of his posterity, or the fact that he had seven hundred wives and three hundred concubines. All these things are mentioned in Samuel and Kings, of which the author or authors appear to have been impartial. The writer of the Chronicles was not only partial to Judah but hostile to Israel, as may be seen by comparing 2. Ch. XX, 35-37, with the 1. K. 48, 49. The proceedings on the occasion of the discovery of the laws of Moses in 624, B. C. are related very differently in 2. K. XXIII, 4-19, and 2. Ch. XXXIV, 3-7, 33. The author of Kings says, that the idolatrous priests of Judah had vessels for the worship of Baal in the temple, that the Sodomites had houses by the temple, that the cities of Judah had defiled the high places, that the kings of Judah had given horses to the Sun, and that Solomon had built high places for idolatrous worship. All these interesting items the Chronicles discreetly omit to mention. The history of Judah is brought down to 535 B. C. But the third chapter of the First Book gives the descendants of Jehoiakim, brother of king Zedekiah, for twelve generations later, reaching, at thirty years for each generation, down to 360 B. C.

EZRA AND NEHEMIAH.

XI. The book of Ezra gives the history of Judah from 536 to 515 B. C. Nehemiah commences his story at 444 and comes down to 404 B. C. The book of Ezra is evidently a compilation, and not the work of one author. The second chapter is occupied with a genealogy which Nehemiah (VII, 5.) says he found; and that expression means of course that he did not find it among the writings of an earlier prophet. That portion of Ezra between IV, 8 and VI, 18 is in the Jewish Bible written in Chaldaic and not in Hebrew. In Nehemiah XII, 1-26, there is a list of priests down to Jaddua, who, as Josephus says, lived in the time of Alexander the Great.

ISAIAH.

XII. Isaiah began his vocation as a prophet in 759 B. C., and continued to follow his trade during the reigns of Jotham, Ahaz, and Hezekiah, (I. I. VI, 1.) The first part of the book known by his name may have been written by him, but the latter part (XL. LXVI.) was certainly not. There is a strong difference of style between the two parts. The latter portion was written after the captivity, at least one hundred years after Isaiah's death. Cyrus is mentioned by name, and he did not become known to the Jews till 540 B. C.; and Jerusalem and the cities of Judah are spoken of as laid waste, as they were during the captivity, (XLII, 24. XLIV, 26, 28. XLV, 1, 13. LI, 3, 17. LII, 4, 9. LVIII, 12. LXIV, 9, 11.). The passages XIII, 1, XIV, 23, were not written by Isaiah. Chapter XXXIX ends in the midst of the history of Hezekiah, and chapter XL begins with something else. The rest of the book appears to be an exhortation to support the Jewish nationality after the return from captivity, which return did not occur till two hundred years after the time of Isaiah.

JEREMIAH.

XIII.   Jeremiah was a prophet from 629 to 588 B. C.. (I. 2, 3.   XL.-XLV.).
Many of the later biblical critics are agreed in regarding the book of Jeremiah
as a collection of older writings, though the greater portion of it may have been
composed by one author.   In LI, 64, it is said—"thus far the words of Jeremiah," and we must of course conclude that the remainder, at least, is spurious.
Chapter LII was not written by the author of XXXVII, XXXVIII, and XXXIX,
the first named chapter being a mere repetition of the last three.

DANIEL.

XIV.   Daniel, says the Scripture, (Dan. I. 1, 6.) was taken by order of Nebuchadnezzar, in the third year of king Jehoiakim, 607 B. C, to be educated at
Babylon for a councillor: but Jeremiah says, (XXV, 1.   XLVI, 2.) that Nebuchadnezzar did not come to the throne till the fourth year of Jehoiakim.   The
author of Daniel says, that "Nebuchadnezzar made an image or statue of gold,
ninety feet high, and nine feet through, to be worshipped:" a rather valuable
image—a more valuable one than any nation of the present day *could* erect.
Daniel is frequently mentioned, in the book named after him, with praise,
(I. 17, 19, 20. II. 12. VI. 4.   IX. 23.   X. 11.) Portions of the original are in
Hebrew, and portions in Chaldee.   The book is supposed to be of a comparatively late origin.

JOB.

XV. Nothing is known of the authorship of Job, but Christian authors are generally agreed that the book would be better out of the Bible than in it. The description in the beginning of Job, of the levee day in Heaven, when God and Satan met on the most friendly terms, and agreed to join to tempt and afflict the good man, is very poetic, but not at all consistent with the Mosaic or Christian theology. A writer in the Westminster Review (Oct. 1853.) says:—
" The book of Job is evidently not orthodox Jewish in its character. The more it is studied, the more the conclusion forces itself upon us, that let the writer have lived when he would, in his struggle with the central falsehood of his people's creed, he must have divorced himself from them outwardly as well as inwardly: that he traveled away into the world, and lived long, perhaps all his natural life in exile. Everything about the book speaks of a person who had broken free from the narrow littleness of the 'peculiar people.' The language, we said, is full of strange words. The hero of the poem is of a strange land, a gentile certainly, not a Jew. The life, the manners, the customs are of all varieties and places—Egypt with its rivers and pyramids is there ; the description of mining points to Phœnicia ; the settled life in cities ; the nomad Arabs, the wandering caravans, the heat of the tropics, and the ice of the north, all are foreign to Canaan, speaking of foreign things and foreign people.

" No mention, or hint of mention, is there throughout the poem, of Jewish traditions or Jewish certainties. We look to find the three friends vindicate themselves, as they so well might have done, by appeals to the fertile annals of Israel—to the Flood, to the cities of the plain, to the plagues of Egypt, or to the thunders of Sinai. But of all this there is not a word ; they are passed by as if they had no existence ; and instead of them, when witnesses are required for the power of God, we have strange un-Hebrew stories of the Eastern astronomic mythology, the old wars of the giants, the imprisoned Orion, the wounded dragon, ' the sweet influence of the seven stars,' and the glittering fragments of the sea-snake Rahab, trailing across the northern sky. Again: God is not the

God of Israel, but the Father of mankind. We hear nothing of a chosen people, nothing of a special revelation, nothing of peculiar privileges; and in the court of Heaven there is Satan, not the prince of this world and the enemy of God, but the angel of judgment, the accusing spirit, whose mission was to walk to and fro over the earth, and carry up to Heaven an account of the sins of mankind."

MATTHEW.

XVI. All that is known of the authorship of the first book of the New Testament is that it was ascribed by the early Christians to Matthew, one of the apostles. The first mention made of it in any book, which has come down to us, is by Papias, Bishop of Hierapolis, who said in 116 A. D.,—"Matthew wrote the divine oracles in the Hebrew tongue." Tradition says that it is the same book. Grey says: "It is the general tradition [mentioned by Papias, Irenæus, Origen, Epiphanius, Jerome and Chrysostom] of the early church, that Matthew wrote in Hebrew, which tradition is our only reason for supposing that Matthew wrote at all." Milman, a very high authority among the Christians says: (Affiix to note 153, Ch. XV, Milman's edition of Gibbon's Rome.) "The general opinion of learned biblical writers is that the genuine gospel of Matthew was written in Hebrew. This gospel was addressed to the Jews, whom the author appears to have considered the only people entitled to salvation (Matth. X. 5. XV. 24); and of course a gospel for their benefit, written by one of their own race, ought to have been written in their own language. The original ancient gospel now exists only in the Greek: and the name of the translator, the faithfulness and date of the translation and the date of the loss of the original are alike unknown."

The date of the composition of Matthew's gospel is a matter of dispute. The orthodox say that it was written and published within five or six years after the crucifixion of Jesus, but their only evidence is their belief that the faithful would not be left a longer time without a gospel. Hennell contends that the contents of the book show that it was written between 66 and 70 A. D.—33 or 37 years after the death of Christ. Chapter XXIV written in the prophetic style, agrees with events up to that time, and disagrees with them thereafter. The events prophesied [the prophecy being made after the event had occurred] in XXIV. 4. 5, happened about 55 A. D. (Josephus, War. II. 13.). In XXIV, 6, wars are foretold which happened in 66 A. D. (Josephus, War. II. 16). The seventh verse foretels famines, pestilences, and wars, which are mentioned by Josephus (War IV. 8, 9.), and Tacitus (Ann. XVI. 13.), as having happened about 65, 66, and 70 A. D. Verse ninth foretels the persecutions, which began 64 A. D. In verse tenth it is said that a false prophet would come, and one came about 68 A. D. (Jos. War, VI. 5.). The preaching of the gospel to all nations is promised in the fourteenth verse, and the churches planted by Paul did not flourish extensively till about 60 A. D. The abomination of desolation mentioned in verse fifteenth refers probably to the entrance of Cestius into Jerusalem, and his attack on the temple A. D. 66. In verse sixteenth the Christians are advised to leave the city, and many of them fled about 56 A. D. In verse twenty-second, the term " elect" is used ; a word frequent in the late day of the Epistles, but not natural in the time of Jesus. Here the successful prophecy ends. In verses twenty-ninth and thirty-fourth the writer foretells the near approaching darkening of the Sun, the falling of the stars from Heaven, the mourning of all the tribes of men, and the gathering of the elect from all the four winds, which events were to come to pass in that generation.

MARK.

XVII. The second book of the New Testament is said by the tradition of the Church to have been written by Mark, a companion of Peter. Papias, Irenæus, Clement of Alexandria, Origen, Eusebius, Epiphanius, Jerome, and Chrysostom, Christian fathers living between 116 and 398 A. D. mention this tradition. The tradition further says that Peter approved of the gospel after it was written. Mark evidently copied from Matthew : compare,

Matthew IV. 18, with Mark I. 16.
    "   VIII. 2,   "   I. 40.
    "   IX,   "   II. 14.

Matthew XIII. 1,   with Mark IV. 1.
   "   XIV. 22,   "   "   VI. 45.
   "   XIII. 33,   "   "   IV. 33.

The last twelve verses of Mark's gospel, as we now have it, were not contained in many of the early copies, as we learn from several of the fathers of the Church; and we have no positive information that those verses were in any copies till several hundred years after Christ.

LUKE.

XVIII. The authorship of the gospel of Luke, and of the Acts, is ascribed to Silas, sometimes called Luke, a companion of Paul. He is mentioned in Acts XV. 40. XVI. 3, 4, 6. Col. IV. 14. 2 Tim. IV. 11. Philem. 24. The first mention by tradition of Luke, as the author of these books, is by Irenæus 178 A. D. and Origen 230 A. D., and Jerome 392 A. D., have the same tradition. Luke is said to have written in Greece; and he is supposed to have written soon after Mark, (about 70 A. D.) and to have copied freely from him as well as Matthew. Compare—

Luke   IV. 1-12   with   Matthew IV. 1-11,
  "   IV. 38-44   "   "   VIII. 1-4   with   Mark I. 40-45.
  "   V. 18-38   "   "   IX. 2-8   "   "   II. 3-22.
  "   VI. 1-11   "   "   "   "   II. 23. III. 6.

To account for the similarity of the first three gospels, Eichhorn supposes that they must all have been derived from one original Aramaic document. Mill says:—"Nothing is plainer to me than that Luke borrowed the very phrases and expressions of Matthew and Mark, nay whole paragraphs, word for word." Wetstein says:—"That Luke took many things from Matthew, and more from Mark, appears on collating them." Michaelis remarks:—"It is wholly impossible that three historians, who have no connection, either mediate or immediate with each other, should harmonize as Matthew, Mark, and Luke do."

2

JOHN.

XIX. The fourth book of the New Testament claims (**XXI.** 24. **XIX.** 26.) the disciple whom Jesus loved for its author: and tradition, of which the earliest record is found in Irenæus, A. D. 178, says it was written at Ephesus by the Apostle John, after Matthew, Mark, and Luke had written. Fabricius, Le Clerc, and Hennell think it was written about 97 A. D. According to Hennell " this gospel appears to be the attempt of a half educated but zealous follower of Jesus, to engraft his conceptions of the Platonic philosophy upon the original faith of the disciples." Elsewhere the same critic says :—" The first three gospels agree very well in the style of the discourses attributed to Christ, which were chiefly parables and short pithy sayings. They represent him as beginning his public preaching in Galilee, proceeding after some time to Jerusalem, and suffering there. The chief topic dwelt upon is the approach of the Kingdom of Heaven: and they contain much concerning the fall of Jerusalem. But the gospel of John is of a very different character. The discourses of Christ are here long controversial orations, without any parables. He is made to journey from Galilee to Jerusalem and back again many times: the kingdom of Heaven is nearly lost sight of, the fall of Jerusalem never alluded to, and we have instead of these several new subjects, viz :—the incarnation of the word or *logos* in the person of Christ; his coming down from Heaven, his relationship to the Father; and the promise of the comforter or Holy Spirit. Also, with a few exceptions, a new set of miracles is attributed to Christ."

REFLECTIONS ON THE AUTHENTICITY.

XX. We have thus cursorily examined the authenticity of the principal books of the Bible, and we have seen that it is highly probable that some of them were not written in their present shape by their reputed authors. There is little more than a weak presumption in favor of the authenticity of any of the books, while there are numerous and weighty evidences to the contrary in regard to most of them. Whether the books were published during the authors' lives, and then received as inspired, and extensively published, is also very doubtful. It should be remembered that this question of the authenticity of the books of the Bible is an important one, and very different from the question whether the works ascribed to Thucydides or Homer were really written by such persons as Thucydides and Homer are represented in our books to have been. The poetry of the Iliad is equally pleasing to us, whether we know the author's name or not. The discovery that he wrote to gratify a tyrant, to flatter a friend, to slander an enemy, or to falsify history would not destroy the value of his poem, which depends for its rank upon its merit as a work of art. In regard to Thucydides, the knowledge that he had written his history falsely would detract from its value; but provided it be true, we care little how base his motives, or what the name of the writer, or his place of residence. The history and the epic do not furnish rules for our conduct: we are not inclined to believe the historian and poet act from base motives: they are, as classes, great and high-minded men, and when one of their number stooped to baseness, he was always properly denounced by his brethren. A bad poem has never been palmed off as good, nor was an able and elaborate, but entirely false historical work ever palmed off upon the public as true. The historian has few motives to write falsehoods, and many motives to induce him to tell the truth. It is entirely different with the priest. Large numbers of priests have existed and do exist in nearly all countries on earth; they teach many creeds, most of which are inconsistent with each other and must necessarily be false; the priests know the falsity, but are base enough to make every effort to increase their power by driving the people deeper into superstition, and for this purpose they use the basest frauds. That such has been the history of the priesthood in all ages and countries every one will acknowledge, except so far as it concerns his own faith. Now one of the frauds most common and most profitable has been the forgery of books claiming to be inspired by God, and to have been written by the hand of some man of former times, reputed to have been a great saint: for the success of one such fraud may cast the greater portion of the political power, and the wealth of a nation into the hands of a few men.

The knowledge that such forgeries have been frequently committed, and that every such forgery, if successful, may be considered as increasing and confirming the power of the priests, does not necessarily prove that every book claiming to be a divine revelation must be fraudulent : but it should make us scan the testimony very closely and accept nothing as inspired without conclusive proof.

PRESERVATION.

XXI. Has the Bible been preserved in purity as written ? If it were given as a revelation of truths most important to man, otherwise unattainable by him, and necessary to be believed in their purity to save the human race from everlasting torments—if it were given, as alleged, by a special inspiration, contrary to the ordinary course of nature—and if were intended for the instruction and salvation of all men subsequent to the time when it was first published on earth, it is but reasonable to believe that the divine goodness and omnipotence, so much praised in the book, would have provided that the revelation should be preserved in perfection as originally communicated. If we consider the condition of society, when the books of the Bible were first published, and for many centuries afterwards, the want of printing type, the great labor—even extending throughout a whole year—of making a manuscript copy of the Scriptures, the paucity of all kinds of books, the liability of books to be destroyed, the ignorance of copyists, the strong probability that they would make some errors in copying a long work—all these things considered, it would be a miracle if the Bible had come down to us word for word as written : and if such should appear to be the case on examination, that fact alone will furnish very strong evidence in favor of the theory that the book is a divine revelation. But if on the other hand, it has been allowed to take its chance with ordinary human works, and like them has suffered losses of important portions, and has had numerous passages corrupted, we shall be justified in entertaining very strong doubts, whether it be a divine revelation.

The ancient Jews and the early Christians asserted most positively that the Scriptures accounted holy among them, had been preserved in the most perfect purity, the copyists and translators being under the supervision of the Holy Spirit, so that a mistake or error was impossible : and similar views continued to be upheld by a great many, even until a very late period. Justin Martyr said nothing more than what appeared entirely probable to the early Christian Church, in asserting that when the Septuagint translation of the Hebrew Scriptures into Greek was made at Alexandria, the seventy learned translators were shut up separately in small cells, without the possibility of the slightest communication with each other, and when all had concluded, each his translation, their works were found to agree throughout, not only in word but in letter ; and for the truth of this story, the veracious Justin does not hesitate to vouch.

But the faith in the perfect preservation of the gospels has been disappearing rapidly of late. No learned Christian writer pretends to uphold now the chronology of the Hebrew version of the Bible ; numerous errors are charged to the transcribers. It is a well-known fact that in the twelve hundred manuscript copies of the New Testament, which are now in existence, and have come down from ancient times, there are one hundred and fifty thousand different readings ; * and it is probable that there are at least as many variations in the ancient copies of the Jewish books. The Samaritan and Greek translations from the Hebrew differ very materially from the original in many places. The great majority of these variations are evidently mere trifles, affecting only the letter and not the spirit of the book, but other of the variations cause important differences of meaning. Besides, there is no method of knowing which copy is correct, or indeed whether any one of them is preserved exactly as it was in the first century of the Christian era. Not only are the books, which we have, diminished in value by numerous corruptions, but many books spoken of in the Bible as inspired—by implication if not direct assertion—have been entirely lost. The following list gives the names of twenty lost books, with the passages in the Old Testament where they are mentioned.

1. Book of the wars of Jehovah. Num. XXI. 14.
2. Book of Jasher or Righteous. Josh. X. 13. 2. S. I. 18.
3. Book of the Constitution of the Kingdom. 1. S. X. 25.

---

* Palfrey's Evidences of Christianity. Lect. V.

4. Solomon's Three Thousand Proverbs. 1, K. IV. 32. V. 12.

5. Solomon's Thousand and Five Songs. 1. K. IV. 32. V. 12.

6. Solomon's Book on Natural History. 1. K. IV. 32.

7. Book of the Acts of Solomon. 1. K. XI. 41.

8. Chronicles of the Kings of Israel. 1. K. XIV. 19. XVI. 5, 20, 27. XXII. 39.

9. Chronicles of the Kings of Judah. 1. K. XV. 7.

10. Chronicles of King David. 1. Ch. XXVII. 24.

11. Book of Samuel the Seer, (perhaps part of the present Book of Samuel). 1. Ch. XXIX. 29. 2. Ch. IX. 29.

12. Book of Nathan the phrophet. 1. Ch. XXIX. 29. 2. Ch. IX. 29.

13. Book of Gad, the Seer. 1. Ch. XXIX. 29. 2. Ch. IX. 29.

14. Prophecy of Ahijah. 2, Ch. IX. 29.

15. Visions of Iddo. 2. Ch. IX. 29.

16. Book of Shemaiah. 2. Ch. XII. 15.

17. Book of Jehu. 2. Ch. XXIX. 2.

18. Historical book of Isaiah, the prophet. 2. Ch. XXVI. 22.

19. Sayings of Hosea. 2. Ch. XXXIII. 19.

20. Lamentations. 2. Ch. XXXV. 25. This could not be the Lamentations of Jeremiah, because the missing book contained an Elegy on King Josiah, not contained in Jeremiah.

In addition to these positive evidences, there are many strong presumptions going to show that the Bible has not been preserved in perfect purity. The first of these presumptions is founded upon the probability that transcribers would make mistakes, even while endeavoring to copy carefully and conscientiously. The second presumption is founded upon the probability that the early manuscripts were altered from base motives, to support the doctrines or advance the interests of the forger. The establishment of the early Christian churches was immediately followed by the rise of numerous sects among them, who engaged in the bitterest disputes with each other. They differed as to whether circumcision, sacrifice, the passover, pilgrimages to Jerusalem, and the Sabbath should be observed: whether any but Jews were entitled to salvation; whether matter was eternal; whether Christ was a man or a god, or a union of both; whether Mary was a virgin after giving birth to Jesus; whether God was three or one; whether salvation was obtained by faith, or works, or grace; whether Satan would live forever; whether the world would be burned up in that generation: and a great many similar questions, equally foolish, and equally beyond the possibility of proof; but all raised to a great importance by the popular belief that the rejection of the truth, even in small points of religion, would be punished by everlasting torments in hell. The advocates of the different sects did not hesitate to change the Scriptures to manufacture authorities in their own favor. The extent of the changes no one knows: but it is certain that a great many religious sects, differing widely in their tenets, pretend to prove their doctrines from different portions of the same book.

The evidences and instances of the early forgeries are too numerous to be given in full, but a short space will suffice to make a strong point. Celsus, who lived about 230 A. D., the earliest writer against Christianity of whose writings we know anything, complained that the Christians were continually changing and correcting their gospels. Origen replied to Celsus, and said that he knew of none who altered the gospels, except the Marcionites, the Valentinians, and perhaps the Lucanas. Eusebius said that the followers of Artemon presumed to alter the Scriptures. What evidence Origen and Eusebius had for believing that sects, to which they did not belong, and which they were bound to oppose, had altered the Scriptures, does not appear. It is pretty plain that the gospels differed, and had been made to differ by fraudulent means, but where the fraud was, whether on one or both sides, must remain a matter of conjecture. Origen, the most learned Christian of his time, doubted the authenticity of Hebrews, James, 2 Peter, 2 John, 3 John, and Jude. Of course by expressing a doubt of their authenticity he meant to say that they were probably forged; and he had much information in regard to the matter, such as no person in this age possibly can have. Eusebius received as genuine only the evangels of Matthew, Mark, Luke, and St. John, the epistles known as 1 John, 1 Peter, and Revelation. Mosheim says, "the greatest and most learned doctors of the fourth century were without exception disposed to deceive and lie, whenever the interests of religion required it." Hallam remarks in his History of the Middle Ages, (Ch. VII.) that "many of the peculiar and prominent characteristics in the [Catholic] faith and discipline of those ages, [from the fifth to the tenth century] appear to have been introduced or sedulously promoted for the purposes of sordid fraud." Neander writes, in his history of the early Christian church, "the next ecclesiastical writers who come after the apostles are the so-called apostolical fathers, who came from the apostolical age, and-most were the disciples of the apostles. * * * The writings of the so-called apostolic fathers are, alas! come down to us for the most part in a very uncertain condition, partly because, in early times, writings were counterfeited under the names of these venerable men of the church, in order to propagate certain opinions or principles, partly because those writings, which they had really published, were adulterated, and especially so to serve a Judæo-hierarchical party which would fain crush the free evangelical spirit. We should here in the first place name Barnabas, but it is impossible to believe the epistle ascribed to him to be authentic. * * * After Barnabas we come to

Clement, perhaps the same whom Paul mentions. (Phil. IV. 3.) He was a bishop of Rome at the end of the first century. Under his name we have one epistle to the church of Corinth, and the fragment of another. The first is genuine but is not free from important interpolations. * * * Under the name of this Clement two letters have been preserved in the Syrian churches. * * * These epistles altogether bear the character of having been counter-feited in the latter years of the second or third century, partly in order to enhance the value of celibacy, partly in order to counteract the abuses which rose up under a life of celibacy."

If there was such a disposition to forgery among the early Christians, and if so many forgeries were committed in religious books, as is represented, it is no more than reasonable to believe that attempts would be made to tamper with the gospels. I have already remarked that the last twelve verses of Mark were not contained in some of the early copies of that gospel, and were considered by many as a forgery. Gibbon* remarks that " the word ' which' in 1 Tim. III. 16, was altered to ' God' at Constantinople in the beginning of the sixth century, and this fraud with that of the three witnesses is admirably detected by Sir Isaac Newton."

A third presumption against the theory that the Bible has been preserved in perfect purity is in a tradition contained in the Apocrypha, a work of no little authority in such matters. Esdras (XIV. 21 of his second book) says, " Thy law is burned ; therefore no man knoweth the things which thou hast done or the works that are to begin. But if I have found grace before thee, send down the holy spirit into me and I shall write all that hath been done in the world, since the beginning, which were written in thy law, that men may find thy path, and that they which will live in the latter day, may live." And in verse 45 he says, " And it came to pass that when the forty days were fulfilled, that the highest spake, saying, ' the first, that thou hast written, publish openly that the foolish and unworthy may read it: but keep the seventy last, that thou mayest deliver them only to such as be wise among the people.' " Whether this be true or false, it must necessarily raise doubts in regard to the purity of our present gospels. Irenæus said it was the prevalent belief among the Chris-tian fathers in the second century that Ezra had republished the lost and corrupted books of the old Jewish law. It is stated in 2 Mac. II. 13, that Nehe-miah found and gathered the books.

Not only was there a strong disposition to corrupt the gospels, but there were excellent opportunities, since all the copies were made by hand with the pen ; and, worst of all, the frauds once committed were almost out of the reach of detection. There were few learned men among the Christians, their copies

---

* Note 17 to Ch. XLVII. of the Decline and Fall.

of the gospel were few, some of the books were not received as inspired for several centuries after their composition, and were not carefully preserved, and when accepted as inspired were received with a reverence that did not stop to doubt at the most wonderful or unreasonable doctrines or statements contained in a "gospel." Home, Bengel, Kennicott, Houbigant, Adam Clarke, and Markland, who have all written comments upon the Bible much esteemed by various Christian churches, are agreed that the copyists of the Scriptures have accidentally or intentionally erred in copying different passages. Eichhorn says, "Our four gospels in their present shape were not in use and were not known till the end of the second century; previous to that time it is supposed that other gospels were in circulation, allied to those which we now have, but not the same." Morell gives it as his opinion that "with few exceptions there is not an entire book in the whole of the Old Testament, with respect to which we can determine, with complete accuracy who was the author—when it was written—at what time received into the canon of the Scripture—and on what especial grounds. The sum and substance of our certain knowledge (leaving out mere Jewish tradition) is that the different books were collected together sometime after the Babylonish captivity, accepted by the Jews as divine writings, and read accordingly in the synagogue. Now under such circumstances as these, how are we to stand forth and maintain the inspiration of the Jewish writings on the hypothesis, either that they were all dictated by the spirit of God or written by express commission from Heaven? Only let it be affirmed that either of these notions is necessary to complete the conditions of a truly inspired book, and what chance have we of being successful in proving the inspiration of the Old Testament against the aggressions of the skeptic?"

Besides all this the books now included in the Bible were only a few of those published and at one time received as inspired; and the selection of our inspired gospel for us, and the rejection of the uninspired, all having been previously of equal authority, was made by rules, and for reasons, unknown to us, in a dark age, by men whom we know to have been filled with debasing superstitions, and to have been parties to numerous and gross frauds. The selections were made about 300 A. D., in the very atmosphere of priestly fraud.

ORIGINALITY.

XXII. Were the doctrines of the Bible original with the authors of that book? If they were, there is a strong presumption that it is of a higher than human origin. The doctrines taught in the book under consideration may be classified under three heads: 1. Rules of religious action. 2. Rules of moral action. 3. Rules of political action. The Bible was not written till men had lived many centuries upon the earth, nor till many studious and great men had thought deeply and written wisely of religion, morality, and civil government. These are subjects upon which original ideas are scarce, and he who would in this day compose an entirely new set of practicable rules for the action of men under any circumstances in which they might be placed, would be almost entitled to recognition as an inspired prophet. If on the other hand it appear that the ideas advanced in the Bible are not original, we shall be justified in presuming that the book is a mere fraudulent human compilation. Where would be the necessity or propriety of revealing from heaven something that was previously known among men? It has been said that to induce men to observe the laws of morality, it was necessary that they should believe that these laws were directly sanctioned by the Almighty God, that their violation would be visited by his wrath and eternal vengeance, and that, to give this sanction, a revelation was required. This argument may be worthy of consideration, though it might be used as well in favor of a counterfeit as of a genuine revelation. At least no one will deny that it would be far more satisfactory to believers to have an entirely original revelation than to have a mere rehash of long-recognized truths. Unfortunately for the claims of the Bible to be a God-given revelation, it does not contain one important doctrine of a general character which can be proved to be original, while there is conclusive proof in regard to most of the ideas, and strong evidence as to the remainder, to show that they were learned by the Hebrew prophets and Christian apostles from the priests and philosophers of the Heathen nations, or from that general sense of right and propriety which is common to all naturally intelligent peoples.

There was a wonderful similarity between the religious doctrines and ceremonies of the Jews and Egyptians—a similarity too great by far to permit any reasonable man to believe that those nations derived their creeds and forms from different sources. This similarity will reduce us to a dilemma—we must believe either that the Egyptians copied from Moses, or that the latter copied from the former ; and if the Hebrew law-giver be proved to have obtained his ideas from the Egyptians, we can hardly be expected to believe that he got them from Jehovah. Now for the question whether the Jews copied from the Egyptians or the Egyptians from the Jews. It was the common belief among the most intelligent of the ancient Greeks that the kingdom of Egypt, with its civil and religious forms, reached back into the most remote antiquity, far earlier than any other nation near the Mediterranean. Such was the opinion of Solon, one of the most learned men of his time, and he formed his opinion after con-versing with the priests of Memphis. Herodotus says that when he visited Egypt, the priests took him into a large consecrated chamber, and there showed him the wooden statues of all the high priests of the kingdom, three hundred and forty-one in number, going back consecutively from his time to the founda-tion of the monarchy ; and these statues had been made in the life-time of the respective originals, " who were all men and the sons of men." The Egyptian priests said the Greeks in their religion were children,—a remark indicative of high civilization and long culture—a remark such as the philosophers of this day make of the ancient Greeks—and a remark which our forefathers four or five hundred years ago were not sufficiently cultivated to make.

The Egyptians had an elaborate religious creed and a complex ceremonial. Kenrick says : "Superstitiously attached to their sacred institutions, and pro-fessing a religion which admitted much outward show, the Egyptians clothed their ceremonies with all the grandeur of solemn pomp; and the celebration of their religious rites was remarkable for all that human ingenuity could devise to render them splendid and imposing. They prided themselves on being the nation in which originated most of the sacred institutions afterwards common to other people." If the history of Abraham and his descendants, as given in Genesis, be true, the Jews when they entered Egypt were a few score of rude shepherds, who had never dwelt in houses, or had a permanent place of resi-dence, who were unskilled in all the higher arts of civilized life, ignorant of letters, and destitute of enlightened, clear or positive ideas of religion or govern-ment. At this time (1700 B. C.) Egypt was already a kingdom of long standing, containing a dense and prosperous agricultural population, long accustomed to dwell in houses, skilled in the arts of peace and war, familiar with the use of hieroglyphical letters, and living under social, political and religious systems among the most complex ever devised by man. These facts are not denied and cannot be controverted ; and they are in substance asserted by all the great and celebrated men who have investigated the antiquities of Egypt. Wilkinson observes, "It is indeed a remarkable fact that the first glimpse we obtain of the history and manners of the Egyptians, show us a nation already far advanced in all the arts of civilized life; and the same customs and inventions that prevailed in the Augustan age of the people' after the accession of the eighteenth dynasty are found in the remote age of Osirtasen, the cotemporary of Joseph, nor can there be any doubt that they were in the same civilized state when Abraham visited the country." In the midst of this polished nation the Hebrews lived, poor, rude, engaged in an occupation particularly degrading in the eyes of the Egyptians, and finally reduced to unconditional slavery. Moses was born on the bank of the Nile, he was bred in the family of the Pharaohs, and he could not have avoided learning much of the politics and religion of the Egyptian kingdom. The author of the Acts, writing ostensibly by divine inspiration, says, "Moses was learned in all the wisdom of the Egyptians." Under the leadership of Moses, the Jews escaped from Egypt, and after they entered Arabia, their chief gave them a code of laws, which are found to bear a wonderful resemblance to the laws of the land they had left. Under these circumstances, what reasonable man can believe that the Egyptians copied from the Jews? The former, a long-established and prosperous nation before the Jews existed, powerful, civilized, particularly priding themselves on the antiquity of their religious institutions,—could they in the height of their prosperity, while the children of Israel were still always at war or in captivity with the Philistines, have copied the institutions of a hostile and despised and enslaved race, which had no laws until after it escaped from the brick-yards of the Nile. If there were any room for doubt, it would be removed by an examination of the existing monuments of the ancient Egyptians. The paintings and sculptures on the temples, obelisks and pyramids preserved for nearly, if not . quite, four thousand years, confirm in the most explicit language the assertion of Wilkinson, that the customs of the country were the same long before the time of Moses as they were when Solon and Herodotus visited Memphis to learn wisdom, and returned to their native land with the opinion that the Egyptians were not only the most ancient but also the wisest of nations. Let us now examine whether, and in how far the religious institutions, ceremonies and ideas of the Hebrews and Christians resembled the institutions, ceremonies and ideas of the Egyptians and of other peoples.

Moses gave to his followers a sacred book, but before Abraham was born, the Egyptian priests had had their sacred books. The holy Vedas of the Bramins were written, as Sir William Jones thinks, about 1500 B. C., near the time of Moses. There were also sacred books in China and Persia in ancient times,

and there is no evidence that they did not exist as early as the Pentateuch.
The books of Moses contained an account of the creation of the universe, the
early history of the human race, the origin of the Jewish people, the genealogy
of the principal families, a code of political, social and religious laws and prophecies of future events. The sacred books of the Egyptians and other nations
contained similar matter. Diodorus Siculus tells us that many of the ancient
lawgivers, for the purpose of securing the supremacy and permanence of their
laws, pretended that the latter were of divine origin.

The Jewish legislator established a priesthood with great wealth and political
power, and made the priestly office hereditary in one family or tribe, as had
been done many centuries earlier in the valleys of the Nile, the Euphrates and
the Ganges.

Solomon erected a temple to the Lord one thousand years before Christ, but
temples to the gods were common in Egypt, Chaldea, Phoenicia and Hindostan,
many ages previous to that time. Ruins of religious edifices built while the
Jews were as yet unknown, are still standing on the sites of Memphis and
Thebes. In 1 S. V. 2, it is said that the Philistines had a temple to Dagon
before the time of Solomon. Bishop Kitto gives it as his opinion, from the description of the holy of holies, that that place " was an adytum [a secret apart-
ment] without windows." According to 1 K., VIII. 12, " The Lord said he
would dwell in a thick darkness." The Egyptian temples had an adytum
without windows, for the accommodation of their divinities.

Among the Israelites, and in accordance with the Mosaic laws, there were
men who were prophets by profession; there were also prophets among
heathen nations—the Egyptians, Greeks, Phoenicians, Persians and Chaldeans. Herodotus, who lived 460 years before Christ, wrote: "The art of
predicting future events in the Greek temples came also from the Egyptians
and it is certain that they were the first people who established festivities,
public assemblies, processions, and the proper mode of communing with the
Deity." Yet we learn from Homer that some of the Grecian oracles were
already celebrated at the time of the Trojan war (1100 B. C.)

The Jews had an Ark of the Covenant, (Josh. III., 13; 2 S., XV. 24; 1 Ch.,
XV., 2, 15,) a box in which the Lord was supposed to make his home; and so
sacred was it, that according to Moses, its mere touch was death to all but the
priests. This ark was copied from the Egyptian ark, sacred boat or great shrine,
which was carried in procession by the priests, as the Mosaic ark was borne by
the Levites. The gods of the ancients were supposed to travel considerably,
and to be entitled to the most honorable conveyance known. In the hills and
plains of Greece, a chariot was the most honorable mode of conveyance, and in
the Grecian pictures, the gods are represented in their chariots. But the settled

portion of Egypt was confined to the bottom land of its great valley, subject to overflow every year, and intersected with large and numerous canals. There chariots were little used, and boats were the more ancient and honorable means of conveyance; and, accordingly, the gods of Egypt were painted as sitting in boats and carried about in procession in boats. Moses did not see why his divinity could not travel in a boat as well in Judea as in Egypt, and therefore he just adopted the boat shrine. The Ark of the Covenant had at the ends two "cherubim," little figures composed of a chubby child's face with a pair of wings. There were similar guardians on the Egyptian arks;* but it is supposed by some that these figures were intended originally to represent a sacred beetle, the scarabæus.

The religious ceremonies of the Hebrews bore a remarkable resemblance to those of the Egyptians. The Jews considered Jerusalem a holy city, (Is. II., 2; Ps. LXVIII., 15,) and attributed great religious merit to pilgrimages thither. In the valley of the Nile there were holy places also. The great temple of Aremis, at Bubastis, is said to have been visited by 700,000 pilgrims annually.

The Egyptians offered sacrifices of vegetables and animals to the gods, and so did the Jews.† The priest of both nations slew the sacrificial animals in the same manner, by cutting the throat. The Egyptians preferred red oxen, without spot, for sacrifice; and Moses directed the selection of a red heifer, (Num. XIX., 2.) The custom of the scapegoat (Lev. XIV. 21.) was common to both nations. A sacred fire was kept continuelly burning in the temples of Thebes as well as in Judea., (Lev. VI., 12, 13.) The Egyptian priests took off their shoes in the temples, and Joshua took off his shoes in a holy place, (Josh. V. 16.) The Egyptian priests danced before their altars, and the same custom prevailed in Jerusalem, (Ps. CXLIX., 3). The practice of circumcision, claimed by Moses as a divine ordinance, communicated to Abraham, is proved by the monuments of Egypt, according to Wilkinson, to have been fully established there, at a time long antecedent to the arrival of Joseph. The Egyptians had their unclean meats, including pork, as well as the Jews. The Egyptians annointed their kings and priests long before there were any kings or priests in Israel. The Urim and Thummin (Ex. XXXIX., 8, 10; Lev. VIII.,8,) which play a stupid part in the books of Moses and Jo. Smith, were once not inappropriate

---

* Kenrick says: on the model of an Egyptian shrine, "the ark of the covenant of the Hebrews appears to have been constructed, which contained the tables of the law, the pot of manna, and the rod of Aaron. The mixed figure of the cherubim, which were placed at either end and overshadowed it with their wings, has a parallel in some of the Egyptian representations, in which kneeling figures spread their wings over the shrine."

† See Appendix, note 4.

figures of Re, the god of light, and Thmei† the god of justice, worn on the breasts of Egyptian judges.

Moses taught the existence of only one God, or at least the Jews of a late period believed in and worshipped only one God. The Egyptian people worshipped many gods, but the priests of Egypt as well as of ancient India were monotheists. There was one doctrine for the initiated, another for the vulgar. The deity was called "I am" in Hebrew; and the same term is applied to the deity in the ancient Hindoo "Menu," and was applied by the Phœnicians to their great god. The Jews held the name Jehovah in great reverence, and the common people were prohibited to speak it. except on very rare occasions; and the Egyptians held the name "Osiris" in similar reverence. Even Herodotus, after having been at Memphis, when writing about that divinity, would not use his name. Moses represented Jehovah as having a human shape, coming down ʼto earth, visiting and conversing with men, causing all the occurrences of nature by immediate efforts of his will, frequently performing miracles, and empowering men to do miracles, and to foretell the future, choosing individual men and a particular nation to be his favorites, and establishing certain families to be kings and priests of his "peculiar people" for ever. Such ideas were familiar to all the ancient nations about the eastern shore of the Mediterranean. Jehovah led the armies of Israel to battle: and the gods of the Greeks, Phœnicians, and Egyptians were also reputed to be terrible in warring for their worshippers. The Hebrew Scriptures, in some passages, exhibit a high conception of the divine attributes. According to Robertson, the following was the idea of God, as expressed by the ancient Bramins:—"As God is immaterial, he is above all conception; as he is invisible, he can have no form: but from what we behold of his works, we may conclude that he is eternal, omnipotent, knowing all things, and present everywhere." Moses represents many of the most important events of the early history of the world to have happened in or near Judea: and almost every ancient nation held the same views in regard to its own soil. An orator in the Island of Crete, on a public occasion, once spoke thus: † "Upon this Isle all the arts were discovered. Saturn gave you the love of justice and your peculiar simplicity of heart. Vesta taught you to erect houses. Neptune taught you to build ships. You owe to Ceres the culture of grain, to Bacchus that of the vine, and to Minerva that of the olive. Jupiter destroyed the giants which threatened you. Hercules delivered you from the serpents, wolves, and other noxious animals. The authors of so many benefits, admitted by you to divine honors, were born on this soil and are now occupied in laboring for your happiness." Cory, in the preface to his "Ancient Frag-

---

* In Greek Themis, the goddess of justice.
† So given in Barthelemy's Anacharsis.

ments," says: "In ancient times it was the prevailing custom of all the nations, including Egypt, India, Phœnicia, and Greece; to appropriate to themselves, and assign within their own territorial limits, the localities of the grand events of primeval history, with the birth and achievements of the gods and heroes, the deluge, the origin of the arts, and the civilization of mankind."

The history of Creation, as given in Genesis, is a mere compilation of ancient traditions prevalent in the East, and similar traditions are given by Sanchoniathan, an old Phœnician author. Moses informs us that Abraham was the chosen favorite of Jehovah, and was to be the father of the chosen people. This name Abraham is probably derived from the Hindoo Brahm, * the great spirit, the origin of all things, the creator of all other existences. Abraham was called Abram until late in life, according to Gen. XVII. 5, and he is said to have come from Ur of the Chaldees, a point east of Canaan, either on the Euphrates or farther east—possibly Hindostan itself, the home of Braminism. His name, his birth place, and his position as father of the chosen people, all suggest a derivation from the Hindoo Brahm. In Ex. VI. 3, it is said, that "God was not known to Abra am, Isaac, and Jacob by the name of Jehovah." This is probably true, for Jehovah was a Phœnician word, and the Jews did not learn the Phœnician, or as we now call it the Hebrew tongue, till they returned from Egypt, and settled in Canaan among the Phœnicians.

Thus we have gone over the most prominent points wherein the ideas advanced in the Old Testament resemble the ideas accepted among many nations existing during the time of the Jews. Although Moses evidently derived his principal doctrines from the Egyptians, yet the latter nation had many usages and principles of religion and politi s, which the Jews did not see fit to adopt. The Egyptians believed in the immortality of the soul, in future rewards and punishments, in the adoration of numerous animals, and in the worship of idols. It is a matter of wonder that Moses rejected the doctrine of a future life; but his creed was certainly purer and higher on most points than the creeds of the heathens of western Asia.

Next in order comes the consideration of the question whether the doctrines taught in the New Testament were original with Christ and the Apostles?— The immortality of the soul, and future rewards and punishments, were not taught in any portion of the Old Testament, and not even hinted at in the books of Moses, but were inculcated by Jesus, after they had long been accepted among the Hindoos, Egyptians, and Greeks. We have to this day the works of Plato and Cicero, in which those great philosophers discussed the question of a future life before the beginning of the Christian era.

---

* Brahm, derived from the same root as the Latin word *primus*, (first), the Celtic word *priomh* (chief), and the Gothic word *frum* (origin, beginning). From this last word our "from" is derived.

The dogma that God is threefold in his nature, or three in one, was familiar to the Egyptians, but was rejected by the Jews, and was adopted by the Christians, who made Jesus the second person of the Godhead. The doctrine of the Trin ty, the triune nature of the deity, was familiar to the Hindoos. Tennemann, in his "Hist ry of Philosophy," sp aks thus of the ancient Braminical doctrine in regard to God. "The supreme being of the Hindoos is Brahm,—incomprehensible by any human understanding: pervading and comprehending all things. Originally he reposed in the contemplation of himself; subsequently his creative word has caused all things to proceed from him, by a succession of continued emanations. As creator he is named Brahma; as the preserving power, Vishnou; as the destroyer and renovator of the forms of matter, Siva. These three relations of the divine being constitute the trinity of the Hi doos." Braminism was older than Buddhism, and the latter was established at least six hundred years before Christ. * That the Egyptian creed was older than the faith of the apostles is not to be denied. Wilkinson mentions the Egyptian trinity thus: "The great gods of Egypt were Neph, Amun, Pthah, Khem, Sate, Maut, Bubastus, and Neith, one of whom generally formed, in connection with other two, a triad, [Trinity] which was worshipped by a particular city or district, with a peculiar veneration. In these triads, the third member proceeded from the other two; that is, from the first by the second—thus, the intellect of the Deity, having operated on matter, produced the result of these two under he form and name of the world, and on a similar principle appear to have been formed most of their speculative combinations. The third member of a triad, as might be supposed, was not of equal rank with the two from whom it proceeded; and we therefore find that Khonso, the third person in the Th ban triad, was not one of the great gods, as were the other two, Amun and Maut: Horus, in the triad of hilæ, was inferior to Osiris and Isis; and Anouke to Neph and Sate, in the triad of Elephantine and the Cataracts."

The New Testament teaches that Jesus was the second person of the Godhead, a God, and that he was born of a virgin, impregnated only by the Holy Ghost, or third person of the Godhead, that he lived in the shape of a man for thirty-three years on earth, was crucified on a charge of crime by the officers of Rome, and by his death and suffering atoned for the sins of mankind. The idea of such a redeemer is nowhere advanced in the Old Testament, bu it was famili r to many heathen nations of antiquity. According to Ritter, " the doctrine of Buddhism [established 600 B. C., in Hindostan] contains nothing but the main idea of the heroic poems of the Bramins, fully understood and consequentially carried out—that is, that a man freeing himself by holiness of co duct from the obstacles of nature, may deliver his fellow men from the cor-

---

* Dr. Ritter in his History of Ancient Philosophy, chap. II.

ruption of their times, and become a benefactor, redeemer of his race, and also become a supreme God—a Buddha." Wilkinson says: "At Philæ, where Osiris [an Egyptian Divinity, who came down to earth to battle with Typho, the evil spirit] was particularly worshipped, and which was one of the places where they supposed him to have been buried, his mysterious history is curiously illustrated in the sculptures [made 3,600 years ago] of a small retired chamber lying nearly over the western Adytum of the temple. His death and removal from this world are there described; the number of twenty-eight lotus plants points out the period of years he was thought to have lived on earth; and his passage from this life to a future state is indicated by the usual attendance of the Deities and Genii, who presided over the funeral rites of ordinary mortals. He is there represented with the feathered cap, which he wore in his capacity of Judge of Amenti, and this attribute shows the final office he held after his resurrection, and continued to exercise toward the dead at their last ordeal in a future state." Again: "Osiris was called 'the opener of truth,' and was said to be 'full of grace and truth.' He appeared on earth to benefit mankind, and after having performed the duties he had come to fulfill, and fallen a sacrifice to Typho, the evil principle, (which was at length overcome by his influence, after leaving the world,) he arose again to a new life, and became the judge of mankind in a future state." * Herodotus saw the tomb of Osiris at Sais, nearly five centuries before Christ. Similar redeemers were worshipped in other lands, and like Jesus many of them were born of virgins. Grote, speaking of the early legends of Greece, remarks that "the furtive pregnancy of young women—often by a god—is one of the most frequently recurring incidents in the legendary narrative." St. John speaks of Christ as the "*Logos*," the word. Millman † admits that the term "*logos*" was a term in frequent use in Greece and Egypt before it was used by St. John. The meaning of the "logos" and of the trinity which makes three gods of one god, and one god of three gods is exceedingly dark, but there is a ray of light in Abel Remusat's description of a Hindoo trinity of a god, his law or word, and the union of both.

The Christians abandoned the ceremonial law of Moses, and adopted baptism and prayer as important portions of their new system; but in these matters they only followed the Essenes of Judea, and the Therapeutæ of Egypt; sects described by Josephus and Philo. The Essenes exalted the merit of humility and religious contemplation, and the contempt of worldly goods; they often lived with their property in common, and in these points they were imitated by

---

* According to the New Testament Christ is to be the judge of men in the next world.

† Note to Gibbon's Rome.

the Christians. The Essenes were a sect of Judaistic Buddhists, having evidently derived many of their ideas from India ; and they gave tone to the new Christian Church. The Christians soon needed a ceremonial for their worship, and they found it among the Buddhists. * Huc was astonished to find that the ceremonies of the Buddhist priests in Mongolia and Thibet were scarcely to be distinguished from those of the Catholic Church. In the centre of Asia, he found heathen monks, nuns, and priests, with gowns and surplices, and shaven crowns, with beads and bells, lighted candles and smoking incense, genuflections, chants and prayers, and masses for the dead, and all t..e tedious trickery of Rome. Since Buddhism is much older than Christianity, we must believe that the Catholics have stolen their ceremonies, until there be some evidence to the contrary, and we know of none as yet.

But it is claimed that the great merit of the New Testament is in its moral teachings, which are not only perfectly pure, but are also entirely original. These moral teachings are contained in such expressions as "Love thy neighbor as thyself," "Love is the fulfilment of the law," "Return good for evil ;" and "all that ye would that men should do unto you, do ye even so unto them, for this is the law and the prophets." The fact that such phrases are made the foundation to claims of originality or peculiar merit, shows the ignorance of the people, and the unscrupulous policy of the clergy. The doctrine that love is the fulfilment of the law, taught in the New Testament with much emphasis, and the chief merit of the book in the eyes of many, is as old as human society. It was taught by Plato in almost the identical words ascribed to Jesus. We still have the writings of the great teacher of the Academy, wherein he says "Love † is peace and good will among men, calm upon the waters, repose and stillness in the storm, the balm of sleep in sadness. Before him all harsh passions flee away, he is the author of soft affections, destroyer of un· gentle thoughts, merciful and mild, the admiration of the wise, the delight of the gods. Love divests us of alienation from each other, and fills our vacant hearts with overflowing sympathy : he is the valued treasure of the unfortunate, and desired by the unhappy, (therefore unhappy because they possess him not,) the parent of grace, of gentleness, of delicacy : a cherisher of all that is good, but guileless as to evil ; in labor and in fear, in longings of the affections, or in soarings of the reason, our best pilot, confederate, supporter and savior." It so happens that St. John, who only of the Evangelists, lays a peculiar stress upon the all-sufficiency of love, had an opportunity of becoming thoroughly indoctrinated in Platonism, by his long residence among the Greeks at Ephesus. St. John was the only one of the Evangelists who taught that

---

* Huc's Travels in Tartary, Vol. 1, Ch. V. Vol. 2, Ch. II, III.
† See Mackay's Progress of the Intellect, V. 21.

Christ was the *logos* of which Plato had said so much. Christianity is only a corrupted Platonism grafted upon the Mosaic Law.

Men were always possessed with a mental constitution similar to our own: the rudest savages have the same affections and passions which actuate citizens of enlightened nations. In all ages women have been found to love their children; friends have been ready to aid each other at great cost to themselves; soldiers have been willing to sacrifice themselves for their country. The disposition to act kindly and justly to others is born with all men, and he who claims originality for expressing it is a shameless impostor. Long before Christ, philosophers had taught that men should give to others the treatment they desired for themselves. Confucius expresses the sentiment in almost the very words used by Jesus five hundred years later. Thales * (600 B. C,) taught that we must " do nothing which we would blame in another." Isocrates † (400 B. C.) says: "Treat your parents as you would wish your parents to treat you." "Let your most secret acts be as though you had all the world for witnesses. Do not expect that reprehensible words will be forgotten ; you may hide them from others, but never from yourself. Devote your leisure hours to hearing counsel from the wise; alleviate the sufferings of the virtuous poor; the rec llection of charity well applied is one of the most precious forms or wealth. If you should be clothed with a high office, let your subordinates be upright men, and when you leave your posi ion, let it be with honor rather than with wealth." There is nothing more elevated in all the New Testament than the following from the Enchiridion of Epictetus: "Remember that you must behave at life as at an entertainment. Is anything brough around to you, put out your hand, and take your share with moderation. Doth it pass by you, do not stop it. Is it not yet come, do not stretch forth your desire towards it, but wait till it reaches you. Thus do with regard to children, to a wife, to a public office, to riches, and you will some day be a worthy partner of the Feast of the Gods. And if you do not so much as take things which are set before you, but are even able to despise them, then you will not only be a partner of the Feast of the Gods, but a sharer in their Empire also."

The doctrines of Socrates, Plato, Aristotle and Cicero, in regard to the conduct of men toward each other, will suffer nothing by a comparison with the teachings of Jesus. Herder says that the morality of the ancient Bramins was pure and elevated. Sir Wm. Jones has expressed his admiration of the spirit of the institutes of Menu; and Dr. Arnold speaks in high praise of the greatness of soul exhibited by the Stoics. No chastity can ever surpass that of Lucretia;

* Diogenes Laertius, Lib. I. sec. 35, 36, quoted in Barthelemy's Anacharsis, Ch. XXVIII.

† Quoted in Barthelemy's Anacharsis, Chap. XXVIII.

no honesty that of Aristides; Washington's disinterestedness was not purer than that of Timoleon; and on a comparison of the conduct of Socrates and Jesus, during trial and execution, the latter can certainly claim no pre-eminence. And yet we are asked to believe that Christ was the author of the teaching—" Do to others as you would have them do to you." The demand is preposterous. It would be equivalent to asking us to believe that in the ages before Christ, and in the lands where his teachings are unknown, there was and is no honesty, no truth, no friendship, no peace, no human society; that all men were then and are there liars, thieves and murderers; that, in fact, man is entirely wanting in the knowledge of what is right, or the disposition to do it, or both, until he has heard and believed the words of Jesus. The influence of the priestly lies in regard to the originality of Christ's teaching of the all-sufficiency of love, is so great that many, knowing their falsity, dare not declare it. The Rev. Mr. Milne, in the preface to his translation of the Chinese "Sacred Edict," expresses a fear that he shall be condemned for furnishing proof that before Jesus was born, a morality as pure as his was inculcated in the Celestial Empire. Milman is one of the few Christian authors who have had the manliness and honesty to acknowledge that the New Testament morality was not new. Indeed, many of the moral precepts in that book, upon which so much stress is laid, were contained in the Old Testament. Moses said: "Love thy neighbor as thyself," (Lev. XIX., 18, 39); and Micah asked, (VI. 8,) "What doth the Lord require of thee, but to do justly and to love mercy, and to walk humbly with thy God." A comparison of the following passages will show how the authors of the New Testament made use of the milder portions of the Jewish Scriptures:

Compare Mat. V. 3, 4, 5,	with	Prov. XV. 32, XXIX. 23, Micah. VI. 8.
		Ps. CXLVII. 3, XXXVII. 11, Is. LXI. 1–3
" " V. 6, 8,	"	Is. LVIII. 10, XXXIII. 15, Ps. XXIV. 3.
" " V. 16,	"	Prov. IV. 18.
" " V. 38, 39,	"	Prov. XX. 22, XXIV. 29.
" " V. 42,	"	Ec. IV. 5, Deut. XV. 8.
" " VI. 11,	"	Prov. XXX. 8.
" " VI. 13,	"	1 Ch. XXIX. 11.
" " VI. 14,	"	Ec. XXVIII. 2.
" " VI. 19, 20,	"	Ec. XXIX. 11.
" " VI. 25,	"	Ps. LV. 22.
" " VII. 12,	"	Tobit. IV. 15.
" " XVIII. 17,	"	Ec. XIX. 19.
" " XXII. 40,	"	Deut. IV. 5, Lev. XIX. 18.
" Luke XII. 19,	"	Ec. XI. 19.

Jesus may be entitled to all the honor of having been the first teacher of the doctrine of passive submission to all wrong and oppression ; and a proper view of the circumstances in which he was placed will leave no doubt that this doctrine, so singular and slavish to us, was natural and even absolutely necessary to him.   He was determined to claim to be the Messiah foretold by the Hebrew prophets and long awaited with anxiety by the Jewish nation—the Messiah, the descendant of David, who should be their king, break the yoke of the Gentiles, and restore Judea to her former wealth and power.   The Messiah of popular expectation was to be necessarily the enemy of the Romans ; but Jesus soon found that it was useless to think of revolting against Rome.   The Jews were so restless under the Roman yoke, so ready to revolt, and the Romans were so quick to punish any one suspected of sedition, that Jesus was compelled for the purpose of saving his own neck to inform both Hebrews and Romans by a public declaration of his doctrine, that his kingdom was not of this world, and that it was a sin to resist the powers that be, since they all are ordained of God ; and to make his doctrine consistent, he forbade his followers to resist evil.

The teaching that belief in Jesus as the Son of God is the highest virtue or merit before the Almighty is not original.   Crishna, a Hindoo divinity, says : " Works affect me not, nor have I any expectations from the fruit of works. He, who believeth me to be even so, is not bound by works." *

Thus I have considered the claim of the writers of the Bible to the originality of the principal ideas advanced in that book ; I have endeavored to prove the negative, and the reader must form his own opinion whether I have succeeded.   If he agree with me that the doctrines of the Bible are not original, perhaps he will ask, (as Strauss asks about the later Jewish notions in regard to the angels and their names) were these ideas false so long as they existed among the Gentiles ?   And have they become true by adoption in the Jewish [and Christian] mythology ?   Or have they been true through all time ?   And have idolatrous people discovered truths of such an elevated character sooner than the people of God ?

---

* Mackay's Progress of the Intellect, V. 6.

TRUTH OF DOCTRINES.

XXIII. Are the doctrines advanced in the Bible true? If not, the claims that that book is divinely inspired must be abandoned. It is not sufficient that some of the doctrines should be true, or that there should be that defective approximation to truth which characterizes many human compositions. No book can deserve to be considered a revelation from heaven, unless every doctrine in it be not only true but accompanied by evidence of its truth carrying conviction to all intelligent minds. The Bible claims to be inspired by God, and it must be strictly examined in proportion to the extravagance of its pretensions. Christ affirmed the divine authority of the Old Testament, (Mat. V. 17, 18, XV. 4–7, XXII. 31, XXIV. 15, &c.) Some of the New Testament writers affirmed their own inspiration, (1 Cor. VII. 39, 40; 1 Thes. IV. 6–8, V. 23, 28; 2 Pet. III. 1–4, 14–16; 1 John, IV. 4–6). The inspiration claimed for the Bible is a superhuman wisdom, or rather a divine wisdom, given by God himself to his prophets for the instruction of men. Dr. Knapp defined it to be "an extraordinary divine agency upon teachers, while giving instruction, whether oral or written, by which they were taught what and how they should write or speak." Christians dispute among themselves whether the inspiration of the Bible be plenary or partial; whether Jehovah dictated the very words, or whether he inspired the writer with the idea and left the latter to find their own language, and that perhaps faulty. Plenary inspiration was the received doctrine of the whole Christian church until of comparatively late years, and was not abandoned until the assaults of skepticism made it untenable. The same change of opinion in regard to the nature of inspiration occurred with the Grecian oracles. "When superstitious people," says Neander, "thought that the God himself inhabited the priestess of the Delphic oracle, and spoke through her mouth, so that everything literally came from Phœbus himself, and when, on the contrary, the infidels tried to turn this representation into ridicule, and quoting the bad verses of the Pythian prophetess, laughed at the notion of this coming from Apollo, Plutarch thus replied—'The language, the expression, the words, and the metre, come not from God but from the woman. The God only presents the image to her mind and lights up in her soul the lamp which illumes the future. The God uses the soul as an instrument, and the activity of the instrument consists in the property of representing as purely as possible what is communicated to it. It is impossible that it should be repeated perfectly pure,—nay, without even a large admixture of foreign matter.' "

The apostles held that the very words of the Old Testament were dictated by Jehovah, as appears from the following passages :

" God, who at sundry times and in divers manners, spoke in times past unto the fathers by the prophets." Heb. I. 1.

Paul speaks of " the word of God." Heb. IV. 12.

" God spake by the mouth of David." Acts IV. 25.

The Holy Ghost spake by Esaias the prophet. Acts XXVIII. 25.

The first testimony usually adduced by the advocates of the Bible to prove the truth of its doctrine, is that furnished by the miracles and prophecies of the Hebrew prophets and of Christ and his apostles. These miracles and prophecies will deserve a little consideration.

MIRACLES.

XXIV. In regard to the miraculous evidence adduced to prove the truth and divine origin of the Bible, I shall make the following points :—1. Miracles are an impossibility. 2. If miracles were wrought, man could never distinguish them from the works of human skill. 3. The miracles related in the Bible were never wrought. 4. If the Bible miracles were wrought they would not suffice to prove the doctrines of the Bible to be true.

And first, *What is a miracle?* Hume defines it to be " a transgression of the laws of Nature by a particular volition of the Deity, or by interposition of some agent." It is such a transgression as necessarily exhibits superhuman power. If an act appear to be a transgression of known laws, but be really in conformity with laws unknown, then it is no miracle, any more than many acts which learned and skilful men do every day, appear to the ignorant to be miracles.

The ability to foretell eclipses, and to describe, a moment after their occurrence, events happening in far distant countries, would appear to the savage to be in violation of the laws of Nature and therefore miraculous, but we know that they are in accordance with natural laws.

Secondly, *What evidence will suffice to prove a miracle?* None. There is no record in history that any man ever had sufficient evidence to believe any act to be a miracle. It is impossible to know whether the laws of Nature be violated, because man can never be certain that he knows all the laws of Nature. The savage is laughed at who believes a civilized man to be possessed of miraculous power when he throws a dead body into convulsions with a galvanic battery, or when he, by means of a telescope or a magnetic telegraph, discovers what is going on at a great distance; yet we bear the same relation to Christ which the savage bears to civilized man. If Jesus were to appear in California and perform all the miraculous acts ascribed to him in the New Testament, he would acquire little credit for the possession of supernatural power. If he turned water into wine, he would be called a good juggler; if he cured the blind and lame, and raised the dead, he would be esteemed as an unequalled physician; if he caused the heavens to grow dark, he would be accounted a great meteorologist; if he rose up to heaven, he would have the credit of having invented a flying machine. But as for any pretension of ability to violate the laws of Nature—why the thing is ridiculous. If a man were to order the sun to cease forthwith to shine in clear noonday, and if the sun should so forthwith cease to shine, that man would not be entitled to any more credit than the man who can foretell an eclipse. Their powers would be equally miraculous to a man who knows nothing of astronomy. If, however, it be insisted that the restoration of a dead man to life suffice to prove miraculous power, then ought not a good juggler's trick, well performed, prove as much? To breathe fire is as inexplicable by natural laws (as they are generally understood by educated men) as to cure the blind and lame by a word.

But let it be granted that certain acts, inexplicable by natural laws as usually understood, shall be considered as miracles, what evidence shall suffice to prove these miraculous events? The evidence should be either that of the senses or the best secondary evidence possible. It has been said that "a miracle is no miracle at second-hand;" and it truly would be a difficult matter to satisfy a man by hearsay-testimony that his neighbor had eaten two hundred pounds of tenpenny nails for breakfast with a beneficial effect upon his system. But if such an event could be proved by secondary evidence, that evidence ought to show that the alleged miracle was performed in the presence of many sensible and unprejudiced witnesses, that those witnesses recorded the circumstances of the miracle and published the records at the place and near the time of the per-

formance of the miracle, that those records agreed with each other in the essential points, and that the records were received with respect if not with credit.
That the evidence should prove this much, at least, will be clear to all who are
familiar with history, and who know that several instances have occurred where
the evidence went quite as far as demanded, and yet nobody believes in the pretended miracles, or even thinks seriously on the subject.*

In considering the reports of miracles in ancient times—for no sensible man
believes that any are performed now-a-days—it should be remembered that the
ancients were not acquainted with the natural sciences, and were incompetent
to form clear ideas of the weight of testimony. If a man solemnly asserted that
he had seen a priest raise a dead man to life, his assertion was considered sufficient proof of the event, because every body at that time believed in the power
of working miracles and in the daily occurrence of special providences. It is
only by education that a man learns to judge of probabilities. A child can be
induced to believe almost anything, and the men of ancient times—many even
of the most intelligent—were but children as compared with the men of this
age. The Emperor Julian, one of the earliest writers against Christianity, did
not deny the miracles of Christ, because he did not doubt them. He supposed
that miracles were performed every day. The books of Moses gravely tell us
that the Egyptian priests changed their rods by a word into serpents; and
another biblical writer says that the Witch of Endor raised the dead Samuel
from his grave and caused him to speak to Saul.

Some of Dr. Middleton's remarks on the pretended miracles of the early
Christian Church, will apply quite as well to those of the prophets and apostles:
"Whatever be the uncertainty of ancient history, there is one thing at least
which we may certainly learn from it—that human nature has been always the
same; agitated by the same appetites and passions, and liable to the same
excesses and abuses of them in all ages and countries of the world: so that our
experience of what passes in the present age will be the best comment on what
is delivered to us as concerning the past. To apply it, then, to the case before
us: there is hardly a single fact [fraudulent miracle] which I have charged
upon the primitive times, but what we still see performed in one or other of the
sects of Christians of even our own times. Among some, we see diseases cured,
devils cast out, and all the other miracles which are said to have been wrought
in the primitive Church; among others, we see the boasted gifts of Tertullians'
and Cyprian's days, pretended revelations, prophetic visions and divine impressions. Now, all these modern pretensions we readily ascribe to their true
cause, to the artifices and craft of a few, playing upon the credulity, the superstition and the enthusiasm of the many, for the sake of some private interest."

---

* See Appendix, note 5.

When we read, therefore, that the same things were performed by the ancients, and for the same ends of acquiring a superiority of credit, or wealth or power, over their fellow creatures, how can we possibly hesitate to impute them to the same cause of fraud or imposture?

"In a word, to submit our belief implicitly and indifferently to the mere force of authority in all cases, whether miraculous or natural, without any rule of discerning the credible from the incredible, might support indeed the faith as it is called, but would certainly destroy the use of all history, by leading us into perpetual errors, and possessing our minds with invincible prejudices and false notions both of men and things. But to distinguish between things totally different from each other, between miracle and nature, the extraordinary acts of God and the ordinary transactions of man, to suspend our belief of the one, while, on the same testimony, we grant it freely to the other, and to require a different degree of evidence for each in proportion to the different degrees of their credulity, is so far from hurting the credit of history, or of anything else which we ought to believe, that it is the only way to purge history from its dross, and to render it beneficial to us, and by a right use of our reason and judgment, to raise our minds above the low prejudices and childish superstitions of the credulous vulgar."

Were the miracles reported in the Bible actually performed? The Christian will answer in the affirmative, and in support of them say that the testimony of the word of God is sufficient. But we are now considering whether the Bible is the word of God, and whether the miracles prove it to be so. If the miracles are to prove the inspiration, it will not do to make the inspiration prove them. They must be examined precisely on the same principles as we would examine similar stories in profane books. Let us examine the record of the miracles.

The confusion of tongues is reported by a person who confesses that he knew nothing of the event from his own knowledge, and hearsay testimony will not do for a miracle. We must have at least as good evidence to gain a seat in Heaven as to gain a case in law. Philologists are agreed that the varieties in the languages of the people of Western Asia and Europe were brought about by slow corruptions, proceeding from natural causes only.

The report of the plagues of Egypt (Ex. VII., VIII.,) was not written or published till long after the alleged date of the events.

The report of the arrest of the sun at Joshua's command to permit him to kill the Amorites, (Josh. X., 12–14,) has no title to credence. Such an event could not have happened without a record being made of it in China, Persia, India, and Egypt—countries where astronomy was studied, where observations were taken, and where records were preserved, but where no record is to be found of this miracle. The Chinese books make a genuine report of an eclipse which occurred five hundred years before the time of Joshua.

Joshua stopped the sun; but Isaiah compelled that luminary to turn round and travel backward for more than half an hour in time, and ten degrees in distance, (Is. XXXVIII., 7. 8; 2 K., XX. 8-11). This miracle is reported to have happened only 700 years before Christ; but it wants the confirmation which it would have had, if true, in the records of China, Hindostan, Egypt and Greece.

Matthew (IV. 18, 19) and Mark (I. 16-20) say that Jesus selected Peter as an apostle while the latter was fishing in the sea of Galilee. Luke (V. 1-11) tells of the calling, and *adds* a miraculous draught of fishes. John makes another addition of a miraculous fire to cook the fish, and he also changes the date of the event, and makes it happen after the resurection. John wrote after Luke, and Luke after Mark and Matthew. Hennell remarks: " In such instances the gradual enhancement is very different from wilful falsehood, since the additional particulars doubtless seemed no less probable in themselves than edifying to the Church." It has been by some writers supposed that the Evangelists referred to different miracles, but that supposition is contradicted by similarity of the circumstances as related by the different authors. The scene was at the Sea of Galilee: Peter, James and John were present; they were fishing; Jesus promised that Peter should fish for men; the fishermen forsook all to follow him; when Jesus came they had caught nothing; and Jesus commanded the casting of the net.

Matthew (III. 16,) and Mark (I. 10,) say that when John baptized Jesus, he saw the spirit descending like a dove. Luke (III. 22) says that the spirit descended in a bodily shape like a dove. John (I. 32) adds, that this had been foretold by John the Baptist.

The miracle of turning water into wine, at the marriage in Cana, is reported only by John, (II. 1), though " it did manifest forth the glory" of Jesus. John says: " When they wanted wine, the mother of Jesus saith unto him—' They have no wine.' " On this, Hennell observes: " There is no reason why Jesus should be applied to for wine, which it was the duty of the host to furnish; but however unnatural the application in reality, it was quite natural on the part of the writer who was to prepare the way for the event." Yet even after this miracle, Jesus' relatives, who were present, did not believe on him.

Matthew says (VIII. 15) that Christ healed Peter's wife's mother, and " the fever left her, and she arose and ministered unto them." Mark says, (I. 31), " immediately the fever left her, and she ministered unto them." Luke (IV. 38, 39) says: " it was a great fever," and " immediately she arose and ministered unto them." " Now, the variations," as Hennell remarks, " though perhaps made innocently, are important; for the reality of the miracle depends upon the greatness of the fever and upon the patient's exhibiting immediately some visible sign of recovery, such as rising."

The miracle of the casting out of the demons loses nothing in its progress. Matthew (VIII. 16) says "They brought unto him *many* that were possessed with demons; and he cast out the spirits with his word, and cured all that were sick." Mark says, (I. 32): "They brought unto him *all* that were diseased, and them that were possessed with demons, *and all the city was gathered together at the door*, and he healed *many* that were sick of divers diseases, and cast out many demons, and suffered *not* the demons to speak, because they knew him." Now hear Luke (IV. 40): "*All* they that had any sick with divers diseases brought them unto him, and he laid hands on *every one* of them, and healed them, and demons also came out of many, crying out and saying: 'Thou art Christ, the Son of God;' and he rebuking them, suffered them not to speak, for they knew that he was Christ." Luke's story is clearly marked by the characteristics of priestly fraud.

In Matthew IX., 2–8, a miraculous cure of palsy is related. Christ said to the afflicted man: "'Arise, take up thy bed and go unto thy house;' and he arose and departed to his house." Mark says (II. 12): "And *immediately* he arose, took up the bed and went forth, *before them all*." Luke (V. 25) says: "And immediately he arose up before them, and took up that whereon he lay, and departed to his own house, *glorifying God*."

The miraculous cure of the issue of blood, as related by Matthew, (IX. 20) is considerably stretched by Mark, (V. 25).

Matthew (XIV. 15–22), Luke (IX. 12), and John (VI. 11) tell of a miraculous feeding of five thousand persons; and in Matthew XV. 38, and Mark VIII. 9, it is said that four thousand persons were miraculously fed. These accounts are evidently confused reports of the same tradition or event. That the same event is referred to is clear, because the narratives agree with each other in the order of the speeches and events, and nearly of words; because, according to the latter story, the actors do not remember the first miracle, but ask—"Whence have we bread in the wilderness to satisfy so great a multitude?" and Jesus, in his answer, shows a like unconsciousness of any similar occurrence, because the event occurred near the sea of Galilee in each case; and because, after each miracle, Jesus sends the multitude away, and passes over the sea. Matthew evidently thought that there were two separate miracles, (XVI. 9, 10); while, according to John, (VI. 26, 30–32), both Jesus and the people speak as though there had been no miracle.

Matthew (VIII. 5), and Luke (VII. 1–10), relate the circumstances of a miraculous cure of a Centurion's servant. John relates a similar cure of the son of a nobleman or ruler. All say the event happened at Capernaum soon after the sermon on the mount, and relate the miracle in similar terms, and ascribe nearly the same words to Jesus. Everything goes to show that the Evangelists referred to the same event or report. Matthew describes the sick person in Greek as a *pais* or boy. Luke supposed the boy to be a servant, and called him *doulos*, a servant : and John supposed the boy to be a son, and called him *vios*, a son.

Mark (X. 46–52) relates the miraculous and immediate cure of a blind man by Jesus, while the latter was going *from* Jericho. Luke (XVIII. 35) tells of a cure of a blind man while Jesus was going *to* Jericho. John (IX. 6–11) adds, that the miracle was not immediate, and that the man did not see till he had gone to the pool of Siloam. Matthew has two miraculous cures of two blind men, (IX. 27, XX. 30), in the place of Mark's one cure of one blind man. The expressions and incidents are so similar that they must have been confused accounts of the same affair.

Matthew tells (XVII. 18) of the miraculous and immediate cure of a lunatic; but Mark (IX. 25) says the cure was not immediate.

The barren fig tree, cursed by Christ, withered immediately according to Matthew, (XXI. 19), but Mark says it was found withered the next day.

Luke (XXII. 51) says that Malchus' ear, cut off by Peter, was healed forthwith; but Matthew, (XXVI. 51), Mark (XIV. 47) and John (XVIII. 10) make no mention of the healing.

The assertion made by Luke, (XXII. 43), that an angel appeared in the garden to *strengthen* Jesus (the God) in preparation for the crucifixion, is not corroborated by Matthew, (XXVI. 36), Mark (XIV. 36), or John (XVIII. 1).

John says there was a voice from Heaven (XII. 28, 29), but some thought it was thunder.

Matthew (IX. 18), Mark (V. 22), and Luke (VIII. 41), record the recall of Jairus' daughter to life. These three authors admit that they were not present, but say that John was there. He, however, says nothing about it in his evangel.

The raising of the widow's son at Nain, told by Luke (VII. 11–15), is not mentioned by the other evangelists.

The miracle of recalling the dead Lazarus to life, as narrated by John XI. 43, was the most splendid of all the miracles. The writer does not profess to have been present on the occasion, and the narrative is indirectly contradicted by Matthew (XX. 29–XXI. 1), and Mark (X. 46–XI. 1), and Luke (XIX. 1–37). Hennell says: "Neither Matthew, Mark nor Luke appear to have had any knowledge of the affair; for they are not only silent concerning it, but their accounts do not easily admit of its introduction. John puts the supper at which Lazarus sat after his resurrection, one day before the public entry into Jerusalem. But Matthew, as well as Mark and Luke, makes it appear that Jesus made his entry into Jerusalem on coming direct from Jericho, a distance of about twenty miles; and that after this he took up his abode at Bethany. John's story of Lazarus requires, therefore, another previous abode at Bethany, which breaks in violently upon the order of events in Matthew, whose narrative seems to exclude the possibility of Jesus having already resided for some time so near to Jerusalem as fifteen furlongs. (See Mat. XIX. 1; XX. 18, 29; XXI. 1). The supper at Bethany also is related by Matthew long after the entrance, although he is not precise as to the date, (XXVI. 6). This supper is proved to be the same one at which John says Lazarus was present, by the alabaster box of ointment, and the speech of Judas for the poor. Yet Matthew and Mark seem quite ignorant of that which John says attracted the Jews—the presence of the revived Lazarus. The story of Lazarus seems again to be forced upon the attention of the first three Evangelists, when they relate the entrance of Jesus into Jerusalem, and the conduct of the multitude; for John says that the people bare record of his having raised Lazarus. But here, also, they make not the slightest allusion to it. It is impossible to conceive any plausible reason for this concealment, when the same three Evangelists appear so willing to relate all the miracles they were acquainted with, and actually relate some that were said to be done in secret. That they had all forgotten this miracle so completely, that it did not once occur to them whilst relating the connected circumstances, cannot be imagined; and if any miracle deserved a preference in the eyes of narrators disposed to do honor to Christ, or even to give a faithful account of him, it was this. The Acts and the Epistles no where allude to this story, although it would have afforded Paul a very good instance of the resurrection of the body, (1 Cor. XV. 35). The first mention, therefore, of the most public and decisive of the miracles, appears in a writing published at Epesus, sixty years afterwards—a distance both of time and place, which rendered it easy to publish fictitious statements without fear of contradiction.'"

The transfiguration of Christ is mentioned by Matthew (XVII. 2.), Mark (IX. 2.), and Luke (IX. 28.), but neither one of these was present, while John, who is reported to have been present, says nothing of it. The three Evangelists, who speak of the transfiguration, say that Jesus cautioned those present to keep the event a secret.

Matthew's story (XXVII. 63,) of the guard at Christ's tomb bears the mark of fiction. The Pharisees are made to say:—"We remember that deceiver said while he was yet alive, after three days I will rise again." From John XX. 9, it appears that Jesus never said so even to his disciples. The guard story is not alluded to in any other portion of the New Testament. The disciples did not expect a resurrection (Luke XXIV. 11. Mark XVI. 11. John XX. 29. Matthew XXVIII. 17.), and how should the Pharisees?

The Apostles are said to have been gifted miraculously with the power of speaking various languages, (Mark XVI. 17. 1 Cor. V. 23, XII. 10). Hennell says: "There is no evidence that the Apostles had acquired supernaturally the use of other languages. That generally spoken throughout the eastern provinces of the Roman Empire was the Greek; and owing to the continual intercourse with Roman tax-gatherers and soldiers, even the lower classes of Jews dwelling in towns could not but acquire some rude knowledge of it. Campbell acknowledges that the Greek of the New Testament is a 'barbarous idiom.' 'If any one contends,' says Erasmus, 'that the Apostles were inspired by God, with the knowledge of all tongues, and that this gift was perpetual in them, since everything which is performed by a divine power is more perfect, according St. Chrysoston, than what is performed either in the ordinary course of nature, or by the pains of man, how comes it to pass that the language of the Apostles is not only rough and unpolished, but imperfect: also confused and sometimes even plainly solecising and absurd; for we cannot possibly deny what the fact itself declares to be true.' "

Such are the records of the miracles which deserve a special notice, and not one is sustained by clear and unexceptionable evidence. Hennell objects to the miracles ascribed to Christ:—" That he puts himself on a level with Jewish exorcists, (Mat. XII. 27); that hrecognised the attempts of others as real miracles, (Mark IX. 38, 39,): that he admits there is more difficulty in some miracles than in others (XVII. 2,); that he required faith beforehand, (Mat. IX. 27, 2. Mark VI. 5,); that his answers were of such a nature as to dismiss applicants without injury to his credit, whatever might be the result, (Mat. VII. 13. IX 29. XV. 23, 28. Mark X. 52. John IX. 7). In Matthew and Mark the more decided miracles—such as raising the dead, curing the blind, &c., are admitted to have been done in secret, (Mat. VIII. 4. IX. 30. Mark V. 43. VII. 36.) The miracles were chiefly performed among the country people of Galilee, according to Matthew and Mark. Jesus refused to perform miracles before the Pharisees or learned persons, (Mat XVI. 1-4. Mark VIII. 2. John II. 18, VI. 30.) In most of the narratives the saying of Jesus and the incident leading to it, form the most conspicuous part, and the accompanying miracle is but a brief echo; and none of those on whom the miracles were said to be performed come forward themselves to attest them in the subsequent part of the history, or play any conspicuous part in the affairs of the Church. Besides these things many of the witnesses of Christ's miracles did not believe in him, as appears from the record, (Mat. XI. 20. Mark VI. 52. John VII. 5, XI. 45, 46, XII. 37).

It has already been seen that there is no evidence that any portion of the

New Testament was published at Jerusalem during the generation in which the miracles of Christ are reported to have been done. Neither is there any satisfactory proof that the authors of the New Testament witnessed the miracles; and thus it may be said that two absolutely essential links in the chain of evidence necessary to make a miracle credible, are wanting. But if it were granted, that all four of the Evangelists had personally witnessed the miracles, and had published their evangels on the ground forthwith, the question would arise, is the testimony of four men, not known to us personally, sufficient to prove a miracle? Would the testimony of four priests, that they had seen a marble statue of the Virgin weep watery tears and roll its eyes in agony, carry conviction to the minds of ordinary men? Certainly not, and yet why should more faith be yielded to the assertions of priests of old than to those of the present day? Hume in his "Essay on Miracles," after explaining the evidence that should be required to prove a miracle, continues:—"I am the better pleased with the method of reasoning here delivered, as I think it may serve to confound those dangerous friends or disguised enemies to the Christian religion, who have undertaken to defend it by the principles of human reason; our most holy religion is founded on faith and not on human reason; and it is a sure method of exposing it, to put it to such a trial as it is by no means fitted to endure. To make this more evident, let us examine those miracles related in Scripture; and not to lose ourselves in too wide a field, let us confine ourselves to such as we find in the Pentateuch, which we shall examine according to the principles of these pretended Christians, not as the word or testimony of God himself, but as the production of a mere human writer and historian. Here then we are first to consider a book presented to us by a barbarous and ignorant people, written in an age when they were still more barbarous, and in all probability long after the facts which it relates, corroborated by no concurring testimony, and resembling those fabulous accounts, which every nation gives of its origin. Upon reading this book we find it full of prodigies and miracles. It gives an account of a state of the world and of human nature entirely different from the present, of our fall from that state, of the age of man extending to near a thousand years, of the destruction of the world by a deluge, of the arbitrary choice of one people as the favorites of Heaven—and that people the countrymen of the author—and of their deliverance from bondage by prodigies the most astonishing imaginable. I desire any one to lay his hand upon his heart, and after a serious consideration, declare whether he thinks that the falsehood of such a book, supported by such testimony, would be more extraordinary and miraculous than all the miracles it relates; which is however necessary to make it be received according to the measures of probability. What we have said of miracles may be applied without any variation to

3

prophecies; and indeed all prophecies are real miracles, and as such only can be admitted as proof of any revelation. If it did not exceed the capacity of human nature to foretell human events, it would be absurd to employ any prophecy as argument for a divine mission or authority from Heaven. So, that upon the whole, we may conclude that the Christian religion was not only at first attended with miracles, but even at this day cannot be believed by any reasonable person without one."

Perhaps the reader believes in these miracles of the New Testament; and in that case, for the sake of consistency, he should also believe that miracles are done now-a-days. It is said that the testimony of miracles was necessary to establish Christianity, but that being established the necessity has passed away. The Bible speaks of miracles and divinely inspired prophecies being made every day, or at least frequently, during the whole time covered by the record, more than fifteen hundred years—during a great portion of which time the faith of the people in the divine origin of the Church was not more firm than at present. The skeptical tendency of the present age is evident to all intelligent men; the Bible is losing ground every day; and why should not miracles be done to maintain, as well as to build up a creed? Why were there no miracles done in Europe during the French revolution, when thirty millions of enlightened men deserted the Christian Church, and desecrated the temples of the Lord with heathen mockeries? But when was Christianity established? It gradually extended from the crucifixion of Christ till the beginning of the last century, when it began to lose ground. About the year 1700 then, should be considered the date of its establishment, and yet no enlightened person will consent to believe that the power of working miracles existed until the beginning of the eighteenth century. There is no place to draw the line short of 1700 A. D. But the New Testament does not authorise any line to be drawn. Jesus is represented to have said, (Mark XVI. 17, 18):—"These signs shall follow them that believe: in my name shall they cast out devils: they shall speak with new tongues: they shall take up serpents: and if they drink any deadly thing it shall not hurt them: they shall lay hands on the sick, and they shall recover." The meaning of this sentence is plain—the miraculous power was to follow the faithful forever; and there is nothing in the New Testament to contradict this interpretation. Stephen, Philip, and Paul, who were neither apostles nor disciples of Christ, performed miracles, (Acts VI. 3, 8. VII. 8. XIII. 11. XIV. 8. XIX. 11). Nearly every one of the celebrated fathers of the Christian Church previous to the seventh century recorded or credited a number of miracles. Among those fathers who did so record or credit miracles, were Papias, Justin Martyr, Irenæus, Theophilus, bishop of Antioch, Tertullian, Minucius Felix, Origen, Cyprian, Arnobius, Lactantius, Basil, Chrysostom, Gregory of Nyssa, Diony-

sins, bishop of Alexandria, Athenagoras, Eusebius, Augustine, Hesperius, Athanasius, Epiphanius and Theodoret. All of these persons have been honored with the title of Saint by the Catholic Church, among the members of which during their time, they had no superiors in intelligence or ability; and most of them left writings of importance to show that the gospel is now preserved as it was in their time. These numerous authors, whose works have far better evidences for their authenticity than there are for the reputed evangels of Matthew, Mark, Luke, and John, corroborate each other in regard to the power of the Church to perform miracles, and in regard to the frequency of miracles; and if these two points be well established, there can be little difficulty about accepting particular miracles. But when the nature of the miracles witnessed by these saints is explained, our faith in both saints and miracles must become faint. Chrysostom, Basil, Jerome, and Augustine, four of the greatest men of the primitive Church, exalt the miraculous power of relics, and it was by these saints as a class, that monkery, the worship of relics, the invocation of saints, prayers for the dead, image worship, the sacraments, the sign of the cross, and the use of consecrated oil were introduced. Gibbon, in the "Decline and Fall," * has occasion to say:—"The grave and learned Augustine, whose understanding scarcely admits the excuse of credulity, has attested the innumerable prodigies which were performed in Africa by the relics of St. Stephen; and this marvellous narrative is inserted in the elaborate work of the City of God, which the bishop of Hippo designed as a solid and immortal proof of the truth of Christianity. Augustine solemnly declares that he has selected those miracles only, which were publicly certified by persons who were either the objects or the spectators of the power of the martyr. * * * The bishop enumerates above seventy miracles, of which three were resurrections from the dead in two years, and within the limits of his own diocese. * * * The knowledge of foreign languages was frequently communicated to the contemporaries of Irenæus, though Irenæus himself was left to struggle with the difficulties of a barbarous dialect, whilst he preached the gospel to the natives of Gaul. * *
* The miraculous cure of diseases of the most inveterate or even of preternatural kind, can no longer occasion any surprise, when we recollect that in the days of Irenæus, about the end of the second century, the resurrection of the dead was very far from being considered an uncommon event: that the miracle was frequently performed on necessary occasions, by great fasting and the[?]at joint supplication of the church of the place, and that the persons thus restored[?] to their prayers had lived afterwards among them many years." all

What may be proved by a miracle? A miracle may prove that the doer had supernatural power to do the miraculous act. If a man should do many mi-

---

* Chap. XXVIII

racles, it might be inferred that he possessed and would continue to possess the supernatural power of working such miracles as he had wrought. But the possession of *that* supernatural power would not suffice to prove the possession of all supernatural powers, or of any other superhuman powers. It would not prove him to be sharper sighted, wiser, or more learned than other men. It would not prove that everything he should say would be true. There is no necessary connection between a man's truthfulness and power: and this doctrine is repeatedly recognised in the Bible, where it is said that bad men or idolators have wrought miracles. Then it follows that miracles cannot prove the Bible to be true. Morell says:—"Miracles had nothing immediately to do with inspiration; miraculous powers on the one side are no positive proof of their agent being inspired: thus inspiration on the one side is admitted to exist, where no miraculous powers have been granted. * * * It appears that the one gift was not necessarily connected with the other; that miracles while they evinced a divine commission did not prove the infallibility of the agent as a teacher; that they were in fact separate arrangements of Providence, each having its own purpose to perform, and each requiring a special capacity to perform them. The one demanded an extraordinary physical power—the other a mental and moral enlightenment: and so little are those two qualities regarded in the Bible, as vouchers for each other, that the former is often described as being exercised by evil men, and even by Satan himself." If miraculous evidence cannot prove the Bible to be true, it follows that any appeal to such evidence is discreditable, and unworthy of an upright and dignified source, not to speak of an immediate divine one.

PROPHECIES.

XXV. The Bible is said to contain many prophecies,—predictions of events undiscoverable to human foresight when the predictions were made,—and therefore proof that the prophets were possessed of superhuman knowledge; that they were divinely inspired, and that their teachings as explained in the Bible were true. Before a prophecy be received as of divine origin, it should appear on examination that the prophecy, including the date of the promised fulfilment, was expressed in clear terms; that it was made before the event foretold; that the event foretold was not discoverable to human foresight; and that the special prediction, as well as all others from the same source, was literally fulfilled. There have been pretended prophets in all ages, and in all countries, professing to be possessed of divine knowledge, and teaching very different religious doctrines; and their impostures were maintained by delivering their oracles in ambiguous phrases, which could be interpreted either way to suit the event. Nearly five hundred years before Christ, the Athenians sent to the heathen oracle at Delphi, to learn how they could best resist the great invasion of the Persians, who were approaching. The oracle advised the Athenians to trust in wooden walls. This advice was not explicit, but the Athenians understood it to be a promise that they should succeed by relying upon their navy; and the Greeks were all convinced, by the battle of Salamis, of what they never doubted before, that the oracle of Delphi was possessed of more than human foreknowledge. Grote relates the following instance of ancient prophecy:—"Crœsus sent to inquire of the Oracle of Apollo at Delphi, whether he should undertake an expedition against Cyrus. The reply was that if he did, he would subvert a mighty empire. He sent again and enquired whether his empire would be durable. The reply was:—'When a mule shall become king of the Medes then thou must run away.' Crœsus attacked Cyrus, was defeated, made a prisoner, and his kingdom was subjected to the Medes and the Persians. He accused the Oracle with falsehood, but the reply was that:—'When the god told him he would subvert a mighty empire, it was his

duty to inquire which empire the god meant? and if he neither understood the
meaning nor chose to ask for information, he had himself to blame for the result.
Besides, Crœsus neglected the warning given to him about the acquisition of the
Median kingdom by a mule.   Cyrus was that mule—son of a Median mother, of
royal breed, by a Persian father, at once of a different race and of lower position.'
This triumphant justification extorted even from Crœsus himself, a full confession that the sin lay with him, and not with the god."   One more example
of a supposed divine prophecy, of which thousands could be produced.
We quote now from Gibbon :—" In a very long discourse on the evidences of
the divine authority of the gospel, which is still extant, Constantine [the Emperor who first made Christianity respectable and legal in Rome] dwells with
peculiar complacency on the Sibylline verses and the fourth eclogue of Virgil.
Forty years before the birth of Christ, the Mantuan bard, as if inspired by the
celestial muse of Isaiah, had celebrated with all the pomp of oriental metaphor
the return of the Virgin, the fall of the serpent, the approaching birth of a god-
like child, the offspring of the great Jupiter, who should expiate the guilt of
the human kind, and govern the peaceful universe with the virtues of his father :
the rise and appearance of a heavenly race, a primitive nation throughout the
world, and the gradual restoration of the innocence and felicity of the golden
age. The poet was perhaps unconscious of the secret sense and object of these
sublime predictions, which have been so unworthily applied to the infant son
of a consul or a triumvir ; but if a more splendid and indeed specious interpretation of the fourth eclogue contributed to the conversion of the first Christian
Emperor, Virgil may deserve to be ranked among the most successful missionaries of the gospel."   Such are the records of an infinitely small portion of
the fraud and credulity of former times : and when it is known that men have
been frequently misled in a certain road, all subsequent passers-by should exercise an especial vigilance to avoid falling into the same error.

ALLEGED PROPHECIES OF JESUS.

XXVI. The Apostles believed that the strongest proof of Christ's divine mission was contained in the fulfilment of a large number of prophecies, by his coming, (Luke XXIV. 25, 44; Acts III. 18; XVII. 2–11; II. 16; VII. 52; VIII. 35; X. 43; XIII. 27; XVIII. 28; XXVI, 22; XXVIII. 23; 1 Cor. XV. 3). Jesus appealed to the prophecies for proof of his mission, (John V. 39; Luke XXIV. 25–27). "The greatest proofs of Jesus Christ," says Pascal, "are the prophecies, and thus God foreordained; for the fulfilment of the prophecies is a miracle subsisting from the beginning of the church to the end. * * * If one man alone had made a book predicting successfully the time and the manner of the coming of Jesus Christ, the evidence would have been infinite. But in the Bible there is much more. Here was a succession of men for four thousand years, who constantly, without variation, arise one after another, to predict the same event. The announcement is made by an entire people, which subsists for four thousand years to bear testimony to Him, and from that testimony they could not be turned by any threats or persecution."

We will examine these wonderful prophecies, beginning with those upon which the great Pascal laid so much stress.

Matthew says, (I. 23): "Now all this was done that it might be fulfilled, which was spoken of the Lord, by the prophet, saying, behold a virgin shall be with child, and shall bring forth a son, and they shall call his name Emmanuel, which being interpreted is God with us." The reference is undoubtedly to Isaiah VII. 14, "Therefore the Lord himself shall give you a sign: behold a virgin shall conceive and bear a son, and shall call his name Immanuel. Butter and honey shall he eat, that he may know to refuse the evil and choose the good. For, before the child shall know to refuse the evil and choose the good, the land that thou abhorrest shall be forsaken of both her kings." Isaiah evidently spoke of his own times and of his own child, (VIII. 3, 4). Such is the first of the boasted prophecies of Christ in the Jewish Scriptures, appealed to in the New Testament, and all the rest are no better. The allusions by the Evangelists to prophecies in the Old Testament of the coming of Christ, are so numerous and so plainly erroneous, that they scarcely deserve to be considered separately.

Matthew's second reference (II. 6) to a Messianic prediction in the Hebrew Scriptures, speaks of a promised "ruler in Israel." The alleged prophecy was in Micah, (V. 2), but the latter author spoke of a ruler to deliver "us from the Assyrians." Christ was neither a ruler in Israel nor a conqueror of the Assyrians.

Matthew (II. 15) finds his third big trump in Hosea (XI. 1), who says, "When *Israel* was a child, then I loved him, and called my son out of Egypt." It might be a question whether the writer of Matthew could possibly have claimed this as a prophecy of Christ, under the delusions of superstitious ignorance, free from any consciousness or suspicion of fraud. Hosea is plainly speaking of the Jewish nation alone. Strauss says: "Not a little courage was necessary to apply the first part of that sentence to the Jews under Moses, and the latter part to Jesus, but Matthew did it."

Matthew (II. 17), says that Jeremiah (XXXI. 15) in speaking of "Rachel weeping for her children," foretold the weeping of the women of Judea for their children massacred by Herod. The Hebrew priest was really writing of the sorrows of his people in the Babylonian captivity. Everything goes to show that the pretended prophecy was an allusion to the past.

Matthew says (II. 23) that Christ was a Nazarene, in accordance with prophecy. There is no parallel passage in the Bible. In Judges XIII. 7, it is said that Samson "shall be a Nazarite to God," but there is no perceptible connexion between Christ and Samson, so far as such a prophecy is concerned.

Matthew (III. 2) says: "For this [John the Baptist] is he that was spoken of by the prophet Esaias, saying, "The voice of one crying in the wilderness, Prepare the way of the Lord, make his paths straight." This passage is found in Isaiah (XL. 3), but there is nothing to mark the sentence as peculiarly applicable to any one person, and it might as well be applied to any pretended forerunner of a pretended Messiah, as to John the Baptist. The writer of Isaiah in writing the verse, meant evidently to " give a joyful exhortation to the Jews on their return from captivity."

There is a reference in Matthew IV. 13 to Isaiah IX. 1 as prophetic, but the Hebrew evidently referred to the past time of Josiah. Compare Isa. VIII. 19—IX. 7, with 2 K. XXIII. 24, 25.

Matthew says, (VIII. 16, 17), "that it might be fulfilled which was spoken by Esaias the prophet, saying, Himself took our infirmities, and bare our sickness." Isaiah says, (LIII. 4): "Hereby he hath borne our griefs and carried our sorrows; yet we did esteem him stricken, smitten of God, and afflicted." Everything alludes to something in the past—nothing to fix the application upon a' person in the future; nothing to distinguish whether the bearer of the sorrows was or was to be, a king, a savior, a prophet, or a nation itself. Was Jesus "smitten of God," afflicted by himself?

Matthew (XII. 13) quotes Isaiah (XLII. 1): "Behold my servant, whom I have chosen: my beloved, in whom my soul is well pleased. I will put my spirit upon him, and he shall show judgment to the Gentiles," &c. The servant in this case could not well be a person of the Godhead, while it might be applied very properly to the Jewish people as a body. See Isa. XLI. 8; XLII. 19, 25; XLIII. 1.

The Evangelist (Mat. XIII. 14) applies to his own time a saying evidently written by Isaiah (VI. 9), with reference to the time preceding the captivity. See VI. 1–11.

A saying of Isaiah (XXIX. 13) that the devotion of the Jews to their religion was only outward, intended to refer to ancient time, is tortured (Mat. XV. 7) into a prophecy. There is nothing to show a prediction peculiarly applicable to Christ or his times, while in chapter XXX. of Isaiah the people are reproved for seeking assistance from Egypt.

Mat. XXI. 4, "All this [the entry into Jerusalem] was done that it might be fulfilled which was spoken by the prophet, saying, Tell ye the daughter of Sion, behold thy king cometh unto thee, meek and sitting upon an ass, and a colt, the foal of an ass." The alleged prophecy is found in Zechariah (IX. 9), and refers to Zerubbabel. See Zech. III. 8, 9—IV. 6-10—VI. 11-13.

Matthew (XXVI. 31) says: "Then saith Jesus unto them, all ye shall be offended because of me this night, for it is written, I will smite the shepherd, and the sheep of the flock shall be scattered abroad." The alleged prophecy is found in Zechariah XIII. 7: "Awake, O sword, against my shepherd, and against the man that is my fellow, saith the Lord of Hosts; smite the shepherd, and the sheep shall be scattered; and I will turn mine hand upon the little ones." The writer refers to the miseries of the captivity, as appears very plainly from the context, more particularly the two verses following those quoted. The phrase, "the man that is my fellow," means the man that resides in Jerusalem, the fellow citizen of Jehovah.

"All this [the arrest of Jesus] was done," says Matthew, (XXVI. 56), "that the Scriptures of the prophets should be fulfilled." There is no such prophecy in the Jewish Scriptures.

Matthew says, (XXVII. 9), that the thirty pieces of silver paid for the treachery of Judas, and the potters' field were foretold by Jeremiah. The only corresponding passage is in Zechariah, (XI. 12, 13), but there is nothing to give the passage a prophetic character, or to make it applicable to Christ. Besides the story of the thirty pieces of silver and the potters' field rests entirely in the faith of Matthew, who finds in them a fulfilment of prophecy.

Such are the prophecies so confidently appealed to by Matthew, and not one of them has a clearly prophetic character, or can be restricted in its meaning to Christ, or was understood among the Jews to have the meaning given to it among the Christians. The prophecies appealed to by the other Evangelists are similar in character, and they do not deserve a lengthy consideration. If, however, any one be curious to see the passages in Mark, Luke, John and the Acts referring to prophecies in the Old Testament, he can find them by the following references:

Compare Mark I. 2, with Malachi III., IV.
"　　　　Mark XV. 28, with Isaiah LIII. 12, XIII.
"　　　　Luke I. 69, II. 32, with Isaiah XLII. 6, XLIX. 6, XIII.
"　　　　Luke IV. 17, 18, with Isaiah XLI. 1, 4.
"　　　　Luke VII. 27, with Malachi III. 1.
"　　　　Luke XXIV. 27, 44, John I. 45, with Deut. XVIII. 15, Hosea VI. 1, 2.
"　　　　John VII. 41, with Micah V. 2, 6.
"　　　　John XII. 37, with Isaiah LIII, 2 Ch. XXXVI. 20, 21.
"　　　　John XIX. 24, 28, 29, with Ps. XXII. 16, 18, LXIX. 21.
"　　　　John XIX. 33–36, with Ex. XII. 46.
"　　　　John XIX. 37, with Zech. XII. 10.
"　　　　John XX. 10. No parallel passage.
"　　　　Acts I. 16, 20, with Ps. LXIX, CIX.
"　　　　Acts II. 16, with latter part of Joel.
"　　　　Acts II. 25, with Ps. XVI., CXXXII. 11.
"　　　　Acts III. 24, 25. No parallel passage.
"　　　　Acts IV. 25, with Ps. IL, LXXXIX. 20, 27.
"　　　　Acts VIII. with Is. LIII.
"　　　　Acts X. 43. No parallel passage.
"　　　　Acts XIII. 27, with Dan. IX. 26.
"　　　　Acts XIII. 32, with Ps. II., LXXXIX.
"　　　　Acts XV. 15, with Amos IX. 11, 12.

The errors of the New Testament writers in the allusions to these passages as prophecies, are so evident, that the Church has been sorely troubled to get over them. About a century ago, Whiston, an ardent believer, and the successor of Sir Isaac Newton in his mathematical professorship, published a book to prove that the Jews, during the early ages of the Christian Church, had fraudulently altered the passages of the Old Testament referred to as prophecies of Christ, by the Evangelists. The skeptics replied, that if such were the fact, the Old Testament was not reliable on any point. Whiston's theory was widely received as correct, until a comparison of all the ancient copies of the Jewish Scriptures showed them to be all alike in the alleged predictions. Another theory was that the Old Testament passages referred to had two meanings, one historical and the other prophetic. Palfrey, (Ev. Ch. Lec. XVIII), who has a great deal to say on this question, admits, (and the same thing has been admitted by some of the ablest Christian authors): "The New Testament writers did sometimes interpret the Old Testament erroneously." He also says: "The theory of a double sense, less esteemed now than formerly in any quarter, appears to me to be justly liable to the charge of violating all the principles of language, and of being in fact the theory of no definite sense whatsoever."

PROPHECIES OF A ROYAL MESSIAH.

XXVII. It is not to be denied that many of the Old Testament writers foretold the coming of a Messiah, an anointed person, who was to be not a religious teacher or reformer, but a king destined to relieve the Jews from captivity and restore the nation to its former prosperity and greatness. Accordingly, the Messiah was not to come from the stock of Levi—the family of priests who were to serve the Jews as divine intercessors forever, and were to have Jehovah for their exclusive inheritance—but from the stock of David, the royal family, who had furnished all the kings of Judah subsequent to the time of Saul, and to whom the throne of Judea had been promised as an eternal possession. The Evangelists do not refer to, or lay any stress upon, the true prophecies of the Messiah; (Is. II. 2–4; Jer. XXXI. 31–40; Ezek. XI. 19–29; XXXVI. 26–38; Micah. IV. 1–10; Haggai, II. 6–9; Zech. XII. 10–XIV. 19; Mal. III. 1). The Evangelists do lay particular stress upon the fact that the Messiah was to be a descendant of David, and they attempt to show that Jesus was a descendant from their great king; but their showing fails completely in its purpose. If we accept the New Testament as true, there is not the slightest proof that Jesus had a particle of the blood of David in his veins. Matthew and Luke give each a genealogy to show the descent of Jesus, but these genealogies are irreconcilable with each other, and, if true, they prove only that Joseph—who was in nowise related by blood to Jesus—was the descendant of David. Matthew begins at Abraham, comes down through David, and says

"Jacob begat Joseph, the husband of Mary," (L. 16). Luke begins at Jesus, supposed to be "the son of Joseph, which was the son of Heli," through whom the genealogy, with names almost entirely different from those given by Matthew, is carried up to David, and thence to Adam. But it is asserted that Matthew means to say that Heli was the father, not of Joseph, but of Mary. This theory might avoid the difficulty of the inconsistencies, as well as account for the Davidical blood of Jesus, but unfortunately there is no proof to support the theory. The Evangelists could not have used plainer language, than they have used, in a straightforward narrative to assert the descent of Joseph from David. Matthew tells us (I. 20) that an angel appeared to Joseph and said, "thou son of David," and Luke says (I. 27) that Jesus was born of "a *virgin* espoused to a man whose name was Joseph, *of the house of David.*" The blood of Joseph, about which so much is said, has nothing to do with the matter, if Jesus was not his natural son; while there is not a word in the New Testament, at least not one now known to the writer, to show that Mary was of the house of David. It has been thought by many free-thinkers that Jesus never laid claim to divinity; he certainly does not make any such claim expressly or by necessary implication in the words ascribed to him by the Evangelists; and the inconsistency about his Davidical descent just referred to, may be explained by supposing that the gospels were written by persons who believed Jesus to be a man, and were subsequently corrupted to make him a God.

PROPHECIES OF ISAIAH.

XXVIII. The fifty-third chapter of Isaiah is generally looked upon by the Christian church, and has been declared by Paley, to contain the clearest and strongest prophetic passages in the Old Testament, evidently foretelling the advent, character and fate of Jesus. Before and after this chapter the Hebrew priest speaks of Jacob or Israel, and it is reasonable to suppose, if the context will admit the supposition, that his subject is the same in all these chapters, and that he would not change from history to prophecy and from prophecy to history, without some clear intimation. The first verse of chapter fifty-two begins by speaking of the "servant" of the Lord, interpreted to mean Jesus, who was no servant, if he was a God. The Septuagint translation, made 270 B. C., differs slightly from the Hebrew version, and says, "Jacob is my servant," thus showing very plainly that the ancient Jews saw no prophecy of a Messiah in that passage. Chapter fifty-second goes on to describe the servant as mute, humble and firm in his faith, and so the Israelites were during their captivity. In verse nineteenth the servant is described as "blind," which Jesus was not. In verse twentieth he is said to see without observing, and to open his ears without hearing; and these terms cannot be applied to Christ. In verse twenty-second the servant is said to be "robbed and spoiled." In chapter fifty-third the writer describes him in captivity like a plant on a barren soil, "despised," "rejected," "smitten of God," "wounded for our [the Jews'] transgressions," "silent in his affliction, cut off from the land of the living, [Judea] buried with the wicked, [in Babylon] whom it pleased the Lord to bruise, but who should see his seed, and whose days should be prolonged There is, in fact, in the whole chapter not a verse which may not be applied a appropriately to the Jewish nation as to Jesus.

PROPHECIES OF DANIEL.

XXIX. The eighth chapter of Daniel is reputed to contain some of the most remarkable prophecies in the Bible. Hennell says, it gives "an account of a vision of a ram with two horns, which was smitten by a he-goat having a notable horn between his eyes, which horn being broken, four other notable horns came up toward the four winds of heaven. The chapter itself informs us that by this was meant the conquest of the kings or kingdoms of Media and Persia, by the king of Grecia; the first great horn being the first king, viz.: Alexander the Great, and the four notable horns after him, four kingdoms, which shall stand up out of the nation, but not in his power, i. e., plainly the four Macedonian monarchies of Thrace, Macedon, Syria, and Egypt. So far this vision is clear, and commentators agree. But Daniel sees coming out of the four notable horns a little horn, which plays a very conspicuous part, and to determine who the little horn is, forms the great problem of the book of Daniel. Josephus understood it to mean Antiochus Epiphanes; according to Jerome it was Antiochus as a type of Anti-Christ. Sir Isaac Newton thought it meant the Romans. Bishop Newton thought it meant first the Romans and afterwards the popes." Many biblical critics believe that the book of Daniel was written after the time of Alexander.

REVELATIONS.

XXX. The only book in the Bible making pretensions to be purely prophetic, is Revelations, and it is the most obscure portion of the Scripture. No interpretation has ever been offered that could find acceptation among any large portion of the Christian church. Nearly every prominent commentator on the Bible has had his own theory of the meaning of the Apocalypse, and these theories have been in many cases most inconsistent with each other. Alexander says that the book is "deeply mysterious,"—that is to say, nobody knows what it means. Milman candidly confesses "it is to be feared that a history of the interpretation of the Apocalypse would not give a very favorable view either of the wisdom or of the charity of the successive ages of Christianity." Sir Isaac Newton, a very devout Christian, acknowledges that there are no true prophecies in the Bible, when he says, "God gave these [Revelations] and the prophecies of the Old Testament, not to satisfy men's curiosity by enabling them to foreknow things, but that after they were fulfilled they might be interpreted by the event; and His prescience, not that of the interpreter, be then manifested thereby to the world."

FALSE PROPHECIES.

XXXI. There are many false prophecies in the Bible; and that fact, once established, would suffice to destroy all faith in the successful predictions, if there were any. We shall give the principal of the false biblical prophecies within as small a compass as possible.

Jehovah repeatedly promised that the family of David should possess the throne of Judea forever. See 1 K. II. 33; VIII. 25; 1 Ch. XVII. 12–14, 23; XXVIII. 4; 2 Ch. VI. 16; Ps. LXXXIX. 4, 29, 36; CXXXII. 12.

The prophet says in 1 Ch. XVII. 12, "he [Solomon] shall build me an house and I will establish his throne forever." " I will settle him in mine house, and in my kingdom forever; and his throne shall be established forever more." Solomon, in his prayer at the dedication of the temple, (1 K. VIII. 25) said, "Therefore now, Lord God of Israel, keep with thy servant David my father that thou promisedst him, saying there shall not fail thee a man in my sight to sit on the throne of Israel." David said on a previous occasion, (1 Ch. XXVIII. 4) "Howbeit the Lord God of Israel chose me before all the house of my father to be king over Israel forever." Christian writers claim that these passages were intended to foretell only the everlasting dominion of Christ, the descendant of David, the religious reformer, the usurper of the place of the Levites. Such an interpretation may be necessary in those who pretend to believe that the Bible is the word of God, but it unfortunately is not supported by the letter or spirit of the Old Testament. Besides, where was the throne of David for five centuries before Christ? And where will be the dominion of Christ in a century from this time? Probably not in any enlightened country.

Jehovah and Canaan should be Israel's forever. Moses represents his deity as saying to Abram, "I will give to thee and to thy seed after thee the land wherein thou art a stranger, all the land of Canaan for an everlasting possession, and I will be their God." Gen. XVII. 8; XIII. 15; Ps. CV.

Jerusalem should be the seat of the Lord forever. 2 Ch. XXXIII. 4, 7; Ps. CXXXII. 4.

The Levites should minister to the Lord forever. 1 Ch. XV. 2.

The Israelites should dwell in Jerusalem forever. 1 Ch. XXIII. 25.

Judah should possess Hebron forever. Josh. XIV. 9.

Solomon's temple should be holy forever. 1 K. IX. 3; 2 Ch. VII. 16; XXXIII. 7.

All nations should be afraid of Israel. Deut. XXVIII. 10.

Israel should be high above all nations in name and in praise and in honor. Deut. XXVI. 19.

No king after Solomon should have such wealth and honor as he had.* 2 Ch. I. 12

Judah and Israel should unite. Ezek. XXXVII. 22.

The Israelites should be as numerous as the dust of the earth. Gen. XIII. 16.

The Levites should be perfect. Deut. XVIII. 13.

Nineveh should be immediately destroyed. Jonah III. 4, 10.

Rome should be totally destroyed. Rev. XVIII. 22.

Damascus should be a city no more, but should be reduced to a "ruinous heap." Is. XVII. 1.

Egypt should be conquered by Nebuchadnezzar. Jer. XLIII. 11; Ezek. XXIX. 19; XXX. 12; XXXII. 11, 12.

"No foot of man shall pass through it, [Egypt] nor foot of beast shall pass through it, neither shall it be inhabited for forty years." Ezek. XXIX. 11.

Jeremiah cursed king Jehoiakim and foretold that his dead body should be cast out to the dogs, and that he should have none to sit on the throne of David. Jer. XXII. 18, 19; XXXVI. 30. Jehoiakim, after death, "slept with his fathers, and Jehoiachin, his son, reigned in his stead." 2 K. XXIV. 6.

Jeroboam should die by the sword. Amos VII. 11. Compare with 2 K. XIV. 29.

Tyre should be destroyed within seventy years. Is. XXIII. 11, 17. That city was large and prosperous for more than 300 years after the alleged date of Isaiah's book.

Mount Seir shall be perpetual desolation. Ezek. XXXV. 9.

Jehovah said, "I will wipe Jerusalem as a man wipeth a dish, he wipeth it and turneth it upside down." 2 K. XXI. 13.

There should "no more be a prince of Egypt," and the idols of the Egyptians should be destroyed. Ezek. XXIX. 30. There were princes of Egypt for more than 300 years after Ezekiel, and idols still longer.

Jehovah should scrape the dust from Tyre and make her like the top of a rock, according to some writer who interpolated the book of Ezekiel. Tyre was destroyed 300 years after Ezekiel.

Isaiah foretold (Ch. XIII.) that Babylon should never be inhabited, but should be the abode of wild beasts. Babylon was a great city for several centuries after Isaiah's time.

Christ's kingdom was to appear at Jerusalem during the first century. Mat. XXIV. 30–34; Mark XIII. 29, 30; Luke XVII. 22–37; XIX. 11; XXIV. 21; XXI. 5–36.

This prediction of the immediate coming of Christ is the most important prophecy in the Bible. It is clear as language can make it, and the sincere Christians of the first century were constantly looking for doomsday, like the crazy Millerites in our own times. Matthew says, (XXIV. 30, 31,) "And then shall appear the sign of the son of man in heaven; and then shall all the tribes of the earth mourn, and they shall see the son of man coming in the clouds of heaven with power and great glory, and he shall send his angels with a great sound of a trumpet, and they shall gather together his elect from the four winds, from one end of heaven to the other." * * * " Verily I say unto you, This generation shall not pass till all these things be fulfilled." (V. 34). Mark and Luke are equally explicit.

THE MORALITY OF THE BIBLE.

XXXII. After the miraculous evidence, as it is styled, was attacked so successfully that it lost most of its weight, the advocates of Christianity placed their main reliance upon the testimony furnished by the " perfect morality " of the Gospel in favor of the divine inspiration of its authors. Little praise is given however to the moral precepts of the Old Testament, or rather the subject is studiously avoided, for the very good reason that the Hebrew prophets had very crude notions of human rights and duties.

Moses legalized slavery. In Leviticus, XXV. 44–46, he says, of " the heathens that are round about you," and " of the children of strangers that do sojourn among you" " shall ye buy" and " they shall be your bond-men forever; but over your brethren, the children of Israel, ye shall not rule over one another with rigor." It appears from Exodus, XXI. 7, that Hebrew women were held in perpetual slavery, and the inference may justly be drawn from Deuteronomy (XXI. 14) that the enslaved Hebrew women, if not married to their masters, might be legally sold to any Israelite.   There are many passages going to show that slavery existed among the Hebrews, that it was recognised by the priests as lawful and right: and the Bible in no place expressly forbids human bondage. This omission to forbid slavery is in itself equivalent to an acknowledgment that the institution is proper.   The Bible claims to be a complete guide for all the moral actions which man is called upon to perform.   Such a guide cannot be complete unless it expressly forbid those great sins which are most common among men.   Moses saw fit to denounce murder, theft, perjury, blasphemy, idol-worship, Sabbath breaking, and many minor and even insignificant offences, but slavery is repeatedly mentioned without a word of discountenance.

Polygamy and concubinage were both sanctioned by the practice, and not forbidden by the law of the Jews. See Gen. XX. 17; XXX. 39; Ex. XXI. 8; Num. XXXI. 3, 17, 18; Deut. XX. 13; XXI. 11; Judg's XIX. 2; 2 S. III. 2; XX. 3; 2 Ch. XI. 21; 1 K. XI. 3.   In the eighteenth chapter of Leviticus, Moses takes occasion to spend his wrath very freely upon those who indulge in unlawful amorous delights, but there is nothing said against the possession of scores of wives or concubines.

The Jewish law allowed, and Jewish custom required the nearest relative of a man who had been killed, to follow and assassinate the homicide, even if the latter was excusable or even justifiable in the killing.   Kitto* remarks: " The Mosaical law (Num. XXXV. 31) expressly forbids the acceptance of a ransom for the forfeited life of a murderer, although it might be saved by his seeking an asylum at the altar of the tabernacle, in case the homicide was accidentally committed, (Ex. XXI. 13; 1 K. I. 50; II. 28).   If, however, after Judaism had been fully developed, no other sanctuary had been tolerated but that of the temple at Jerusalem, the chances of escape of such a homicide from the hands of the avenger ere he reached the gates of the temple, must have become less in proportion to the distance of the spot, where the murder was committed, from Jerusalem; six cities of refuge were therefore appointed for the momentary safety of the murderer, in various parts of the kingdom, the roads to which were kept in good order to facilitate escape.   Thither the avenger durst not follow him, and there he lived in safety until a proper examination had taken place before the authorities in order to ascertain whether the murder was a wilful act or not.   In the former case he was instantly delivered up to the *goel*, or avenger of blood, against whom not even the altar could protect him, (Ex. XXI. 14; 1 K. II. 29); in the latter case, though he was not actually delivered into the hands of the *goel*, he was, notwithstanding, not allowed to quit the precincts of the town, but was obliged to remain there all his lifetime, or till the death of the high priest."

---

* Popular Cyclopedia of Biblical Literature, by Bishop Kitto.

There are a few precepts of a high morality scattered through the Pentateuch, but they are completely lost in the great mass of grosser matter. The teaching, "love thy neighbor as thyself" is most effectively contradicted, and its influence for good destroyed, by its insertion in the midst of such a multitude of priestly rules as are contained in Leviticus. The pervading spirit of the Old Testament is wrong. The book was the work of rude men in a rude age, when every tribe in Western Asia had its exclusive language or dialect; when, for want of a common language, and in the absence of commercial relations, there was little friendly intercourse between foreign nations, and when each tribe had its separate priesthood which found its interest in discouraging all mixture with foreign nations. The Bible has no regard for the rights or feelings of the Gentiles; they might be held in bondage forever, their land and cities might be taken, the men, if obstinate, were to be slaughtered, and even the friendly strangers in Jerusalem might be swindled into buying for provision the meat of animals that had died by disease. The Jews, though the favorites of Heaven, were governed according to a code far more bloody and illiberal than that which prevailed among the more civilized nations of the same ages. Morell acknowledges that " an imperfect morality is plainly discernible throughout the period of the Old Testament dispensation, and frequently embodied too in the Old Testament Scriptures. The fierce spirit of warfare, the law of retaliation, the hatred of enemies, the curses and imprecations poured upon the wicked, the practice of polygamy, the frequent indifference to deception to compass any desirable purposes, the existence of slavery, the play, generally speaking, given to the stronger passions of our nature—all these bespeak a tone of moral feeling far below that which Christianity has unfolded." Even if the writings of Moses and the other Jewish prophets had not expressly taught the Hebrews to systematically violate the rights of the poor and strange persons, yet the lineaments in which Jehovah and his favorites are painted would be enough to show that no high morality could prevail where these Scriptures were received as divine. The Mosaic Deity was a cruel, blood-thirsty, vindictive, changeable, deceitful character, who delighted in slaying tens of thousands to avenge a fancied insult, or in leading his blind worshippers to slay the males and married women and carry off into captivity and concubinage the unprotected virgins of some heathen tribe.

The morality of Jesus is full of mildness and universal love and charity. A common expression among Christian writers is, that his moral precepts are sufficient in themselves to prove his divine mission and to entitle the Bible to our belief and reverence. Many of the greatest and purest free-thinkers have not hesitated to declare that there were no rules of moral conduct equal to those contained in the Sermon on the Mount. Hennell, Franklin, Strauss, Rousseau,

Goethe, Voltaire, Paine and Rammohun Roy, while opposing the Christian Church, have all expressed their admiration of the moral character of Jesus.*

.And yet, in the face of all this authority, I venture to contend that the moral teachings of Jesus are highly objectionable, and that no man can live by them, or should endeavor to live by them. They are indeed mild and kind in spirit, but they err as much in inculcating humility, as did Moses upon the other side in encouraging his followers to hate and despise and avoid all Gentiles. The founder of Christianity could not tolerate the old Hebrew law of "an eye for an eye," and "a tooth for a tooth," and blood for blood—even if the first blood had been shed accidentally or justifiably; but he taught that the child must submit to the parent, the wife to the husband, the servant and the slave to the master, and the subject to the ruler; and all this unconditionally. His teaching will appear more clearly from the texts:

Children must obey their parents—Eph. VI. 1; Col. III. 20.

Servants must obey their masters—Eph. VI. 5–7; Col. III. 22; 1 Tim. VI. 1; Titus II. 9; 1 Peter II. 11.

"Servants obey *in all things* your masters." Col. III. 22.

"Let as many servants as are under the yoke count their own masters as worthy of all honor." 1 Tim. VI. 1.

"Exhort servants to be obedient to their own masters, and to please them well in all things." Titus II. 9.

"Servants be subject to your masters with all fear; not only to the good and gentle, but also to the froward." 1 Peter II. 18.

The word translated "servants," in these passages, is *douloi* in the original Greek; and *douloi* was applied to all servants, but more particularly to hereditary slaves, of whom there were a great number at the time and place in which these Scriptures were written.

Wives must obey their husbands. Eph. V. 22–24, 33; Col. III. 18; Titus II. 5; 1 Peter III. 1. "The head of every man is Christ, and the head of the woman is the man." 1 Cor. XI. 2.

The people must obey the priests: Mat. X. 14; Luke X. 16; 1 Cor. IV. 1; Gal. VI. 1; 1 Thess. IV. 8; 1 Tim. V. 17; Heb. XIII. 7, 17. In the verse last cited, Paul says: "Obey them that have the rule over you, and submit yourselves, for they watch for your souls, as they that must give account."

Subjects must obey their rulers.

"Let every soul be *subject* unto the higher powers: For there is no power but of God; *the powers that be are ordained of God*: [Tyrants, demagogues and fools included]. Whosoever therefore resisteth the power, resisteth the ordi-

* See Appendix, Note 6, for quotations from Hennell, Franklin, Rousseau, Goethe, Voltaire, Paine and Rammohun Roy.

nance of God; and they that resist shall receive to themselves damnation."
Rom. XIII. 1, 2.

"He [the ruler] is the minister of God to thee for good.' 'Rom. XIII. 4.

"Put them in mind to be subject to principalities and powers, to obey magistrates." Titus III. 1.

"Submit yourselves to *every ordinance of man* for the Lord's sake: whether
it be to the king as supreme; or unto governors as unto them that are sent by
him." 1 Peter II. 13, 14.

"Fear God. Honor the King." 1 Peter II, 17.

Men must never resist evil or oppression.

"I say unto you that ye resist not evil; but whosoever shall smite thee on
thy right cheek, turn to him the other also. And if any man will sue thee at
law, and take away thy coat, let him have thy cloak also. And whosoever shall
compel thee to go a mile, go with him twain." Mat. V. 39–42.

"Unto him that smiteth thee on one cheek, offer also the other; and of him
that taketh away thy goods ask them not again." Luke VI. 29, 30.

"Being persecuted, we suffer it." 1 Cor. IV. 12.

"Christ also suffered for us, leaving us an example, that ye should follow his
steps." I Peter II. 21.

These precepts may appear to be very lovely, very beautiful, very poetic, and
very philanthropic; but if put in practice on any large scale, they would be
productive of far more evil than the bloody code of Moses. These precepts are
unqualified; they are not contradicted in any portion of the New Testament;
they are frequently repeated and inculcated with great earnestness, and in
many passages they are made absolute. Peter says: "Submit yourselves to
every ordinance of man." Paul says, "There is *no* power but of God;" and
Christ says, "resist not evil." They never say, "If ye are outrageously oppressed, and can easily relieve yourselves of oppression with little pain to any
one, then ye shall so relieve yourselves"; but they do say, "unto him that
smiteth thee on one cheek, offer the other also." The Evangelists tell us, in
accordance with divine inspiration, that the omnipotent and all-wise God came
down to earth to redeem mankind, and lived like a man among men for thirty
years. If this be true, it is probable that, as is asserted of Jesus, all the actions
of the divinity were examples which mankind should constantly aspire to imitate; and his conduct while on earth should furnish examples for men to follow
in every circumstance in which they could be placed. Jesus, the reputed
divinity, was repeatedly abused and maltreated, and finally he was executed by
his enemies; yet never did he resist evil, although if possessed of omnipotent
power as is claimed, he might have done so with results incalculably beneficial
to the human race. Hence it follows that no Christian can, consistently with

the teachings of his revelation, resist the rod of a tyrant or the lash of a master. It is strange that such doctrine should be extensively received as gospel, particularly among those nations which are the most free and the most ready to defend their rights by force; and perhaps it is almost as strange that any man should ever have promulgated it, but as we have shown (Sec. XXII.) the peculiar circumstances in which Christ was placed, made it necessary for him to preach passive submission. Such doctrines never have been put in practice by any nation and never will be. The Quakers, who are non-resistants almost as thorough in practice as in theory, have been but a very small proportion of the nations where they have existed, and they have existed only in the most enlightened communities and in places comparatively free from the horrors of war. The Puritans of England made perhaps the grandest attempt recorded in history to practice the doctrines of the Bible, but they found that Samuel hewing Agag to pieces before the Lord in Gilgal was a better saint for a people determined to preserve their liberties, than Paul with that outrageous lie, "the powers that be are ordained of God."

It may be said that the earth would soon become a paradise if all men would only practice love to all men and non-resistance to evil. But what folly to talk of this when it never can occur! Gospels should be suited for men as they are. It may also be said that Jesus, in teaching passive submission, meant only to teach a reasonable humility, and to impress as forcibly as possible the importance of the most generous self-sacrifice for the good of others. It might also be said that when Moses told the Jews to slay all the males and married women of the heathen, and save the girls for concubines, he meant only to inculcate a proper spirit of self-defense.

The New Testament permits slavery and polygamy since it does not expressly prohibit them, and since they were lawful under the Mosaic law, and must remain lawful until expressly forbidden. Christianity is a faith which, if followed as strictly as possible, is fit only for slaves, and it was devised by a slave of the great Roman empire, who was wise enough to see that any attempt to resist the Cesars would only end in his own destruction.

TRUTH OF HISTORICAL STATEMENTS.

XXXIII. Some of the statements of the Bible in regard to historical events deserve examination; and the account of creation, and of the antediluvian history of the world will be first in order.

CREATION AND ANTEDILUVIAN HISTORY.

XXXIV. The Mosaic account of creation and the early history of the world require us to believe that:—

1. God never made anything before he made the earth; and therefore he must have spent an eternity in idleness.

2. He made the earth six thousand years ago.

3. He spent five days in making the earth and the animals and vegetables upon it.

4. He made all the other worlds and planets in one day.

5. He made the earth before he made any of the other planets,

6. He made the planets only to mark time for the earth.

7. He made the earth only to serve as a residence for man. The earth as compared with the remainder of the planets is no more than a drop of water is to the earth. What would men say if they should discover that the worms in a particular drop of water had a religious faith, that the universe was made for them, that their drop was made the first of all things, that the Lord spent five

days in creating and perfecting their drop, and only one day in making all the rest of the universe?

8. God made the light two days before he made the sun, moon and stars.

9. He placed a supply of water in the sky. It was very natural for the ignorant to suppose that there is a large body of water where the rain comes from. Philosophy tells us that there is no water in the sky till it begins to fall. Moses put water there, before there was a sun to raise the vapor by evaporation; and yet he would have us believe that there was no rain for sixteen hundred years. (Gen. II. 5. IX. 13).

10. God made the vegetable kingdom before the animal. Geology says that there were no vegetables before the time when the coal beds began to be deposited; while for thousands of years before, many kinds of animals abounded, and their remains are found in the stones below the coal.

11. Man ate no meat for sixteen hundred years, though Abel was "a keeper of sheep."

12. Animals, the same which we have now, ate no meat for sixteen hundred years. (Gen. I. 30. VI. 19, 20).

13. Moses was ignorant that man is an animal.

14. Man was made sinless and happy, and ignorant of right and wrong.

15. Man while ignorant of wrong was persuaded to do wrong by a snake which could speak.

16. Man for doing wrong unconsciously was punished by being made subject to sin and misery. The story that men were formerly without sin and perfectly happy, and were reduced to their present state for some offense to the gods, was a common tradition or myth in ancient times.

17. The naughty serpent, which could talk, was punished by a curse that it and all its kind should for ever go upon their bellies, and eat dust and be hated by man. Did the snakes in Paradise go upon feet or walk upright upon their tails? If they went on their bellies before the temptation, what was the punishment? If they did not go on their bellies, were they snakes? Snakes do not eat dust now, neither are they universally hated. The Egyptians worshipped the asp for many ages.

18. Men before the deluge lived sometimes to be nine hundred and fifty years old, and generally to the age of about seven hundred.

19. After men had increased for seventeen hundred years, Jehovah became so angry at the sins of mankind, that he sent a great deluge to cover the whole earth, (Gen. VI. 17. VII. 19, 22), and kill all men and animals, except a few of each species, which were preserved in an ark. How the ark floated or the animals lived above the tops of the highest mountains, where the most intense and fatal cold now prevails constantly, is not explained. Neither is it explained

what became of the water, for there is not enough now to cover the mountains. Though the water stood upon the earth for ten months, above the tops of the highest mountains, the trees apparently were still flourishing several miles down below. The dove found a fresh olive leaf. Trees now a-days are not so tough in their vitality.

Such are some of the wonderful events recorded by Moses; events for which we can find no parallel since reliable historical records have been made, except in such books as Gulliver's Travels and Sinbad the sailor. An Irish curate after reading Gulliver's Travels said :—" There are some things in that book which I cannot believe." Geologists cannot believe that there has ever been a universal deluge, and astronomers will not believe that the sun and stars were created in one-fifth the time devoted to the creation of the earth.

CHRONOLOGY OF THE BIBLE.

XXXV. The chronology of the Bible teaches that the earth and universe were made about six thousand years ago, but the science of geology says that the earth has existed many millions of years, and astronomy says that many of the stars must have been existing for hundreds of thousands of years, or their light would not yet have reached us, so far are they away. After it was found that geology could not be reconciled with the Bible, the Christians began endeavoring to reconcile the Bible to geology. It is said that the "days" of creation were long periods—perhaps of many millions of years each—but Moses says, those "days" had an evening and a morning, and in Ex. XX, 10, 11, the prophet again speaks of these six days as though they had been ordinary days of twenty-four hours each. If however those "days" were periods of thousands or millions of years each, then God must have rested an equal period, "the seventh day," during which time Adam and Eve lived in Paradise; whereas we know (according to Moses) that Adam could have remained in Paradise for only a short period comparatively.

From Adam to Shem there was a period of one thousand six hundred and fifty-eight years, and in this time there were eleven generations averaging one hundred and fifty years each. From Arphaxad to Isaac was four hundred and ninety years, with ten generations of forty-nine years each. Between Jacob and David, a period of nine hundred and fifty-six years, there were eleven generations of eighty-six years each on an average, showing a wonderful increase in the length of the generations subsequent to Isaac. During this latter period, we have not the years of each generation, as we have during all the rest of the time from Adam down to 600 B. C. Moses says (Ps. XC.) that in his day, the utmost limit of human life was eighty years.

From Solomon to Christ was a period of one thousand years : and of thirty-nine generations of twenty-six years each on an average, according to Matthew, and of fifty-three generations, with nineteen years each, on an average, according to Luke. Moses says (Gen. XLVII. 9) that Jacob was one hundred and thirty years old when he entered Egypt, and that the Israelites were four hundred and thirty years in Egypt, (Ex. XII. 40, 41), but Paul asserts (Gal. III. 17), that the time between the call of Abraham and the departure from Egypt was four hundred and thirty years. Paul is evidently wrong.

According to 1 K. VI. 1, it was four hundred and eighty years after the Exodus that the temple was commenced. The writer of Acts says (XIII. 21), that Saul reigned forty years : David reigned forty years (1 K. II. 11); and Solomon reigned four years before beginning the temple ; and thus we have nine hundred and sixty-six years from the birth of Jacob to the building of the temple, in the year 1011 B. C. In Acts XIII. 20, it is said, there were judges over Israel for four hundred and fifty years, and yet there were only six generations among the forefathers of David during that time.

We are told (1 C. VI. 1, 2, 3) that Moses was the grandson of Kohath, who went with Jacob to Egypt, (Gen. XLVI. 11), and was the contemporary of Korah, (Num. XVI. 1), another grandson of Kohath, and with Nashon (Num. I. 7), the great grandson of Phares, who went with Jacob to Egypt. The Israelites when they went to Egypt numbered there seventy *persons*, (Gen. XLVI. 27). In three generations, or during the lives of Kohath, Amram, and Moses, those Israelites increased from seventy persons to be six hundred and three thousand, five hundred and fifty fighting men, or three millions in all; and in this number, the Levites, one-twelfth of the whole nation, were not counted, (Num. I. 46). The five sons of Judah had increased to seventy-four thousand fighting men, or at the modest rate of a duplication every twenty-five years. During a considerable portion of this time—four hundred years—(see Gen. XV. 13), the Israelites were sorely tasked (Ex. I. 13. V. 5). From Isaac to Solomon, there were twelve generations : from Isaac to Azariah, Solomon's High Priest, there were eighteen generations : and from Isaac to Heman, Solomon's saintly singer, there were twenty-two generations, (1 Ch. VI.); whence it appears that the holy Levites were better propagators before the Lord than those who ate not of the fat of the sacrifices. Ezra (VII. 1–5) was only fourteen generations from Phineas, who was a priest in the time of Moses (1450 B. C.). This would give seventy years for a generation : and yet during less than one-half that period, there were twenty kings on the throne of Juαah.

The difficulties of this chronology, however, do not end with the internal evidence, but are greatly increased by the contradictions of profane history. It is generally conceded among learned Christians that the common version of the Bible is wrong in its chronology. Milman says, " It is greatly to be regretted that the chronology of the earlier Scriptures should ever have been made a religious question." Pritchard, in his "Physical History of Man," says, " biblical writers had no revelation on the subject of chronology ;" and he asserts that men have existed upon earth for hundreds of thousands of years. No learned man pretends to say the earth was made only six thousand years ago. We have incontestable proof, according to such celebrated men as Champollion, Bunsen, Boeckh, Barucchi, Kenrick, Henny, Lesueur, Hincks, Lepsius and Gliddon, that we have Egyptian monuments extending to a time beyond that given as the date of the flood* Geologists of high rank, Lyell, Agassiz and others, have expressed their conviction, founded upon fossil remains and antiquities found buried under numerous strata of the earth's surface, that man has existed on earth for some fifteen or twenty thousand years at least. Lyell says that the Falls of Niagara, and the delta of the Mississippi bear evidence that their respective streams have been running in their present courses for fifty thousand years. To escape from all this, it has been admitted that the chronology of the common version of the Bible is incorrect. If this be so, we must throw away the genealogy of Christ, as given in the New Testament, and with that must go the divine inspiration of the whole Gospel.

---

* See Appendix, Note 7.

STUBBORNNESS OF THE JEWS.

XXXVI. The stubbornness of the Jews, recorded by Moses as a natural occurrence, not caused by any special interposition of Jehovah, if received as true, deserves to be considered as presenting some of the most singular phenomena in the history of the human mind. The march through the wilderness after leaving Egypt was accompanied with a vast number of miracles, of which there were thirty-one of the first magnitude, and all of which were performed in the sight of the whole people; miracles so great that on two separate occasions more than fourteen thousand incredulous and stiff-necked Israelites were killed by the hand of Jehovah. Yet after all these wonders, which were to be seen every month, if not every day, the Hebrew people as a body rebelled against the Almighty God and his ministers no less than eleven times within a few years. Gibbon remarks, " The devout and even scrupulous attachment to the Mosaic religion, so conspicuous among the Jews who lived under the second temple, [from 535 B. C. to 60 A. D.] becomes still more surprising if it is compared with the stubborn incredulity of their forefathers. When the law was given on Mount Sinai, when the tides of the ocean and the courses of the planets were suspended for the convenience of the Israelites, and when temporal rewards and punishments were the immediate consequences of their piety and disobedience, they perpetually relapsed into rebellion against the visible majesty of their divine king, placed the idols of the nations in the sanctuary of Jehovah, and imitated every fantastic ceremony that was practiced in the tents of the Arabs or in the cities of Phœnicia. The contemporaries of Moses and Joshua had beheld with careless indifference the most amazing miracles. Under the pressure of every calamity, the belief of those miracles has preserved the Jews of a later period from the universal contagion of idolatry; and in contradiction to every known principle of the human mind, that singular people seems to have yielded a stronger and more ready assent to the traditions of their remote ancestors than to the evidence of their own senses."

References are here given whereby the accounts of the principal of these miracles and rebellions may be found in the books of Moses.

The Jews believed the first teachings of Moses and Aaron, who sought to rid their tribe from the yoke of the Egyptians. Ex. IV. 30, 31.

Jehovah renewed his promise of favor to Israel. Ex. VI. 4.

He turned the waters of Egypt to blood. Ex. VII. 19.

He covered the land with frogs. Ex. VIII. 6.

He turned the dust into lice. Ex. VIII. 16.

He filled the land with flies. Ex. VIII. 24.

He slew all the cattle of Egypt. Ex. IX. 6.

He covered the Egyptians with boils. Ex. IX. 10.

He sent a fiery hail upon Egypt. Ex. IX. 24.

He filled Egypt with locusts. Ex. X. 13.

He covered Egypt with a deep darkness. Ex. X. 22.

He slew the first-born of every Egyptian family. Ex. XII. 30.

The Israelites murmured. Ex. XIV. 10.

Jehovah sent pillars of fire and clouds to lead the Jews. Ex. XIV. 20.]

Passage of the Red Sea with a great miracle. Ex. XIV. 21.

The Israelites murmured. Ex. XV. 24.

Waters of Marah miraculously sweetened. Ex. XV. 25.

The Israelites expressed their regret that they had not died in Egypt by God's hand. Ex. XVI. 3.

Quails and manna foretold and sent by miracle. Ex. XVI. 4–14.]

The Israelites disobeyed Moses. Ex. XVI. 20, 27.

The Israelites murmured. Ex. XVII. 1.

Water furnished to the Jews by miracle. Ex. XVII. 6.

The Jews conquered the Amalekites by the aid of a great miracle. Ex. XVII. 11, 12.

Jehovah sent a message to the Jews, and they promised to obey. Ex. XIX. 8.

Jehovah descended upon Sinai in fire and smoke. Ex. XIX. 16–18.

The Jews saw, feared, stood afar off and begged Moses to "let not God speak to us lest we die." Ex. XX. 18, 19.

All the Jews promised obedience to all the ordinances of God. Ex. XXIV. 3.

The Glory of the Lord dwelt six days on Mount Sinai, and the sight of it was like a devouring fire in the eyes of the Hebrews. Ex. XXIV. 16.

Moses, Aaron, Nadab, Abisha, seventy elders, and the nobles of Israel, saw God. Ex. XXIV. 10, 11.

While Moses was upon the Mount, the Israelites induced Aaron, (previously consecrated as high priest of Jehovah,) to make the Golden Calf, which they worshipped. Ex. XXXII. 1–4.

Jehovah appeared in a cloud at the Tabernacle door, and the Hebrews "every man at his tent door," worshipped. Ex. XXXIII. 10.

The Israelites willingly brought offerings to the Lord. Ex. XXXV. 20; XXXVI. 5.

They did all that the Lord commanded to Moses. Ex. XXXIX. 32, 42, 43.

The cloud of the Lord by day and his fire by night rested upon the Tabernacle in the sight of all the house of Israel. Ex. XL. 38.

The Glory of the Lord appeared to all the people; and a fire came from before the Lord and consumed upon the altar the burnt offering and the fat; and all the people saw and shouted and fell on their faces. Lev. IX. 23, 24.

The Israelites murmured. Num. XI. 1-6.

They lamented that they had not died in Egypt, and they proposed to return. Num. XIV. 2-4.

Jehovah was exceedingly provoked, and his Glory appeared on the Tabernacle before all the children of Israel. Num. XIV. 10, 11.

Jehovah slew all who spake evil of the promised land. Num. XIV. 36.

Two hundred and fifty princes of Israel rebelled against Moses and Aaron, and the rebels were consumed with all the tribe of Korah; and all Israel that were round-about fled, for fear they should be consumed likewise. Num. XVI. 32, 35.

The next day the Jews murmured against Moses and Aaron for slaying the people of the Lord. [1] Num. XVI. 41.

A cloud covered the Tabernacle, and the Glory of the Lord appeared. Num. XVI. 42.

Jehovah slew 14,700 of the murmuring Jews. Num. XVI. 49.

Every Israelite prepared a rod with his name upon it, and Aaron's rod was miraculously exalted above all; and the people thereupon appealed to Moses and Aaron to be protected from death. Num. XVII. 1-13.

The Israelites murmured and lamented that they had not died in Egypt. Num. XX. 2-5.

The Glory of the Lord appeared to them. Num. XX. 6.

Moses brought water from the rock at Meribah by miracle. Num. XX. 7.

The Jews became discouraged and murmured against Jehovah and Moses, and exclaimed, "Wherefore have ye brought us up out of the land of Egypt to die in the wilderness." Num. XXI. 4, 5.

Jehovah plagued them with fiery serpents, and many died. Num. XXI. 6.

Moses made a brazen serpent and hoisted it upon a pole, and all the wounded who looked upon it were healed. Num. XXI. 9.

Israel committed idolatry and whoredom. Num. XXV. 1, 2.

Jehovah slew 24,000 Jews in a plague for their sins. Num. XXV. 9.

MIRACULOUS POWERS OF WITCHES AND SORCERERS.

XXXVII. The prophets and apostles asserted directly and indirectly the power of witches and sorcerers to perform miracles. See Ex. VII. 11, 22; VIII. 7; Lev. XIX. 31; XX. 6; Deut. XIII. 1; XVIII. 11; Is. XXVIII. 7; Mat. VII. 22; XII. 27; XXIV. 24; Mark IX. 38; Luke IX. 50; Acts VIII. 9; XIII. 6-10; XVI. 10; XIX. 15; 2 Cor. XI. 13; 2 K. XXIII. 24.

THE EXISTENCE OF RACES OF GIANTS.

XXXVIII. Races of giants are frequently spoken of in the Old. Testament. Amos (II. 9) speaks of giants as tall as cedars. Moses says that Og, the remnant of a race of giants had a bedstead fifteen and a half feet long. See Gen. XIV. 5; Deut. II. 10, 11; Josh. XV. 8; XVII. 15; XVIII. 16.

POSSESSION OF THE HUMAN BODY BY DEVILS.

XXXIX. The belief that insanity, epilepsy and some other diseases were caused by the entrance of devils into the human body was common among superstitious people in ancient times, and was received as true by the apostles. See Mat. IX. 32; X. 1, 8; XI. 18; XII. 27, &c.

THE MASSACRE OF THE INNOCENTS.

XL. Matthew says, (II. 16), that when Herod heard of the birth of Jesus, "the King of the Jews," he was troubled, and for fear ordered that "all the children that were in Bethlehem and in all the coasts thereof, from two years old and under," should be slain. Hennell remarks that this wholesale murder "is not mentioned by the other three Evangelists, nor by Josephus, although the latter is very minute in detailing the barbarities of Herod. The conduct attributed to Herod is in itself absurd: he makes no search after the one dangerous child, to whom the visit of the wise men must have afforded a good clue, but slays the children of a whole town and the adjoining country in a mass. It is inconceivable that any fit of anger should lead a politic old king, however tyrannical, to indulge in such useless and costly cruelty. And how could Josephus, who had filled thirty-seven chapters with the history of Herod, omit all allusions to such a wholesale murder? Lardner supposes tha. Josephus wilfully suppressed this fact, which is rather hard upon Josephus, since Mark, Luke, John, and all other historians are as silent as he."

CONTRADICTORY STATEMENTS.

XLI. We have seen that many events in the Bible recorded as having occurred naturally, never did so occur; and now we shall see that there are in the same book numerous contradictory statements, where it is impossible that both sides should be true or divinely inspired.

In one place (Ex. VI. 3) it is said that God was not known to Abraham, Isaac and Jacob by the name of Jehovah. Yet in Genesis (XXVIII. 13) it is said that the Lord appeared to Jacob in a dream and told his own name (Jehovah in the Hebrew Bible). And elsewhere, (Gen. XXII. 14), it is said that Abraham called the place of the proposed sacrifice of Isaac, "Jehovah-jireh ;" and in Gen. IV. 26, it is said, "then men began to call on the name of Jehovah."

Moses says (Gen. XXXII. 19) that Jacob bought the field of Sychem, while Luke says (Acts VII. 15, 16) that Abraham bought it.

There is a discrepancy between Genesis XLVI. 26, 27, and Acts VII. 14, in regard to the number of Israelites who went to Egypt with Jacob : Moses says there were sixty-six, and Luke says there were seventy-five.

In the time of David there were 1,100,000 fighting men in Israel, according to 1 Ch. XXI. 5, 6 ; while, according to 2 S. XXIV. 9, there were only 800,000, showing a difference of thirty per cent.

The number of measures of oil presented by Solomon to Hiram is represented in 1 K. V. 11, to have been 20, and in 2 Ch. II. 10 to have been 20,000.

Was Bashemoth, Esau's wife, the daughter of Elon the Hittite, (Gen. XXVI. 34), or was she an Ishmaelitish woman, (Gen. XXXVI. 2, 3)?

In 1 K. XV. 1, 2, 9, it is said that King Abijam reigned only three years, and died before Jeroboam ; but in 2 Ch. XIII. 1, 2, 20, 21, XIV. 1, it is asserted that Jeroboam died before Abijah, and that the latter waxed mighty, married fourteen wives and begat two sons and fourteen daughters.

We are told (1 K. XV. 33) that there was a war between Asa and Baasha al their days ; but elsewhere (2 Ch. XIV. 1, 6) we learn that in Asa's reign, during at least seven years of Baasha's time, the land had peace. Baasha is represented in 1 K. XIV. 6, 8, to have died in the 26th year of Asa ; but according to 2 Ch. XVI. 1., Baasha built Ramah in the 36th year of Asa's reign.

Did Omri begin to reign in the 31st (1 K. XVI. 23), or in the 27th year of Asa, (1 K. XVI. 10, 15, 16)?

According to 2 Ch. XXII. 2, Ahaziah was forty-two years old when he mounted the throne, but according to 2 K. VIII. 26, he was only twenty-two years old.

There is a discrepancy of ten years in regard to the age of Jehoiachin when he began to reign, between 2 K. XXIV. 8, and 2 Ch. XXXVI. 9.

Did Aaron die on the top of Mount Hor, on the way from Kadesh to the Red Sea, (Num. XX. 28), and also at Mosera on the way from Beeroth to Gudgodah, (Deut. X. 6)?

David numbered Israel at the instigation of Jehovah, (2 S. XXIV. 1). David was provoked to number Israel by Satan, (1 Ch. XXI. 1). David numbered Israel only once.

For the offense of numbering the people, David was permitted to choose one

4

of three grievous punishments proposed by Jehovah; and one of these punishments was either a seven years' famine, (2 S. XXIV. 13), or a three years' famine, (1 Ch. XXI. 11, 12).

The Ammonites are said, in 2 S. X. 6, to have hired one thousand men of King Maacah to fight against Israel, but in 1 Ch. XIX. 7, it is said that they hired thirty-two thousand chariots of Maacah—though there was not that number of chariots in all Western Asia. In the battle seven hundred charioteers were slain according to 2 S. X. 18, and seven thousand according to 1 Ch. XIX. 18.

Abraham did not leave Haran till after the death of his father Terah; (Acts VII. 4). Terah died one hundred and thirty-five years after the birth of Abraham; (Gen. XI. 32). Abraham left Haran when he was seventy-five years old, (Gen. XII. 4).

Jeremiah (XXI. 9) advised the Israelites to desert to the Chaldeans; and he denied (XXXVII. 14) that he gave such advice; and then we are told that he was cast into two different prisons for giving that advice (Jer. XXXVII. 16, XXXVIII. 6).

The author of the book of Joshua (X. 13) quotes the book of Jasher as authority for the arrest of the sun by Joshua, and the author of Kings (1 K. I. 18) quotes the same book to prove the sayings of Saul four hundred years later.

"God did tempt Abraham," Gen. XXII. 1.

"God tempteth not any man," James I. 13.

Saul was much pleased with David before the battle with Goliah, (1 S. XVI. 21, 22). After the death of Goliah David was an entire stranger to Saul. (1 S. XVII. 55). Bayle remarks in his famous article on David:—"It is somewhat strange that Saul did not know David that day, since that young man had played several times on his musical instrument before him, to disperse those black vapors which molested him. If such a narrative as this should be found in Thucydides, or in Livy, all the critics would unanimously conclude that the transcribers had transposed the pages; forgot something in one place; repeated something in another, or inserted some preposterous additions in the author's work. But no such suspicions ought to be entertained of the Bible."

"Joram begat Ozias," according to Matthew (I. 8); but according to 2 Ch. XXII. XXIII. XXIV. XXV. Ozias was the great, great grandson of Joram. Dr. Doddridge supposes that Matthew intended to punish Ahaziah for his wickedness, by leaving his name out!

Did Peter deny Christ to a man (John XVIII. 26. Luke XXII. 58), or to a maid? (Mat. XXVI. 71. Mark XIV. 69).

Matthew says (XXVII. 34) that at the Crucifixion they gave Jesus "vinegar mixed with gall," but Mark (XV. 23) says "wine mixed with myrrh."

Judas repented according to Matthew XXVII. 3, and it is implied in Acts I. 18, that he did not repent. Matthew says he gave back the thirty pieces of silver to the priests; Acts says he did not. Matthew says the priests with that money bought a field to bury strangers; Acts says he bought a field for himself. Matthew says he hanged himself: according to Acts—"He burst asunder in the midst and all his bowels gushed out." Matthew accounts for the designation of the stranger's graveyard, as the field of blood, by saying that it was bought with the reward of iniquity: but Acts says it was because of Judas' tragic death there.

The expulsion of the money changers from the temple took place soon after the baptism of Jesus, according to John (II. 13), but Matthew (XXI. 12) Mark (XI. 15), and Luke (XIX. 45) place the event in the last visit to Jerusalem, and just before the crucifixion.

John (I. 28, 40, 41) says that Jesus called Simon and Andrew, at Bethabara beyond Jordan, in the presence of John the Baptist, while Matthew says (IV. 12, 18) the call occurred at the sea of Galilee after the temptation on the mount and after John was cast into prison.

According to Matthew (III. 16. IV. 1, 2), Mark (I. 11, 12), and Luke (III. 22. IV. 1, 2), Jesus after being baptized by John was forthwith led out into the wilderness, and tempted by the devil during forty days: but John (I. 33, 35' 43. II. 1, 12, 13) completely excludes the temptation. He says that on the first day after the baptism Jesus was with John, on the second day he conversed with Peter, on the third day he attended the marriage in Cana, then he went to Capernaum, and then to Jerusalem, so that it was impossible for him to have spent any forty days in the wilderness.

John the Evangelist (1. 29-34) says that John the Baptist "bare record" of Christ at the baptism:—"This is the son of God." Again, a few days later, and long before the imprisonment of the Baptist, the latter, in a long discourse, is represented saying: "The Father loveth the son, and hath given all things into his hand," (John III. 27): and yet Matthew (XI. 2), and Luke (VII. 18), state that when the Baptist was in prison, he sent two of his disciples to Jesus to learn whether he was really the Christ, or whether he was only the forerunner of a greater? Mark (I. 11) says that at the baptism, there was a voice from Heaven:—"Thou art my beloved son, in whom I am well pleased." How then could John the Baptist doubt, himself being inspired, and having such evidence before him? St. John must have manufactured those speeches; for Apollos, an "eloquent man and mighty in the Scriptures," who was a disciple of the Baptist, knew not Christ, and long after his death was baptising with the baptism of John, when he was converted by Paul, (Acts XVIII. 25; XIX. 3).

Matthew, (IV. 12) and Mark (I. 14) assert that Jesus did not go into Galilee until after the Baptist's imprisonment, but John states (III. 33) not only that Jesus went into Galilee immediately after the baptism and before the Baptist was imprisoned, but even baptised the latter in Judea.

On the morning of the resurrection, says Matthew, (XXVIII. 1), Mary Magdalene and the other Mary went to the sepulchre. According to Mark (XVI. 2) Mary Magdalene, the other Mary, and Salome went. Luke tells us (XXIII, 55. XXIV. 1–10), that Mary Magdalene, the other Mary, Joanna, "and other women," went together to the tomb; and John (XX. 1) says that Mary Magdalene went to the tomb alone.

Matthew states that an angel descended from Heaven and rolled away the stone as the women came. Mark says the stone was rolled away when the women arrived there, and when they entered, they saw a young man clothed in a long white garment, sitting on the right side. According to Luke, they found the stone rolled away, and inside after a little time they saw that "two men stood by them in shining garments." John says, Mary Magdalene found the stone rolled away, and saw two angels "sitting the one at the head, and the other at the feet, where the body of Jesus had lain."

Matthew says that after the two women left the tomb, Jesus met them and requested them to tell Peter and the disciples to meet him in Galilee. Mark states that the young man in white requested the three women to direct the disciples to meet Jesus in Galilee. Luke asserts that the six or more women, finding the sepulchre empty, were told by the "two men in the shining garments," that Jesus had arisen, saying nothing about going to Galilee; and thereupon the woman told the apostles, who disbelieved, and Peter ran to the sepulchre to satisfy himself. John says, the one woman told Peter and John that the sepulchre was empty, whereupon those two "ran both together" to the tomb.

According to Matthew, Jesus met the two women going from the sepulchre, requested them to send the eleven to meet him in Galilee, whither they went, and where he met them, and where "they worshipped him: but some doubted." Mark affirms that Jesus appeared first to Mary Magdalene, who went and told his disciples, and they "believed not." Afterwards he appeared to two of the apostles and these two told the others, who did not believe. Afterwards he appeared unto the eleven as they sat at meat and upbraided them with their unbelief, and "so then after the Lord had spoken unto them, he was taken up into Heaven." Luke states that on the day of the resurrection, Christ appeared to two of the apostles on the road to Emmaus, and had a long conversation with them. That same day he appeared to the eleven at meat in Jerusalem, ate "broiled fish, and of an honey comb," spoke with them for some time; led them out as far as Bethany, and was carried up to Heaven before them. John says, that Jesus appeared in the sepulchre to Mary Magdalene, and the same day in the evening, he appeared to ten apostles, Thomas being absent. Eight days later, Christ met the whole eleven in the same place, and Thomas who then saw him for the first time after the resurrection being somewhat skeptical, stuck his finger into the hole to know whether it was there yet. Afterwards Jesus showed himself to the disciples at the sea of Tiberias. Acts says, Jesus was seen of the apostles for forty days after the resurrection.

There is a remarkable discrepancy between the report given by the four Evangelists of the last words of Jesus to his apostles.

Last words of Jesus, according to Matthew :—"All power is given unto me in Heaven and in earth. Go ye therefore, and teach all nations ; baptizing them in the name of the Father, and of the Son, and of the Holy Ghost. Teaching them to observe all things whatsoever I have commanded you : and lo I am with you always, even unto the end of the world." XXVIII. 18, 19, 20.

Last words of Jesus, according to Mark :—"Go ye into all the world, and preach the gospel to every creature. He that believeth and is baptized shall be saved ; but he that believeth not shall be damned. And these signs shall follow them that believe ; in my name shall they cast out devils ; they shall speak with new tongues ; they shall take up serpents ; and if they drink any deadly thing it shall not hurt them ; they shall lay hands on the sick, and they shall recover." XVI. 15-18.

Last words of Jesus, according to Luke :—"Thus it is written, and thus it behooved Christ to suffer, and to rise from the dead the third day : and that repentance and remission of sins should be preached in his name among all nations, beginning at Jerusalem. And ye are witnesses of these things. And, behold, I send the promise of my Father, upon you : but tarry ye in the city of Jerusalem, until ye be endued with power from on high." XXIV. 46-49.

The last words of Jesus, according to John :—"Peace be unto you ! as my Father has sent me even so send I you. And when he had said this, he breathed on them, and saith unto them, receive ye the Holy Ghost. Whosesoever sins ye remit, they are remitted unto them ; and whosoever sins ye retain, they are retained." XX. 21-23.

Thus we have seen that there are a number of false and contradictory state-ments in the Bible. It requires no argument to show that falsehood and con-tradiction are inconsistent with the theory of a divine inspiration. Paley says : "I know not a more rash or unphilosophical conduct of the understanding than to reject the substance of a story by reason of some diversity in the cir-cumstances with which it is related." We expect human witnesses to contra-dict each other : would the same be expected of divinely inspired prophets ?

We shall now consider whether there are not false and contradictory doc-trines in the Bible.

EXISTENCE OF A PERSONAL CREATOR OF THE UNIVERSE.

XLII. The Bible teaches that a God exists—a personal, conscious Deity, who created and governs the Universe, and exists independently of it. The existence of such a deity is here denied. First, there is no satisfactory proof of his existence; and, secondly, there is proof to the contrary.

Christians argue thus: All human experience teaches that there can be no effect without a cause. The universe must be considered as an effect; it is material, gross, unconscious; it has not, so far as we know, any power in itself which could lead to the harmonious action and the intelligence which pervades all existence. The recognized forces of nature—gravitation, electricity, inertia, heat, animal and vegetable life, and chemical affinity—are dependent for their origin and existence upon matter, and cannot create or destroy it. The exist-ence of the universe can only be accounted for by supposing it to have been created by a Deity independent of it.*

The harmony and adaptation of means to ends throughout the universe proves that it must have had an intelligent creator and governor. No man will believe that a watch could grow by accident. Then how should a man grow by acci-dent, every inch of whose flesh is a thousand times more curious than all the watches in the world? Besides, the natural tendency in man's mind to seek some superior object for worship presupposes the existence of a God, and the general belief in a personal creator proves that the idea is in accordance with the general principles of human reason.

On the negative, it is argued that the universe has not yet been proved to be an "effect;" and if it were, its cause would not necessarily be a deity. To

---

* And yet the Bible does not say that Jehovah made the earth *out of nothing.* The word translated "created," in the first verse of Genesis, is the same word afterwards used to describe the creation of the animals out of material of the earth.

assert that the universe is an effect is to take the question for granted—the question whether the universe was created or existed from all eternity. If the universe must be an effect, would not its creator have been an effect also? And if the creator of the universe had a creator, and he another creator, and so on, there would be no end, and no satisfaction.* The wonderful adaptation of means to ends apparent throughout the universe cannot be denied by any reasonable man, but so far as science has gone she has not been able to find the hand of God. On the contrary, she has proved that the Deity is not the immediate actor, where he was universally supposed to be, by the ignorance and superstition of early ages. The revolutions of planets, the change of seasons, the constant ebb and flow of animal and vegetable life, the thunder, lightning and storm were formerly ascribed to the immediate divine influence, but all are now known to occur in accordance with, and in obedience to, general laws; and the farther scientific investigation has been carried, the greater has been found to be the extent and influence of the general laws. Ignorance and superstition may lead a man to believe in a personal deity, but science certainly does not. She attempts to account for the present shape of the universe, and even to create animal life.

The popular belief proves nothing. The idea that the human soul was immaterial and would exist after death entirely independent of the body, led many to believe that there must be an immaterial personal deity, with whom the soul should take refuge after leaving the body. In another place I shall attempt to show that the soul cannot exist after death; and we have no evidence whatever that spirit can exist independently of matter. If there were a deity such as is represented in the Bible, he would certainly not leave his existence and nature in doubt; whereas history tells us that in such diversity of opinions as prevail in regard to divine existence, more than half the human race must necessarily be wrong.

It is said that the God of the Bible is all-powerful and all-good; but why does evil exist? If Jehovah exist and be all-powerful, he does not wish to prevent evil, and therefore he cannot be good; or if he be good, he cannot prevent evil, and therefore is not all-powerful.†

---

* See Appendix, Note 7.

† The Bible says the devil could do no evil without Jehovah's permission. 1 K. XXII. 22; Job I. 12; II. 6; XII. 16; Ezek. XIV. 9; Mat. VIII. 31; 2 Thess. II. 11; Judges IX. 23.

NATURE OF THE DEITY.

XLIII. *Jehovah is represented in the Bible as a being in the human shape, a visitor and guest with men, oftentimes unjust, cruel, vindictive, deceitful, ignorant and repentant.*

Moses says, (Gen. I. 26, 27), man was created in God's "image" and "likeness." It is evident (Gen. III. 22) that man's mental powers were not considered to be like those of Jehovah until after the fall—if they were so then. The common belief of ancient times was that the gods had bodies like men. If Moses had desired to contradict this idea, he would have done so in express terms, and not have used such a word as "image," never applied to mental, but always to physical likeness.

Jehovah *walked* in the garden in the cool of the day. Gen. III. 8.

"The Lord smelled a sweet savor." Gen. VIII. 21.

"The Lord came down to see the city and tower" of Babel. Gen. XI. 5.

The Lord appeared to Abraham. Gen. XII. 7; XVIII. 1.

Jehovah ate butter, veal and milk. Gen. XVIII. 8.

Jehovah stood at the top of Jacob's ladder. Gen. XXVIII. 13.

Jacob saw "God, face to face." Gen. XXXII. 24–30.

"God went up from him [Jacob] in the place where he talked with him." Gen. XXXV. 13.

God spoke with a voice. Ex. III. 2.

"Then went up Moses and Aaron, Nadab and Abihu, and seventy of the elders of Israel; and they *saw* the God of Israel; and there was under his feet, as it were a paved work of sapphire stone, and as it were the body of heaven in its clearness, and upon the nobles of the children of Israel he laid not his hand. Also they *saw* God and did eat and drink." Ex. XXIV. 9–11.

"The Lord spake unto Moses face to face, as a man speaketh unto his friend." Ex. XXXIII. 11.

The Lord said unto Moses, "And I will take away mine hand, and thou shalt see my back parts." Ex. XXXIII. 23.

There arose not a prophet since in Israel like unto Moses, whom the Lord knew face to face. Deut. XXXIV. 10.

The Lord appeared twice unto Solomon. 1 K. XI. 9.

Jehovah had particular days for receiving company. Job. I. 6 ; II. 1.

He also had particular angels to wait upon his person. Luke I. 19.

Jehovah said to himself, "Go to, let us go down and confound their [the Babelites] language." Gen. XI. 7.

"And the Lord went his way as soon as he had left communing with Abraham." Gen. XVIII. 33.

Palfrey* speaks as follows of the narrative in the eighteenth chapter of Genesis :

"Jehovah journeying like an opulent traveller with two attendants, approaches Abraham's tent in the heat of noon, and accepts his hospitable offers of water for his feet, and refreshment for his hunger. In recompense of this entertainment, he makes a promise to his attentive hosts of that blessing on which their hearts are most set, while he rebukes Sarah for her incredulity and the indecorons levity of its expression. The interview over, he proceeds on his way towards Sodom, and tells Abraham, who has respectfully accompanied him, that his purpose is to see whether tidings which have been brought to him of the iniquity of that place, are well founded. Like an obliged and grateful guest, he listens patiently, as they walk, to Abraham's solicitations for mercy for his neighbors. He sends his servants forward to make the scrutiny on which he is intent; and the truth of the unfavorable reports being ascertained by their experience, he proceeds to the accomplishment of his work of vengeance, sparing only the family in which his messengers had found safety and protection. What intelligent friend to the Divine Mission of Moses will be prepared to say that such views of God and of his agency as are presented in these particulars, were set down by him as just representations?" Compare this eighteenth chapter of Genesis with the fourteenth chapter of Numbers, which Palfrey says was inspired.

Jehovah is represented in the Bible as cruel and bloodthirsty.

The Lord hath sworn that he will have war with Amalek from generation to generation. Gen. XVII. 16.

He slew 500,000 men of Israel. 2 Ch. XIII. 15–17.

He sent a pestilence to destroy 70,000 Israelites. 1 Ch. XXI. 15.

He vexed Israel with all adversity. 2 Ch. XV. 6.

He punished his true prophet for being innocently deceived, and permitted the deceiver to go unharmed. 1 K. XIII. 1–25.

---

* Lectures on Jewish Antiquities. Lec. XXIII.

He directed the Jews to slay all the Midianite prisoners, except the virgins, who were to be kept as concubines and slaves. Num. XXXI. 3, 17, 18.

The Samaritan women with child should be ripped up. Hosea XIII. 16.

Jehovah destroyed 185,000 men in one night. 2 K. XIX. 35

He ordered the heads of the people to be hung in the sun. Num. XXV. 4.

He slew 50,070 Bethshemites for innocently looking into the ark. 2 S. VI. 19.

He smote Uzzah for piously putting up his hand to save the ark from falling. 2 S. VI. 6, 7.

He inflicts punishment on the third and fourth generation. Deut. V. 9; Num. XIV. 18; Ex. XX. 5; XXXIV. 7.

He will send a strong delusion to make men believe a lie. 2 Thess. II. 11.

The Old Testament represents the Deity as partial. See Sec. LIV.

The Bible represents the Creator as ignorant and weak.

Jehovah tried to find out what was in Hezekiah's heart. 2 Ch. XXXII. 31.

He sent to have the length and breadth of Jerusalem measured with a tape. Zech. II. 2.

He went to Balaam for information. Num. XXII. 9.

He inquired for information. 2 Ch. XVIII. 19.

He could not conquer chariots with scythes. Jud. I. 17.

The Father of the Universe is depicted in the Hebrew Scriptures as changeable and frequently repentant.

In the fourteenth chapter of Numbers there is a notable instance in which Jehovah was persuaded to change his mind by Moses, and the eighteenth chapter of Genesis contains a similar story.

It grieved the Lord at his heart, and it repented him that he had made man. Gen. VI. 6, 7.

" The Lord repented of the evil which he thought to do unto his people." Ex. XXXII. 12, 14.

Jehovah wavered in his intention. Num. XXXIII. 55, 56.

He repented having make Saul king. 1 S. XV. 10, 11, 35. He had previously given Saul another heart and promised to be with him. 1 S. X. 7, 9.

The Lord repented of the evil he was about to do to Jerusalem. 2 S. XXIV. 16.

He was grieved for the misery inflicted by himself on Israel. Jud. X. 16.

He repented of the evil he had done to Israel. 1 Ch. XXI. 14, 15.

He repented of the evil he was about to do to Israel. Jer. XXVI. 13.

He repented or would repent. James VI. 16, 17; Joel II. 13; Micah VII. 18; Jonah III. 10; Jer. IV. 28; XVIII. 18; Zech. VIII. 14.

Jehovah is triune.

The New Testament is said, by ninety-nine out of a hundred Christians, to teach that God, the only Deity, is one, but is composed of three persons. These three persons are distinct individuals and can act separately from each other. The Virgin Mary was impregnated by the Holy Ghost, (Mat. I. 18; Luke I. 35), and the child conceived was the Son. In the acts of impregnation and conception, the second and third persons of the Godhead acted separately from the Father, and from each other. What the Father was doing in the meantime is not stated. The Son was so far independent of the Father that he was not so much in favor with the latter at one time as at another: (Luke II. 40, 52). The desires of the first and third members of the Divine firm did not always agree. The junior partner said, on one occasion, "Father, if thou be willing, remove this cup from me; nevertheless, not *my* will, but *thine* be done." (Luke XXII. 42). Indeed he frequently used expressions to show that their purposes did not always coincide. (John V. 30; VI. 39; Mat. VII. 21; XII. 50). The Father seems to have been even too indifferent to the feelings of the Son, and the latter, in the bitter agonies of the cross, cried out, reproachfully, "My God, my God, why hast thou forsaken me?" (Mark XV. 34). And yet these three persons are not three persons, but only one. They are the tri-une, the three-in-one God of orthodox Christians, who though they believe in the Trinity, though they assert that belief in the Trinity is necessary to eternal salvation, though they refuse to have any religious fellowship with all who do not acknowledge the Trinity, yet do not pretend to defend that Trinity by reason. They boldly confess that the Trinity is incomprehensible, and, to the natural reason, absurd. But they say it is "a mystery," one of the sacred mysteries, it is beyond reason, and must be accepted without argument.

"And how do I know that it is a mystery?"

"The priest says so."

"Then the priest can tell me any absurd story and say it is a mystery, and I must forthwith believe it; and the more absurd the story, the greater the mystery."

Mystery in revealed religion is only another word for absurdity. The Church says there are mysteries in science and natural religion—but it is not so. There are many unexplained problems, but no mysteries, in the sense of that word as used in regard to the peculiar doctrines of the Christians.

THE IMMORTALITY OF THE SOUL.

XLIV. One of the fundamental doctrines of Christian ty is, that man's soul is immortal. The mind or soul is "the mental strength," * or all the psychological endowments of an animal, including the faculties of consciousness, sensation, reason, memory, desire, will, and the power of harmoniously governing the actions of the muscles. The mind is the function of the brain. The animal body is formed of various organs, such as muscles, bones, nerves, brain, heart, stomach, liver, kidneys, eyes, ears, nose, palate, &c. ; and all of these again are composed of subordinate organs. Every organ has a function. Sight is the function of the eyes, taste of the palate, digestion of the stomach, and mind is the function of the brain. A function is necessarily immaterial. No man has ever cut out a piece of flesh from the human stomach and proved it to be digestion, neither has any man seen the function of sight, or the strength of a muscle. All search for a material mind is in vain.

That the mind is a function is a well established fact of physiology.† Different faculties of the mind have their seats in different portions of the brain. If the back part of the brain (the cerebellum) be destroyed, the animal cannot stand; if the upper and forward part of the brain (the cerebrum) be destroyed, the faculties of reason and memory are lost. If the stomach be injured, the digestive faculty is impaired—if the brain be injured, the thinking faculty will be disordered. The man who gets drunk in his body is drunk in his mind, too : he loses the clearness of his ideas. While the brain is soft in extreme youth, the mind is weak; with old age, the brain frequently decreases in size and solidity, and second childhood comes on. The existence, as well as the vigor of the function, dies with the organ. Digestion ceases to exist with the stomach; there is no sight after the destruction of the eye ; there is no mind after the brain dies.

Man is an animal. He has the same physical organs, and these organs have the same functions, as those of other animals. His flesh and his

* Webster's definition.　　† See Appendix, Note 8.

blood and his brain are constituted of the same materials, and in precisely the same method. The man is apparently far superior in hisorganization and capacities to the dog; but the dog is quite as much superior to the frog as the man is above the dog. The inferiority of many of the higher order of brutes is not to be attributed only to natural mental inferiority,—perhaps less to that cause than to the want of an articulate voice and of hands. A man who should grow up among orang-outangs, without ever seeing any of his own kind, would be little better than a brute ; and yet he would be no worse than a race of animals possessing all the qualities of man except the articulate voice, the hand fitted for grasping, and the erect stature. If man has an immortal soul, the dog must have the same.

THE MORAL ACCOUNTABILITY OF MAN TO HIS CREATOR.

XLV. The New Testament asserts, indirectly if not directly, that man is morally responsible to God for his actions. In other words, the Creator gives his creature certain propensities, and then rewards and punishes him for acting in obedience to them. Different men have different mental constitutions : one is by nature more disposed to be foolish and sinful than another, but Christ would hold them all equally responsible. No man can change his mental constitution ; no amount of wishing, or striving, or praying, will make a brave man out of a great coward, or a wise man out of a great fool, or a high-minded man out of a very base one. Neither can man govern the circumstances in which he is placed ; time and tide will have their course in spite of all his exertions. Natural mental constitution and outward circumstances, both beyond his control, govern him, determine his action, suggest the motives according to which he must act. Man is the slave of motives. He never acts without motives; he cannot act contrary to the motives which appear the strongest to him. He, who feels very hungry, and has a palateable dish within his reach, and has no motive for not eating then and there, must eat, as a mat ter of necessity. Men cannot create motives at their will, and therefore cannot. be morally free or responsible to a creator. The purpose of all action is self-gratification ; the most magnanimous as well as the meanest of all deeds can have but one end—the gratification of the actor. From no point in which the question can be viewed, does it appear that man should be punished or rewarded for the moral nature of his actions. There may be a personal, conscious Deity, but he knows no such distinctions as virtue and vice. All men are as he made them, and equally good before him.* Christ holds men responsible, not only for their actions, but also for their opinions in matters of religion ; as though belief were under the control of the will, and were a matter of merit. According to Christian doctrine a man should desire, not to learn, the truth, but to believe the tenets of the orthodox church, just as they are. But if such a desire were proper, would it be possible for the mind to be governed, in its conclusions, by the desire? Can any man believe that black is white, that fresh grass is red, merely because he knows that such a belief would be rewarded by some great good? Man believes in accordance with the evidence, or his views of the evidence, before him. Man cannot make evidence by wishing, cannot believe without evidence, and therefore he cannot govern his belief according to his desire. But if he could, it would not be consistent with our ideas of human, much less of divine justice, to hold him responsible for his religious opinions. Men ordinarily follow the creed of their parents, and desire to do so. The children of the Bramins, Mohammedans, Buddhists, Confucianists, Parsees, Jews, Greeks, Catholics, Protestants, Skeptics, and Mormons, almost invariably follow the respective religious creeds of their fathers ; and all consider themselves most fortunate in being placed in a situation to learn, what appears to them to be, the only true religion.

---

* See Appendix, Note 10.

IMMEDIATE DIVINE GOVERNMENT

XLVI. The Old Testament represents nearly every occurrence as the imme-diate act of Jehovah, who, according to the old Hebrew doctrine, governed the universe without the intervention of any general laws. He made contracts with Abraham, wrestled with Jacob, and advised with Moses. He came down from heaven to examine into the sins of Adam, Babel, and Sodom. He repeat-edly led the armies of Israel to the battle-field. He slow the Amalekites with stones from heaven, and he stopped the sun in its course, to permit Joshua to destroy the fugitive Gentiles. When Job is smitten, it is not without a previous consultation on the subject, between the Lord of Heaven and Satan; and when Pharoah obstinately refuses to permit the Jews to depart, he acts not from natural stubbornness or blindness, but because Jehovah had hardened his heart for that special occasion. Even women could not become pregnant, on many occasions, without the immediate intervention of the God of Abraham, Isaac, and Jacob.*

These interpositions do not take place now; and, as it would be foolish to believe that a Supreme Deity would change his system of government, we must believe that there never were such interventions. The authority of Moses is worth noting on this point; he only gave expression to the superstition almost universally prevalent in ancient times. Eichhorn says, "According to the language of this book, [the Pentateuch] God produces everything directly, without availing himself of the course of nature and certain intermediate causes. But in this there is nothing peculiar to it. Its conceptions are only like those of the ancient world in general, when it had not been ascertained by long con-tinued inquiry that all events are connected into a series of intermediate causes." Grote remarks, "The perpetual junction of gods and men, in the same picture, and familiar appeal to everpresent divine agency, was in harmony with the interpretation of nature" universal in early ages.†

* See Gen. XX. 18; XXV. 21; XXIV. 1; XXIX. 31; XXX. 17, 22; XXXI 11, 12; Jud. XIII. 2; 1 S. I. 17; IV. 11; 2 K. IV. 16; Ruth IV. 13; Luke L 19.
† See Appendix, Note 9.

THE SCHEME OF REDEMPTION.

XLVII. The Christian doctrine is, that Christ came to enable men, by believing on him, to enjoy everlasting delights in Heaven. Men were originally created immortal, sinless, perfectly happy, and ignorant of the difference between right and wrong. While in that condition man violated a command of his Creator, and he and his posterity forever were in punishment made mortal, sinful, miserable on this earth, and condemned to everlasting pains in a future life. The race existed for two thousand and four hundred years almost without revelation or aid from God, till the publication of the books of Moses, and these were given only to the tribe of Israel. The Jews apparently could be saved by their faith, (Rom. IV. 2; Gal. III. 6; James II. 21, 23; Luke XVI 22); but all the rest of mankind were doomed to hopeless and everlasting damnation. After fifteen hundred years, God sent Jesus, a portion of himself, to earth, to atone by his sufferings for the sin of Adam. Jesus was conceived by a marriageable woman, who was distinguishable in no natural and important point from other women of her age and country. He was carried in the womb and born and bred like other children. He was possessed of a body of real flesh and blood, he was subject to animal wants and desires, and he was fed upon the ordinary food of men. He was circumcised, and he grew in form and spirit to be a man, (Luke II. 40; Mat. XI. 19). He was bred to the trade of a carpenter, (Mark VI. 3), and he was supposed by his acquaintances to be the son of Joseph, (Luke II. 41, 48; IV. 22), and to be a man like other men. He made no claim to be anything more till he was thirty years of age, (Luke III. 23; IV. 24; Mat. XIII. 54; Mark VI. 1; John VI. 42); nor did he, previous to that time, utter a sentence worthy of record. On one occasion his relatives thought him to be crazy, (Mark III. 21, 31). At the age of thirty he proclaimed himself a prophet, but found so little faith at home that he declared "a prophet is not without honor but in his own country, and among his own kin, and in his own house." (Mark VI. 4; Mat. XIII. 57; John IV. 44). He was then looked upon at home as an impostor! Not even his own brothers believed on him (John VII. 5); and they appear to have cared little about him, for they are not mentioned as having been present at his seizure, trial, execution, or resurrection. After his mother had given birth to the Divine Redeemer of men, she yielded to the embraces of a man and had children—merely human sons and daughters. (Mat. I. 25; XII. 16; XIII. 55; Luke VIII. 19; John II. 12; Acts I. 14). After teaching three years, and before he had committed his doctrine to writing, Jesus was arrested on a charge of sedition, tried and executed ; and he, God, died in the midst of great torments. Verily, as Paul says, such things are "foolishness to the natural man."

CONTRADICTORY DOCTRINES.

XLVIII. Two contradictory doctrines cannot both be true; and no book on earth teaches so many conflicting dogmas as the Bible. Moses says there are no future rewards and punishments, no future life, and no devil; he teaches the existence of one single God who should be worshipped by only one nation with peculiar ceremonies—among which sacrifice was prominent—under the ministration of a hereditary caste of priests. The Christian Evangelists teach a future life and future rewards and punishments, a God who is three in one, to be worshipped by all nations, without sacrifice, and without the intervention of a hereditary priesthood. It is a notorious fact that texts can be found in the Bible to prove anything. A large number of Christian sects, differing very widely in their doctrines, all pretend to find the foundation of their faith and the condemnation of that of their rivals in this one book. They dispute whether God be one or three, whether Christ was a man or a God; whether, at the Sacrament of the last supper, the communicants eat and drink the flesh and blood of Christ, or only the apparent bread and wine; whether men can be saved by faith, or by works, or by grace; whether sinners and unbelievers will be punished by everlasting pains in hell; whether there be a temporary hell into which sinners are thrown after death; whether the Pope of Rome has the authority of Christ to act as the Vicegerent of God on earth; whether the priests have the authority to pardon sins and to condemn men to hell; whether there be any priests with authority from Christ; whether kings and masters have a divine right to rule their subjects and slaves; whether baptism be necessary to salvation; whether true believers possess the power of working miracles; whether all the books of the Bible be inspired; and whether the inspiration extend to every word or to the ideas. Let us take up some of the most glaring of the contradictions.

IMMORTALITY OF THE SOUL.

XLIX. The immortality of the soul is one of the chief points of Christ's teaching (Mat. XIX. 16, 17; XXII. 30, 37, 39; Mark X. 17, 21; Luke X. 27, 28; XX. 36; John III. 15). In the fifteenth chapter of 1 Corinthians, Paul holds a lengthy discourse on eternal life. The sanctions of morality—the rewards for the deserving and the punishments for the wicked—are all confined according to the New Testament, to the next world. Everlasting and intense delight in Heaven, or pain in Hell, is to be the portion of every man according to his deeds on earth, and surely that sanction should be enough. The Evangelists in no place promise pleasure in this world to the followers of Christ, or threaten earthly punishment to sinners. On the contrary, the Lord is represented as treating all alike in this world. "He maketh his sun to rise on the evil and on the good, and sendeth rain on the just and on the unjust." (Mat. V. 45). "He is kind to the unthankful and to the evil." (Luke VI. 28).

The Old Testament teaches that the soul dies with the body. A few texts may be found to show that the doctrine of the life of the soul after the death of the body was not unknown, but the weight of authority is all against a resurrection. The silence of Moses in the law in regard to the immortality, is equivalent to an express denial of it. He represents Jehovah as saying that man shall return to the dust whence he came, (Gen. II. 19), and shall not "live forever." No exception is made for the soul. Solomon, the wisest of all men, gifted with even superhuman wisdom (1 K. III. 11), asserts (Ec. I. 4), that man passes away, "but the earth abideth forever;" and again he says, man dies like a *beast*,

(Ec. III. 19, 20); and elsewhere he uses the emphatic language, "the living know that they shall die; but the dead know not anything, neither have they any more a reward; for the memory of them is forgotten. Also their love and their hatred and their envy is now perished : neither have they any more a portion forever in anything that is done under the sun. Go thy way, eat thy bread with joy, and drink thy wine with a merry heart; for God now accepteth thy works. Let thy garments be always white; and let thy head lack no ointment. Live joyfully with thy wife whom thou lovest all the days of the life of thy vanity; for that is thy portion in this life, and in thy labor which thou takest under the sun. Whatsoever thy hand findeth to do, do it with thy might; for there is no work, nor device, nor knowledge, nor wisdom in the grave whither thou goest." Job is not so emphatic, but his denial of the resurrection is equally clear : (VII. 9; XIV. 7, 12; XIX. 26; XXI. 32). David is nearly as plain as Solomon, (Ps. LXXXIX. 48; CII. 11, 12). Isaiah was of the same opinion, (XXXIX. 7, 8).

The Old Testament prescribed a minute code of things to be done, and things to be avoided; the disobedient were threatened with severe punishments, and the faithful encouraged with the promise of great rewards, but all these rewards and punishments were to be administered on this earth. Adam's sin was to be punished in this world only. The punishment of Cain was to be that the earth should not yield her strength to his tillage. (Gen. IV. 12). The wickedness of the Antediluvians was so great that "it repented the Lord that he had made man on the earth, and it grieved him at heart;" yet there is no mention of any punishment except the flood. (Gen. VI. 13). Ham's unlucky eyes were damned by Noah, with Jehovah's consent, in the condemnation of himself and all his descendants to slavery on this earth. (Gen. IX. 25). The people of Sodom were struck with blindness and destroyed with "brimstone and fire." (Gen. XIX. 11, 24, 25). Abraham's willingness to obey the Lord was to be rewarded on earth by the increase of his posterity to be a great nation, with Jehovah for their God and protection. No mention is made of reward in Heaven, (Gen. XXII. 17). The idea of final settlement with man for all his sins and virtues, before he leaves this world, is particularly strong with Moses, and is set forth with great force in the beginning of Deuteronomy. Chapter seventh contains the words of Jehovah conveying assurance to the Jews that obedience to the law of Moses would be rewarded by the fulfilment of the promise to Abraham, (Gen. XVII. 6, 7), and disobedience should be punished with destruction. In chapter twenty-eighth of Deuteronomy, there is a long enumeration of the blessings which Jehovah will bestow upon the Israelites if they shall be true to him, and of the evils which he will inflict if they turn away and neglect his laws and ordinances. The blessings promised are all kinds of earthly prosperity, and the long list concludes thus: "the Lord shall make thee plenteous in goods, in the fruit of thy body, and in the fruit of thy cattle, and in the fruit of thy ground, in the land which the Lord sware unto thy fathers to give thee." The evils threatened for disobedience are the sword, famine, pestilence, "madness, and blindness, and astonishment of heart," consumption, fever, inflammation, extreme burning, blasting, mildew, all the diseases of Egypt, trembling of heart, failing of eyes, sorrow of mind, renewed captivity in Egypt; and, finally, "the Lord shall send upon thee cursing, vexation and rebuke, in all that thou settest thine hand unto for to do, until thou be destroyed." Not a word of Heaven or Hell! It is very clear that Moses was determined not to patronize those institutions. See, likewise, Lev. XXVI. 3, 4, 15–17; Ex. XX. 12; Ps. LVIII. 11.

No Christian author worthy of note, contends that a future life was taught by the Old Testament. * Milman says that Moses was acquainted with the doctrine of the immortality of the soul, but he did not teach it, because it was received among the Egyptians, and because he wished to make his law differ as much as possible from that of the Egyptians. This is the only excuse offered for Moses, and much worse than none at all.

THE MYTH OF PARADISE AND ADAM'S SIN.

L. The author of the Pentateuch, in giving an account of the early history of mankind, thought proper to introduce the myth prevalent among all the ancient nations of western Asia, of a golden age when the earth and nature were inconceivably beautiful, when the whole animal creation was at peace, when men were free from pain and death, satisfied in every want and gratified in every desire without exertion, and perfectly happy and sinless and even ignorant of the distinction between right and wrong. The present condition of man is accounted for by supposing that he violated a command of Jehovah, and for that reason was rendered sinful and mortal, liable to disease and pain, and compelled to live in misery, and to earn his support by his labor. No idea of

---

* Note to the XVth Chapter of Gibbon's Decline and Fall.

punishment in a future life was affixed to Adam's sin, nor is there any hint in any of the writings of the Hebrew prophets that his guilt was to be expiated after death.

In the time of Jesus, the doctrine of the immortality of the soul was adopted by the majority of the people in Judea, and was firmly rooted among that class in which he hoped to make the most of his converts.   Another doctrine had also some prevalence—that man was born wicked, that he was naturally sinful. Christ and his followers connected these two doctrines with the myth of the fall, to which a new interpretation was given.   The chief punishment of Adam was not as represented by Moses, but was the condemnation of all men to hell, from which they could be rescued only by believing on Jesus Christ.

THE ONENESS OF GOD.

LI.   The Deity is considered throughout the Old Testament as a unit, and as single in his nature.   He is generally styled Jehovah; he is sometimes called the "Father," but never the "Son," and the Holy Ghost is never referred to as a distinct personage.   (Deut. IV. 35, 39; V. 7; VI. 4; VIII. 13; XXXII. 39: Ex. XX. 3; Ps. LXXXVI. 10; Is. XXXVII. 16; XLIII. 10; XLIV. 6; XLV. 5; Jer. X. 10).

The New Testament has always been interpreted by the great majority of Christians to teach that God is not single but three persons in one, composed of the Father, the Son, and the Holy Ghost.   The following texts are relied on by the Trinitarians: Mat. III. 16, XVII. 5, XXVIII. 19; Luke I. 35; John V. 18; XIV. 16, 26; XV. 26; XVI. 13; 1 John V. 7; 2 Cor. XIII. 14.   Christ is said to be the maker and preserver of all things, John I. 3, 10; Heb. I. 2, 10; 1 Cor. VIII. 6; Col. I. 16; Rev. IV. 11.   Christ is one substance with God, John X. 30, 38; XII. 45; XVII. 11, 22; XIV. 9.   Christ is the God of Gods, Rom XIV. 9; Phil. II. 9; Col. II. 10, 15; 1 Pet. III. 22; Rev. XVII. 14; XIX. 16.   The Holy Ghost is spoken of as a distinct personage, Mat. III. 16; Mark I. 10; Luke III. 22; John I. 32.

MEANS OF ATTAINING DIVINE FAVOR.

LII. The only passport to divine favor recognised by the Old Testament writers was descent from Jacob; but the Christians asserted that there was no means of salvation except by the faith of Christ. In many passages of the New Testament it is pointedly asserted that belief in Jesus as the Redeemer of mankind is the only means of escaping from eternal hell, (John VI. 40, 47; X. 28; XI. 26; XVII. 3; XX. 31. Acts. II. 38; XVI. 31. Rom. 1. 17; X. 9; XIV. 23. 1 John IV. 2, 6, 15; V. 1, 13). Mark is rather positive when he says (XVI. 16), "He that believeth and is baptised shall be saved, but he that believeth not shall be dammed."

In other passages it is said that love is the fulfilment of the law, or that salvation may be attained by good works, (Mat. V. 44, 45. XVI. 27; XXII. 37, 39, 40; Mark XII. 31; Luke X. 27, 28; XVIII. 22; Rom. XIII. 8, 10; 1 John IV. 7, 16).

Elsewhere it is intimated that neither faith nor works will suffice to wash out the sin of Adam, but that only the grace [or caprice] of God can suffice (Mat XX. 15: Luke XVII. 35; John VI. 27; Acts II. 23; VIII. 16; XV. 11; Rom. II. 4; X. 3; IX. 16; 1 Cor. X. 13; Eph. II. 8; Phil. II. 13; 2 Pet. III. 15). The term "elect" frequently applied in the New Testament to the favorites of Heaven conveys the idea that the divine favor cannot be gained by anything that man can do. All these dogmas are inconsistent with each other, and equally inconsistent with reason.

THE DEVIL.

LIII.   Moses had no devil; he never hints that there is an evil spirit.   His history of the temptation and fall show conclusively that he rejected the doctrine of a devil, which was received in Egypt long before his time, as he must have known.   Eve was tempted by a serpent, "which was more subtle than any beast of the field."   There is no hint that the devil entered, or took the shape of a snake.   Jehovah condemns that reptile as though it had been the sole sinner, to eat dust, and crawl upon its belly, and be hated and persecuted by man for ever.   The temptation having caused the greatest evil in the history of the universe, according to both Hebrew and Christian writers, it follows that Satan must have been the actor, if Moses had been disposed to recognise such a personage.

The devil plays an important figure in the New Testament.

DIVINE FAVORITISM.

LIV.   The Old Testament, claiming to be a divine revelation, was given to the Jews only; they were assured that they were the especial favorites of Jehovah; that he had chosen them, and them alone, to be a holy people before him; that he had no communication with other nations; and that he would be their exclusive God for ever.   They were directed to utterly destroy all opposing Gentiles; they were forbidden to intermarry with foreigners; they were assured that none should ever sit upon their throne, except the family of David, and that none should ever minister to Jehovah, except descendants of Aaron. The peculiar favor of God for Israel is the most prominent of the doctrines of Moses. Gen. XVII. 8, 9; XVIII. 7; XIX. 5; XXVII. 29; Ex. XI. 7; XIX. 6; XXIX. 45, 46; XXXV. 34; Dent. IV. 37; VII. 6, 36; IX. 9; XI. 9-18; XIV. 2, 21; XVIII. 5; XXVI. 18, 19; XXXII. 43; XXVII. 10; Num. XIV. 40; XXVI. 1-14; Ps. XVIII. 19, 20; 1 Ch. XVII. 9, 22; &c.

The New Testament denies the superiority of the blood of Abraham, (John VIII. 33), and asserts that all nations are alike before God; (Mat. XXVIII. 1, 9; Mark XVI. 15; Luke XXIV. 47; Acts XV. 17; Rom. III. 22; Gal. III. 28; VI. 15; Eph. I. 10; II. 14; Col. II. 14). Paul declares Jews and Gentiles to be alike transgressors (Rom. II. 12; III. 20).

GENERAL SPIRIT OF THE LAW.

LV. The general spirit of the New Testament differs greatly from that of the Mosaic law. The Christians disregard the Jewish code in relation to circumcision, sacrifices, the Sabbath, unclean meats, and exalt the virtues of baptism, prayer, and humility. The Old Testament is sanguinary in its teachings, and unfitted to educate any nation to feelings of charity, love, moderation or justice towards the foreigner, the poor or the innovator. The punishment of death was decreed for blasphemy, (Lev. XXIV. 23); for Sabbath breaking, (Num. XV. 32); for idolatry, (Deut. XIII. 6; XVII. 5; Ex. XXII. 20); for filial stubbornness, (Deut. XXI. 18), and for adultery, (Dent. XXII. 22). Nations in the neighborhood of Judea, if idolatrous, were to be destroyed utterly, "smiting them with the edge of the sword," "making no covenant with them, and showing no mercy to them," unless it were to carry off the virgins for concubines, after slaying all the males and married women, (Dent. VII. 12; XIII. 15, 17; Ex. XXXII. 27).

The following quotations from different books will serve to show something of the spirit of the Old Testament:

"Thy foot may be dipped in the blood of thine enemies, and the tongue of thy dogs in the same." Ps. LXVIII. 22.

"The righteous shall rejoice when he seeth the vengeance: he shall wash his feet in the blood of the wicked." Ps. LVIII. 10.

" Do unto them as unto the Midianites, as to Sisera, as to Javon, at the brook of Kison, which perished at Endor ; they became as dung for the earth." Ps. LXXXIII. 9.

"O my God, make them like a wheel, as the stubble before the wind, as the fire burneth the wood, as the flame setteth the mountain on fire. So persecute them with thy tempest, and make them afraid with thy storm." Ps. LXXXIII. 13.

"Let them be confounded and troubled forever; yea let them be put to shame and perish." Ps. LXXXIII. 17.

"I will make mine arrows drunk with blood, and my sword shall devour flesh." Dent. XXXII. 42.

"An eye for an eye," and "a tooth for a tooth," (Ex. XXI. 24; Lev. XXIV. 20) was the rule of conduct toward Jews—but toward Gentiles there was "no mercy."

David, in Psalm CIX., thus hurls his curses at some enemy :

"Let his days be few; and let another take his office.

"Let his children be fatherless, and his wife a widow.

"Let his children be continually vagabonds, and beg; let them seek their bread also out of their desolate places.

"Let the extortioner catch all that he hath; and let the stranger spoil his labor.

"Let there be none to extend mercy unto him ; neither let there be any to favor his fatherless children.

"Let his posterity be cut off; and in the generation following let their name be blotted out."

Christ repealed the eye-for-an-eye and tooth-for-a-tooth doctrine, and prohibited revenge, (Mat. V. 44; Luke VI. 28; Acts VII. 60; Rom. XII. 14). He said nothing of punishing blasphemers, Sabbath-breakers, idolaters, or stubborn sons, in this world, and he directed that the punishment of an adulterer should be inflicted only by sinless persons, which was equivalent to saying that the Jewish law against adultery should not be executed at all, (John VIII. 11). The Jehovah of Moses is a god of battles: the Deity of Paul is a god of peace, (Rom. XV. 33 ; Heb. XIII. 20) ; and yet we are told they are the same God.

"God is *love*." 2 Cor. XIII. 11; 1 John IV. 8.

"The Lord is a *man of war*." Ex. XV. 3.

PERMANENCE OF THE JEWISH LAW.

LVI. There are few points in which the Old Testament is clearer than that the law of Moses was intended to remain in force forever. When Jehovah chose Abraham to be the father of God's people, he used the following very perspicuous words: "I will establish my covenant between me and thee, and thy seed after thee, in their gener,tions, for an everlasting covenant; to be a God unto thee and to thy seed after thee. And I will give unto thee and to thy seed after thee, the land wherein thou art a stranger, all the land of Canaan for an everlasting possession; and I will be their God." (Gen. XVII. 7, 8). Whether Abraham had a bad memory, or whether the covenant was not of sufficient importance for him to keep it before his mind, Moses does not say, though he informs us that Jehovah repeated his promise no less than five different times to Abraham. (Gen. XII. 1-8; XIII. 14-17; XV. 1-5, 13-21; XVII. 1-8; XXII. 15-18). To Isaac the promise was renewed but once, (Gen. XXVI. 2-5), and to Jacob thrice. (Gen. XXVIII. 13-15; XXXV. 10-12; XLVI. 2-3). Jehovah did not expressly state on all these occasions that the covenant should last forever, but that was plainly implied. During the time of Moses the Lord frequently alluded to the promise, which he "sware unto Abraham and Isaac and Jacob;" but when he found out what a stiff-necked race the Jews were, he gave them to understand that the contract was mutually binding, and if they would not observe their share, he would not only not observe his part, but he would give them a hell on earth besides. (Dent. VIII. 20). It was nevertheless very plain that he never intended to entirely fulfil his threat, but purposed to preserve his law to Israel forever, (Ex. XX. 12; XII. 24; XXIX. 42; XXXI. 16; Deut. VI. 2; VII. 9, 16; XI. 21; XII. 19; XVIII. 5; XXVI. 19; XXVII. 26; Lev. X. 15; XXIII. 21; Num. XXXV. 29; 1 Ch. XVII. 9-14, 22; 1 K. VI. 13; 2 K. XVII. 37; Ps. CV. 11; Mal. IV. 4). The threats against the Jews in no place hint a withdrawal or destruction of the Mosaic law, or its repeal to make room for an improved code. Moses said, (Deut. XXVII. 26), "cursed be the man that confirmeth not all the words of this law to do them." Eight hundred and fifty years later, after the Jews had committed nearly all

their great offences against Jehovah and his law, he said to Jeremiah, (XI. 3),
"cursed be the man that obeyeth not the words of this covenant." Besides the
numerous promises that the covenant with Abraham should endure forever,
the only consideration for which—circumcision—was always faithfully observed
by the Jews, there were numerous promises that minor points of the law should
be sacred forever. Thus, Levi should minister forever to Jehovah and be his
heir, (Deut. XII. 19; XIV. 27; XVIII. 5; Num. XVI. 40; III. 10). Offerings
should be made forever, (Ex. XXIX. 42). The Mosaic Sabbath should be observed forever, (Ex. XXXI. 15-17); and the same method for washing, and the
same kind of oil for ointment should be used for ever. (Ex. XXX. 21, 31).

The publication of the New Testament as a divine revelation was an abroga-
tion of the law of Moses. The two systems are at the extremes of all known
religions codes for mildness and severity. It is impossible to reconcile them,
and no author has attempted to do so. The declaration of Jesus that he came
to fulfil the Mosaic law, to every "jot" and "tittle," (Mat. V. 17, 18), amounts
to nothing, when we know that nearly all his acts were in defiance of that law.
The Baptist, who was inspired, (Mat. III. 10; Luke III. 9), said, (Luke VII.
28,) that the axe was to be laid at the root of "every tree which bringeth not
forth good fruit," and the tree specially referred to was the Jewish law. Christ
flatly contradicted the Old Testament as to the mortality of the soul, the nature
of God, the superiority of the blood of Abraham, swearing and divorce, but he
dodged the questions of circumcision, offerings, the Sabbath, and clean meats,
wherein the law was violated by his followers, with his approval.

JESUS A CRIMINAL UNDER THE JEWISH LAW.

LVII. The Christian philosopher is compelled, in defence of his faith, to
assert that it is consistent with the attributes of an all-wise, unchangeable and
perfect God, to publish two different and entirely inconsistent systems of religion; but he would hardly confess that if one prophet were legally condemned
to death under the laws of another, both could have acted by the same divine
inspiration. The Jews claimed that Jesus had forfeited his life by the Mosaic

law; and if upon examination we find that to be the fact, we must conclude that either Jesus or Moses acted without Jehovah's authority.

Jesus affirmed the divine inspiration of the Pentateuch, (Mat. V. 17, 18; XV. 4–7; XXII. 31; Mark VII. 9–15; XII. 26; Luke XX. 37; XXIV. 27; John V. 46).

Jesus claimed to be divine; (Mat. I. 18; VII. 23; Luke I. 35; John VIII. 58; X. 30; XX. 28; Col. II. 2; John V. I).

The claims of Jesus to the Messiahship, to possess the power of forgiving sins, and to be divine, left the Jews, and particularly the priests, no half-way course to pursue. It was their duty to acknowledge him as a true prophet, or to denounce him as an impostor. This would have been their duty if the pretender had confined his mission to lamenting like Jeremiah, or psalm-singing like David, and much more when the prophet proposed to abolish at once the laws given by Jehovah himself. When a man assumed the prophetic character among the Jews, the burden of proof was upon himself. The people were to assume that he was a false prophet, if he did not prove himself to be a true one. The Pharisees and Levites were surely not to blame if Jesus did not convince them of his divine authority; and if he failed to so convince them, it was their duty to punish him as a blasphemer and an impostor.

It was proper to prove divine authority by miracles. (Num. XVI. 29; Ex. IV. 1–30; Jud. VI. 17; 2 K. XX. 8–11; Is. XXXVIII. 7, 8).

Christ refused to perform miracles to prove his divine authority when requested to do so. (Mat. XII. 39; XIII. 58; XVI. 24; Mark VI. 5; Luke XI. 16; John II. 18; VI. 38).

The Jews were not to receive a prophet on trust, but were required to examine into his claims and to judge for themselves. Dent. XVIII. 20–22.

Prophets were required to act in the name of the Lord. Deut. XVIII. 20.

Jesus refused to say in whose name he acted. Luke XX. 8.

The Mosaic law was given to last for ever. See Sec. LVI. of this book.

Jesus said, evidently referring to the Jewish law: "Every plant which my Heavenly Father hath not planted, must be rooted up." (Mat. XV. 13). And he was on friendly terms with John the Baptist, an open enemy to the law of Moses.

Jesus repealed portions of the old law inculcating strict retaliation. (Mat. V. 44; Luke VI. 28). He repealed the Mosaic law in regard to adultery. (Mat. V. 31, 32; XIX. 8, 9; Mark X. 5–12; Luke XVI. 18); and in regard to swearing (Mat. V. 34; James VI. 12); and in regard to resistance to oppression (Mat. V. 39–42). He also taught a new doctrine not authorised by the law of Moses in relation to baptism, (Mat. III. 11, 15, &c.), and in regard to prayer, (Mat. VII. 7, &c.). He frequently exhibited signs of disrespect for the old law (Mat XII. 6 ; V. 22–44; Mark XII. 29–31 ; Luke V. 21 ; VI. 37; XV. 13 ; XIX. 9 ; Rom. XIII. 8, 10 ; John IV. 23).　His whole life and doctrine was an assertion of the insufficiency of the Jewish law.

The Levites were to be the heirs of Jehovah's ministry for ever.　Deut. XVIII. 5.

"The man that will do presumptuously, and will not hearken unto the priest that standeth to minister there before the Lord thy God, or unto the judge, even that man shall die, and thou shall put away the evil from Israel." Dent. XVII. 12.

"Take heed to thyself that thou forsake not the Levite as long as thou livest on the earth."　Dent. XII. 19 ; XIV. 27.

Jesus forsook the Levites ; he denied that they were the heirs of Jehovah's ministry, (Mat. IV. 18–21).　He spoke of them with habitual disrespect, (Mat. V. 20 ; Luke X. 31, 32; XVIII. 10).　And his whole life was a doing presumptuously toward them, and a refusal to hearken to them.

Moses said that Jehovah rested on the Sabbath.　Gen II. 2.

Jesus denied it.　John V. 17.

The Old Testament called down curses on "every man that confirmeth not all the words of this covenant to do them."　Deut XXVII. 26 ; Jer. XI. 3.

Christ did not confirm all the words of that Covenant.

The man that despised the law of Moses should die, (Heb. X. 28).　"Ye shall not add unto the word, [the Mosaic law,] which I command you, neither shall ye diminish aught from it; that ye shall keep the commandments of the Lord your God."　Deut. IV. 2.

Jesus added to and diminished from the Mosaic law.　Moses had directed that even the performance of miracles should not suffice to convince the Jews of the divine authority of any prophet who proposed to lead them to strange gods.　Deut. XIII. 1–5.

Jesus did introduce the worship of a strange god ; a divinity entirely different from the God of Moses ; a worship entirely different from that taught by the Old Testament, and a theory of moral duty entirely different from that of the Pentateuch.

Jesus claimed to be the Messias foretold by the prophets, but he was no king. John XVIII. 36.

The Messias foretold by the prophets was to be a king. Is. XIV. 2 ; XXXII. 1, 18 ; XLV. 14; XLIX. 22; LII. 1–4, 21; LX. 3 ; Ezek XXXVI. 8 ; XXXVII. 23 ; Dan. VII. 14; IX. 25 ; Joel. III. 9 ; Jer. III. 17.

Jesus was a false prophet, and a blasphemer, and a reviler of the Levites, within the meaning of the Mosaic law, and if he did not convince the Israelites of his divine mission, it was their duty to punish him as an impostor.

The punishment of the false prophet, the blasphemer and the reviler of the Levites was death. Deut. XIII. 1–5; XVIII. 20; Lev. XXIV. 23.

Jesus was executed by the Jews for his offences against the laws of Moses; and the evidence of his guilt was so strong that no reasonable man can deny that his conviction and execution were justified by the law.

REVIEW OF INCONSISTENCIES.

LVIII. For all these inconsistencies in the doctrine of the Bible, there is only one excuse; that man in different stages of civilization required different teaching. Archbishop Whately says,—"Any one who regards the Bible, as many Christians do, as *one book*, containing divine instructions, without having formed any clear notions of what does, and what does not, belong to each dispensation, will of course fall into the greatest confusion of thought. He will be like a man who should have received from his father, at various times, a great number of letters containing directions as to his conduct, from the time when he was a little child just able to read, till he was a grown man; and who should lay by all these letters with care and reverence, but in a confused heap, and should take up any one of them at random, and read it without any reference to its date, whenever he needed his father's instructions how to act." The Mohammedans and Mormons, who adopt all the Scriptures of the Hebrews and Christians, would no doubt explain the (if possible, greater) inconsistencies of their books in the same method.

LIX. A divine revelation should be more powerful for good than any mere human teaching; and the apologists of Christianity assert that its practical effects prove its divine origin. They say that civilization and morality have kept equal pace with knowledge of, and faith in, the Bible. Only among Christians have the arts and sciences reached their highest development; only the influence of the Bible has been able to break down the barbarous customs of ancient times, which considered every stranger an enemy, and might equivalent to right. The truths and promises of the Bible, it is said, the hopes of heaven and the fears of hell, have a great and unequalled power in rendering man moral, aiding him to subdue his baser passions, inclining him to justice and morality, and enabling him to free himself from idol-worship, debasing superstitions, and vile propensities. On the other hand, wherever Christianity has not prevailed, there public and private morality have been at a low ebb, the arts of civilized life have languished, political liberty has disappeared or remained unknown, and its place has been occupied by despotism or anarchy.

Illustrations in support of these assertions are not wanting. The Jews were the only people of antiquity who were not worshippers of idols and who possessed an exalted idea of the Deity, and a high morality. The Greeks and Romans of that early time were polytheists and idol-worshippers, they represented their divinities as possessed of the most debased characters, and the most disgusting crimes, now not even to be named in respectable society, were then publicly practised, almost without reproach, by the most prominent and influential men. In our own day, the Bible is better known in England and America than in any other lands, and there accordingly are found governments more free, arts more flourishing, and people more moral than in any other lands. Germany and France, where the Bible is less known, are not so prosperous, yet they are far in advance of all the pagan nations and of Catholic countries, where the people are forbidden to read the Bible, and where the popular faith is loaded down with a multitude of superstitions. Sweden and Denmark are Protestant countries, and the people are moral. Italy and Spain are Catholic, and the people are ignorant and debased. And yet the Turks are a grade lower in civilization, being farther removed from the truths of Christianity, and still beyond them are the Chinese and Hindoos, and in the lowest grade of ignorance and debasement are the idolaters of Africa and the Polynesian Islands. But there is a fearful state to which the superstitious and untaught idolator never reaches, the condition of perfect lawlessness and immorality, the unbridled reign of all that is basest in man's nature, when a nation educated in the truths of Christianity, casts them off and rushes into the arms of a heism. Such was France in 1793, drunk on blood to vomit crime, the horriblest of horrors, a great nation of divine intelligence, struck with atheistic frenzy, denying the distinction between virtue and vice, sending all their best men to the guillotine, and elevating their meanest to the summit of power, and hurling public order, religion, and morality into one general ruin.

There are several complete answers to all this: first, civilization and belief in the Bible do not keep equal pace; secondly, if they did, there is no proof that the former is the effect of the latter; and thirdly, there is strong evidence to show that high enlightenment is generally followed by disbelief in the Bible. Let us see whether Jews and Christians in ancient and modern times have been much superior to the Gentiles and Skeptics? And first for a comparison between the Jews and Greeks—nations which existed about the same time, and between which, partial comparisons have frequently been drawn by Christian writers. All, or nearly all, that we know, is derived from their own books, and on the first examination of these, a notable difference is perceptible. The Hebrew books are all upon religious or historical subjects, and principally occupied with devotional ideas, while the writings of the Greeks are upon all branches of history, philosophy, the fine arts, and the natural sciences. This difference is to be accounted for, partly at least, by the fact that the Jews were a priest ridden nation; all their books were written by priests; all their learning was monopolised by priests; all their opinions were derived from the priests; and it may well be supposed that a hereditary, despotic, superstitious, and corrupt priesthood, would tolerate no light literature. Greece on the other hand had no hereditary, powerful or organized priesthood. Everybody could write books as well as the priests, and could publish in defiance of them.

That the Jews were a rude, blood thirsty, violent people, harsh toward each other, and illiberal and unjust toward other nations, has sufficiently been shown already. Great credit has been claimed for them because of their exalted idea of the Deity, as a unity, who was to be worshipped directly in the idea, and not indirectly, through idols or natural phenomena: but an examination of the Old Testament will show that the Israelites were generally far from pure monotheism. Even the Pentateuch is not free from polytheistic ideas.

" I know that the Lord ['Jehovah' in the original] is greater than all gods."
Ex. XVIII. 11.

"Who is like unto thee, O Lord, [Jehovah] among the gods?" Ex. XV. 11.

"Jehovah is a great king above all gods," Ps. XCV. 3. Compare Gen. VI.
2; 1 K. XXII. 19.; Job. II. 1; Ps. XCVII. 7; Joshua XXIV. 15; Ezek. XX.
7; XXIII. 3; Deut. XII. 2; XIII. 6, 7; XVII. 3; Ex. XXXII. 1; Lev.
XVII. 7.

In all these passages Jehovah is spoken of, as Jupiter might be spoken of
among the Greeks, implying evidently that he was not the sole divinity.
Lessing speaks thus of the polytheistic idea in Judea:—"So far as we can
learn from the Old Testament, the Israelites before the time of the Babylonish
captivity had no correct idea of the unity of God. Otherwise they would not
have given the same name to the false deities of other lands, and they would
not have styled Jehovah *their* God—the God of *their* country, and the God of
their fathers. It is plain that where he is called the only god, the meaning is
that he was the first, the greatest, the most perfect. He recognised the divinities of the heathens as gods, and he claimed to be superior to them in wisdom
and in power. So long as the Jews found no reason to doubt the superiority
of their God, so long they were true to him; but when they saw that another
people, by the providence if its God, surpassed themselves in wealth or power,
just so soon did they go o' whoring after the strange gods, * supposed to be
more powerful. But when the Jews were carried to Babylon, and had their
minds opened as by a revolution, and saw a nation with a purer idea of monotheism and became more familiar with the writings of Moses, th'y became
another people, and were no longer capable of running after strange gods. All
idol-worship was at an end. If this undeniable change in the religious history
of the Jews is not to be thus explained, then it is inexplicable. They might
desert a natural divinity, but they could not desert the only God." As for
polytheism at the present day, there is quite as much of it in the Catholic
Church as among any heathens.

The government of the Jews was one of the most despotic and debasing
which ever existed. A hereditary priesthood, with such influence as the Levites
possessed, must necessarily keep any nation at a low grade of civilization. The
system of castes is said by all philosophers, who have observed its influence, to
be the most damnable invention of tyranny and priestly fraud. It destroys all
sense of human equality and dignity, and makes the many to be the abject
slaves of the few.

---

* This is a very expressive figure, and was frequently used by the holy prophets:—
See Ex. XXXIV. 15; Lev. XX. 5; Deut. XXXI. 16; 2 Ch. XXI. 13; Ps. LXXIII. 27;
Ezek. VI. 9; Hosea IV. 12; Jud. II. 17.

The ancient Jews did nothing for our benefit. They left us no liberal or well-digested laws; no valuable essays on political, moral, social, or religious philosophy; no able historical works; no grammar, no logic, no rhetoric, no great orations, no epics, no tragedies, no comedies, no mathematics, no astronomy, no geography, no mechanical inventions, no great architectural monuments, no statues, no pictures, not even the glory of a great empire. All the peculiar favor of Jehovah, all the miracles, all the prophets with their revelations from heaven did not enable the Jews to rival the unassisted human energy and ability of neighboring heathen nations. Voltaire * remarks:— "Moses changes his ring, before the king, into a serpent, and all the waters of the kingdom into blood; he creates toads which cover the earth; he changes the dust into lice; he fills the air with winged poisonous insects; he strikes all the men and all the animals of the land with frightful ulcers; he calls down storms, hail, and the thunder-bolts to ruin the country; he covers it with grasshoppers; he plunges it into the deepest night for three successive days; he cuts off the first born of animals and men, beginning with the heir of the throne; he passes dry-shod over the bed of the Red Sea, while the waters stand heaped up in mountains on either hand, and after his passage they rush down and overwhelm the army of Pharoah. After reading of all these miracles, the thinking man says, surely the nation for which and by which such wonders are done, is destined to be the master of the universe! But no! They end by suffering famine and misery in arid sands, and after prodigy upon prodigy they all die before seeing the little corner of earth where their descendants were established for a few years."

The Greeks were far less numerous than the descendants of Jacob, [if the numbers given by Moses be correct,] and yet how much do we not owe to Greek civilization? It might almost be said that we owe everything to them. "The beginnings† of all our intellectual civilization, of our poetry, music, history, oratory, sculpture, painting and architecture, of our logical, metaphysical, ethical, political, mathematical and physical science, and of our free political institutions must be traced to the Greeks. They are pre-eminently the aristocracy of the human race. No other nation can ever do for mankind what they did. They found the world immersed in all the darkness of of the oriental form of society. Despotic governments enforcing abject submission to the sovereign, and a prohibition of open discussion in assemblies of chiefs or counsellors; exclusive [and hereditary] priesthoods predominating over the people; in private life polygamy; cruel punishments and bodily mutilations; art massive, shapeless and grotesque; the absence of all literature worthy of the name; no science, no oratory, no drama; no history beyond a meagre chro-

---

* Essay on Miracles.   † Edinburgh Review, January, 1850.

nicle of the genealogies and acts of the kings;—such was the state of the most civilized portion of mankind when the influence of Greek genius began to operate upon the inert mass. It was this which first infused a soul into a lifeless body—it was the Greek Prometheus who stole from Heaven the fire which illuminated and warmed these benighted races; and it was under its excite. ment that they made the first great step out of the stationary into the progress. ive state; that step of which all experience proves the extreme difficulty, even where there is a model at hand to work upon." Not only did the Greeks lay the foundations of all our present intellectual culture, but they carried many of the highest branches of the arts to an excellence which all the millions of Christian European blood—one hundred times more numerous than the Greek kindred—have been unable to surpass. England, Italy, France, Spain and Por- tugal have produced their epic poems, but the Iliad is the greatest of them all. Pindar's heroic odes are the models in their kind. The orations of Demosthenes are superior to the greatest efforts of all later orators. The scanty remnants of ancient Grecian sculpture—many of them mere mutilated fragments—have maintained their pre-eminence of merit in spite of all the genius and labor of modern statuaries. Architects of the present day have scarcely a hope to sur- pass the buildings or improve the proportions of Athenian architecture.

But the Christians delight to dwell upon the moral purity and devout spirit of the Jews as compared with the Greeks. The latter people, and even their most famous and reputable men, were in the daily and notorious practice of debasing vices; and their ordinary conversation, and the common pictures and ornaments in their houses were filled with ideas the most obscene and disgust- ing. That the Greeks were different from us in their notions of decency and propriety, is true; but whether they were more coarse and debased than the Jews is exceedingly doubtful. There is much to testify against the Greeks— their houses, pictures, statuary, household utensils, and books written by uncensored scribblers; but there is no such testimony against the Jews, who have left nothing but sermons and annals written by slavish Levites. Yet even these books do not represent the Jews as having been models of morality. Human sacrifices were frequent in Judea during many centuries. (Ezek. XX. 25, 31; 2 K. XXI. 6; XVII. 17; Jer. XIX. 5; XXXII. 35; Is. LVII. 5). In the sixteenth chapter of Ezekiel, written about 600 B. C., and after, as is represented, the Israelites had enjoyed for nine hundred years the purifying and enlighten- ing influences of the Word of God, Jehovah describes the depravity of the Jerusalemites as nobody ever described the Athenians: "As I live, saith the Lord, Sodom thy sister hath not done, she nor her daughter, as thou hast done, thou and thy daughters." Compare with chapter XIX. of Genesis. The Douay translation says (1 K. XV. 15) that the mother of King Asa was "the princess' in the sacrifices of Priapus and in the grove which she had consecrated to him," and such sacrifices by such a person presupposes a wide-spread devotion to the most obscene rites. The translation made under King James, says (1 K. XV. 12) that King Asa removed "the Sodomites out of the land." The multitude of wives and concubines maintained by David and Solomon, are evidence that the Jewish morals were far from pure. But if it be admitted that the Jews were more devout and quite as pure in matters of amorous indulgence as the most sober communities of modern times, and if it be also admitted that the Greeks were as obscene in word and deed as the Christians have ever repre- sented them, still impartial observers could scarcely say that the Hebrews were the more moral people. Judea was remarkably barren of good and great men. The character of Job commands respect, but he is not said to have been a descendant of Abraham. Of the other biblical heroes, the best are those of whom the least is said. David and Solomon, to whom more space is given in the sacred records than to any other men, were stained with almost every crime. We seek in vain through the whole Bible for characters—for even one character—which may serve as a reasonable approximation to our modern ideal of a high moral nature. According to the sacred records, Israel never had any such men. But among the Greeks there were, in proportion to the total number of their people, multitudes of characters to which we cannot refuse our heartiest admiration—men in whom "greatness of mind seems but second to greatness of virtue"*—men whose moral nobility is unsurpassed in our own times—men whose glorious deeds makes the blood of every student of Grecian history tingle with enthusiastic admiration for them as he reads of their deeds. No prominent man has risen in modern Europe to emulate Timo- leon.†; America produced a rival, but no superior in Washington. The un- paralleled self-sacrifice of Leonidas and his band, the devotion of Socrates to intellectual freedom, and Aristides' exalted purity and sense of justice, must remain as ideal models to all generations of men. The human mind can scarcely conceive a more loveable character than that of Epaminondas. Besides these, there are Solon, Pericles, Pelopidas, Brasidas, Anaxagoras, Plato, Demo- critus, Zeno, Aristotle and Dion—all of them men whose moral natures were unequalled by any of the priests or kings of Israel.

Neither has it been the rule in modern times that morality, popular enlight- enment and national prosperity have depended upon faith in the Bible; but rather the most prosperous nations of the present day—the English, Americans, French and Germans—are notorious for the skeptical dispositions of the great majority of their most intelligent men. In all countries where faith in the Bible

---

* John Foster—" Aversion of Men of Taste to Evangelical Religion."
† See the character of Timoleon as described in Grote's Greece.

is undisturbed by doubt, the grossest superstitions prevail. Milman confesses, "It is idle, it is disingenuous to deny or to dissemble the early *depravity* of Christianity, its gradual but rapid departure from its primitive simplicity and purity, still more from its spirit of universal love." Middleton speaks of "the corrupt and degenerate state of the Church in the end of the fourth century, allowed by the most diligent inquiries into antiquity." On the corrupt state of the Church of late years, no long disquisition is needed for those who have seen much of the world with watchful eyes. The Christian Church is at this moment the grandest humbug in existence: and the majority of its intelligent support-ers know it, but find it a matter of pecuniary profit, and use the Church as they would use any other humbug. The history of Christianity from the time of the accession of Constantine, has been one long series of bickering and war, illiberality and despotism.

"Christianity* was intended to reform the world: had an All-wise Being planned it, nothing is more improbable than that it should have failed: Omnis-cience would infallibly have forseen the inutility of a scheme which experience demonstrates to this age to have been utterly unsuccessful." Peace and good-will, in consequence of the prevalent religion, do not prevail more now among Christian nations than they did among the ancient Grecians, although many of the early followers of the Gospel expected that the dominion of the Bible would soon convert all swords into ploughshares. Lactantius,† the Christian father who wrote just before Constantine was converted to the faith of Jesus, and made it the State religion of Rome, "seemed firmly to expect and almost ventured to promise that the establishment of Christianity would restore the innocence and felicity of the primitive age; that the worship of the true God would extinguish war and dissension among those who mutually considered themselves as the children of a common parent; that every impure desire, every angry and selfish passion would be restrained by the gospel; and that the magistrates might sheath the sword of justice among people who would be universally actuated by the sentiments of truth and piety, of equity and modera-tion, of harmony and universal love."

---

* Shelley : Note to Queen Mab.   † Gibbon's Decline and Fall.

ERRORS OF THE INSPIRED.

LX. Let us consider briefly the errors into which these prophets and apostles and clergymen have fallen—these men who held and hold divine commissions to teach the truth of God to their fellow-men.

And first, for the heroes of the Bible:

Noah cursed Ham and all his descendants to endless slavery for accidentally seeing the parental nakedness: Gen. IX. 22-25.

Noah was a perfect man: Gen. VI. 9.

Abraham was a favorite with Jehovah: Gen. XII. 1-8; XXVI. 5; Luke XVI. 22.

Abraham and Sarah agreed to deceive Pharaoh: Gen. XII. 11-19.

Abraham took a concubine with Sarah's consent: Gen. XVI. 3.

Abraham and Sarah agreed to deceive Abimelech: Gen. XX. 2-5.

Abraham doubted Jehovah's promise: Gen. XXV. 8.

Isaac was a favorite with Jehovah: Gen. XXVI. 2-5, 12, 24.

Isaac and Rebekah agreed to deceive Abimelech: Gen. XXVI. 7-11.

Jacob deceived Isaac and defrauded Esau: Gen. XXVII. 6-30.

Jacob was a favorite with Jehovah: Gen. XXVIII. 13-15.

Jacob practised polygamy and concubinage: Gen. XXIX. 23, 28; XXX. 3, 9.

Jehovah promised to be with Aaron: Ex. IV. 15.

Aaron was appointed Jehovah's high priest forever: Ex. XXVII. 21.

Aaron was possessed of miraculous power: Ex. IV. 28, 30.

Aaron rebelled against Moses: Ex. XII. 2.

Aaron made the golden calf and worshipped it: Ex. XXXII. 1-6.

Moses doubted Jehovah's word: Num. X. 21, 22.

Moses hesitated to obey Jehovah's command: Ex. IV. 10, VI. 30.

Moses requested the Lord to kill him: Num. XI. 10-15.

Moses remonstrated obstinately with the Lord: Num. XIV. 13-19.

Moses lied, pretending to Pharaoh that the Israelites wished to leave Egypt only for the purpose of sacrificing to their God: Ex. V. 1.

Moses directed the Jews to borrow jewels for purposes of fraud: Ex. XII. 35, 36.

Moses smashed the tables of the law, written by Jehovah's own hand: Ex. XXXI. 18, XXXII. 9.

Joshua reproached Jehovah: Josh. VII. 7.

- Gideon doubted the word of the Lord: Judges VI. 13.

Eli erred: 1 S. I. 13.

Jeptha devoted his daughter to death while the spirit of the Lord was on him: Jud. XI. 29–35.

Samuel hesitated to obey Jehovah: 1 S. XVI. 1.

Samuel lied: 1 S. XVI. 5.

Samuel hewed Agag to pieces, before the Lord in Gilgal: 1 S. XV. 33.

Samuel erred: 1 S. XVI. 6.

Jehovah gave Saul a new heart: 1 S. X. 7, 9.

Saul sought to kill David and Jonathan: 1 S. XXI. 33.

David took two hundred Philistine foreskins as trophies: 1 S. XX. 27.

David practiced polygamy: 1 S. XXV. 39; 1 Ch. XIV. 3.

David committed adultery with the wife of Uriah the Hittite: 2 S. XI. 4.

Several months afterwards, David, for the purpose of getting rid of Uriah, sent him to Joab, the general of the Jewish army in war, with a letter, saying, "Set ye Uriah in the fore-front of the hottest battle, and retire ye from him, that he may be smitten and die:" (2 S. XI. 5–15). Joab obeyed, and David soon had Uriah's widow all to himself, and she became the mother of Solomon and the ancestress of Jesus—that is, if the latter was of the blood of David.

David delivered the seven sons of Saul to the Gibeonites to be hung: 2 S. XXI. 8, 9.

David was angry with the Lord: 2 S. VI. 8; 1 Ch. XIII. 11.

David was "a man after God's own heart": Acts XIII. 22; 1 K. XI. 46 IX. 4.

David cut the Ammonites with saws and hammers, and roasted them in ovens: 2 S. XII. 31; 1 Ch. XX. 3, 2.

David ravaged the territory of Achish, whose guest he was, and he slew those whom he robbed, so that Achish should not learn the perpetrator of the wrong: 1 S. XXVII. 8–12.

David gained the chief men by bribes to make him king, and concerted with the traitor Abner to overthrow Ishbosheth, (2 S. III. 12), though the latter was the lawful heir of the throne, and a righteous man: 2 S. IV. 11.

David sent Hushai to betray Absalom: 2 S. XV. 24.

David broke his promise to Mephibosheth: 2 S. IX. 7, XVI. 3, 4, XIX. 29.

David ordered Joab, a faithful man, to be put to death: 1 K. II. 6.

David was a man of blood : 1 Ch. XXII. 8, XXVIII. 3.

Nathan, a holy prophet, erred; 2 S. VII. 3, 4.

Solomon caused the assassination of his brother Adonijah : 1 K. II. 25.

Solomon appointed the assassin to be his priest : 1 K. II. 35.

Solomon had seven hundred wives and three hundred concubines : 1 K. XI. 3.

Solomon committed idolatry : 1 K. XI. 7.

Jehovah was with Solomon : 2 Ch. I. 1.

The Lord gave Solomon more than human wisdom : 1 K. III. 2, IV. 29 ; 2 Ch. I. 11.

The prophet Zedekiah slapped the face of the prophet Micah, in the presence of King Jehosaphat : 2 Ch. XVIII. 23.

Jeremiah damned his luck : Jer. XX. 14–18.

Jeremiah lied : Jer. XXXVIII. 27.

Jonah, a true prophet, tried to run away from Jehovah : Jonah I. 10.

"It displeased Jonah exceedingly, and he was very angry" that Jehovah did not fulfil his authorized prophecy of the destruction of Nineveh : Jonah IV. 1.

Two of the apostles of Christ desired to destroy an unbelieving village with fire from Heaven : Luke IX. 54.

Peter corrected Christ : Mat. XVI. 23.

Peter denied Christ : Mat. XXVI. 69.

Peter cut off Malchus' ear : Mat. XXVI. 51.

Paul damned Alexander, the coppersmith, with polite phrase : he "did me much *evil*—the Lord rewarded him according to his *works*" : 1 Tim. I. 20; 2 Tim. IV. 14.

Paul cursed those who preached a doctrine different from his own : Gal. I. 8, 9.

Paul declared that Peter deserved to be blamed : Gal. II. 11.

The apostles mistook the meaning of the Old Testament : (Acts. II. 14–21, 25–34; III. 18, 21–24; IV. 25, 26; Gal. IV. 24; 1 Cor. X. 4,) and yet the apostles were inspired to explain the true sense and spirit of the Old Testament : (Acts XXVI. 22, 23; XXVIII. 23.)

The apostles differed*: Acts XV. 6–39; Gal. I. 11, II. 14; 2 Peter III. 16. Compare with these : Gal. III., Rom. III., James II.

They disputed, after Christ's predictions of his death, as to who should be the greatest in the coming kingdom : Mat. XX. 24; Mark IX. 35; Luke XXII. 25.

They went so far as to ask for seats at the right hand and at the left : Mat. XIX. 28, XX. 21; Mark X. 37; Luke XXII. 30.

They thought that Christ's kingdom would appear immediately at Jerusalem : Luke XIX. 11, XXIV. 21.

They supposed that the second coming of Christ was to be at the destruction

---

* See Appendix, Note 12.

of Jerusalem by Titus: Mat. XXIV. 33, 34; Mark XIII. 29, 30; Luke XVII. 22–37; XXI. 5–36.

They thought that Jesus would come in that generation : Mat. X. 23, XVI. 28; John XXI. 23; I Cor. VII. 29, X. 11, XV. 51, &c.

They misunderstood the prophecy of the resurrection : Mat. XVII. 9; Mark IX. 31 ; Luke IX. 45, XVIII. 34; John XX. 9; II. 19–22.

Some thought that Christ's body had been removed by the gardener: John XX. 15.

They would not believe the women's story of the resurrection : Luke XXIV. 11.

The conversation of the two disciples on the road to Emmaus is proof that they had never expected the resurrection : Luke XXIV. 11.

The disciples fled when Jesus was arrested : Mat. XXIV. 36.

Christ was buried by a stranger : Mark XV. 43.

As for the clergymen, the priests of the Christian Church, there are undoubtedly some good men among them, but the majority are no better than their predecessors, the Levites, against whom Jesus had so much to say. Byron said of them, that they sought " to merit Heaven by making earth a Hell." Bacon says, " You may find all access to any species of philosophy, however pure, intercepted by the ignorance of divines." The world is indebted to the Christian priests for a long series of wars, persecutions and inquisitions, but it is unnecessary to encumber these pages with the bloody record.

LITERARY MERIT.

LXI. If a book-revelation from Heaven has been given, we must suppose that the book would be written with perfect wisdom, and would contain all the information in regard to religion and morality undiscoverable by human reason, and proper for man to know. Unequalled depth of thought, and simplicity, clearness, and compactness of style should characterise the writings of a divine author; but these are not the characteristics of the Bible. The laws of Moses were certainly composed by no divine intellect, for they are far inferior

in every respect to many mere human codes.   Many passages of Job and
Isaiah, and the Psalms, are well written, but they are not more beautiful than
the writings of uninspired moral poets.   Not a verse can be found in the whole
Bible, for which an equal may not be found in some profane author.

As a whole the book is exceedingly dull, confused and obscure.   There is no
appropriateness, clearness or beauty of plan.   History, prophecy, poetry, and
teachings of morality, ceremonial observances and criminal law are all scattered
about without order or apparent design.   In the Pentateuch alone, the writer
changes from history to the law and from the law to history more than twenty
times.   In some of the historical books long periods are skipped over without
a word, and not unfrequently there are abrupt changes from one subject to
another; and there are frequent repetitions of long passages, where one author
has evidently copied word for word from another.   Examples may be found by
a comparison of the following passages:

Compare 2 S. XXIII. 8–39 with 1 Ch. XI. 10–47.
"   1 S. XXXI. 1–3 with 1 Ch. X. 1–12.
"   2 S. V. 17–25 with 1 Ch. XIV. 8–16.
"   2 S. VI. 1–11 with 1 Ch. XIII. 5–14.
"   2 S. VII. 1–29 with 1 Ch. XVII. 1–27.
"   2 S. VIII. 1–18 with 1 Ch. XVIII. 1–17.
"   2 S. X. 1–19 with 1 Ch. XIX. 1–19.
"   2 S. XXIV. 1–25 with 1 Ch. XXI. 1–27.
"   1 K. VIII. 12–50 with 2 Ch. VI. 1–39.
"   1 K. X. 1–29 with 2 Ch. IX. 1–28.
"   1 K. XII. 1–19 with 2 Ch. X. 1–19.
"   1 K. XXII. 2–35 with 2 Ch. XVII. 1–34.
"   2 K. XI. 4–40 with 2 Ch. XXIII. 1–21.
"   2 K. XVIII. 13, 17–37 with Is. XXXVI. 1–22.
"   2 K. XIX. 1–37 with Is. XXXVII. 1–38; 2 Ch. XXXII. 1–24.
"   2 K. XX. 12–21 with Is. XXXIX. 1–8; 2 Ch. XXXII. 24–33.
"   Ps. XVIII. 2–50 with 2 S. XVII. 1–54.
"   Ps. CV. 1–15 with 1 Ch. XVI. 8–22.
"   Ps. XCVI. 1–13 with 1 Ch. XVI. 23–33.

It has never been claimed that there was any superhuman wisdom in the
Criminal Code of Moses; and as for his law of religious ceremonies far from
being divinely wise, it is only utterly ridiculous.   He would be a singular
Deity who should inspire a prophet to write a gospel containing such sentences
as these:

" And they make coats of fine linen, of woven work for Aaron, and for his
sons, and a mitre of fine linen, and goodly bonnets of fine linen, and linen

breeches of fine twined linen, and a girdle of fine twined linen, and blue, and purple, and scarlet, of needle-work; as the *Lord commanded* Moses." (Ex. XXXIX. 27–29); or these:

"And the priest shall dip his right finger in the oil that is in his left hand, and shall sprinkle of the oil with his finger seven times before the Lord; and of the rest of the oil that is in his hand shall the priest put upon the tip of the right ear of him that is to be cleansed, [of leprosy] and upon the thumb of the right hand, and upon the great toe of the right foot." (Lev. XIV. 16, 17.)

There are many passages in the Old Testament which are inexcusably and even grossly obscene, particularly a passage in Ezek. XXIII. 20. The Song of Solomon is a remarkable production to be included in a gospel. It is said to be an allegory of the love of Christ for the Church, but the literal language is very similar to such as a heathen poet might use in regard to earthly lovers— such as Solomon may be supposed to have written in his idolatrous years to some favorite concubine. The lover says "thou hast doves' eyes;" "thy teeth are like a flock of sheep that are even shorn;" "thy lips are like a thread of scarlet;" "thy neck is as a tower of ivory;" "thy two breasts are like two young roes;" "the joints of thy thighs are like jewels;" "thy navel is like a round goblet, which wanteth not liquor;" [referring of course to the sacramental cup and wine of the Church]; "thy stature is like to a palm tree;" and finally "until the day break and the shadows fall away, I [Christ] will get me to the mountain of myrrh, [what portion of the church is that?] and to the hill of frankincense." Neither is the beloved one taken at random, for Solomon has "threescore queens and fourscore concubines, and virgins without number;" but she is more lovely than them all, "the fairest among women."

She [the church] replies: "my beloved [Christ] is white and ruddy, the chiefest among ten thousand;" "his locks are bushy and black as a raven;" "his eyes are as the eyes of doves by the rivers of waters, washed with milk and fitly set, his cheeks are as a bed of spices," "his lips like lilies dropping sweet-smelling myrrh," "his hands are as gold rings set with beryl, his belly is as bright ivory overlaid with sapphires," "his legs are as pillars of marble set upon sockets of fine gold," "his mouth is most sweet, yea, he is altogether lovely;" "a bundle of myrrh is my beloved unto me; he shall lie all night between my [the Church's] breasts." "He brought me to the banqueting house and his banner over me was love; stay me with flagons, comfort me with apples, for I am sick of love." "Make haste my beloved, and be thou like to a roe, or to a young hart upon a mountain of spices." "Let us get up early to the vineyards; let us see if the vine flourish, whether the tender grape appear, and the pomegranate bud forth; there will I give thee my loves." O, Solomon! Solomon! far was your lecherous soul from thinking that you and your paramour would be converted into symbols of Christ and the Church, and that your song would be circulated and received all over the world as part of the word of God !

To read the Bible intelligibly requires much information, a knowledge of geography, history, chronology, and the arts, besides the Hebrew and Greek languages, in which the books were originally written, and from which no translations have been made by the authority of the alleged divine author. A man cannot read the Bible until he has learned his letters, and cannot appreciate its meaning until his mind has been educated to habits of thought by long training. Far from being simple and clear, the Bible is the most equivocal in meaning of all books, as the multitude of sects may testify, which all seriously believe that their doctrines are taught, and that their doctrines alone are taught, in its pages. That is a very questionable divine revelation which is differently understood by different persons. Indeed many, the most celebrated priests, have declared that the prophets and apostles wrote with two meanings—one apparent the other hidden—one literal, the other figurative. If the literal meaning was foolish or manifestly untrue, they could retreat to the figurative, and twist that in any way to suit themselves. Origen was one of the earliest Christian advocates of the double meaning, and he said :—" Were it necessary to attach ourselves to the letter, and to interpret the law after the manner of the Jews or of the populace, I should blush to say aloud that it is God who has given us such laws; I should find even more grandeur and reason in human codes, such as those of the Athenians, Lacdæmonians, and Romans." Gibbon, in speaking of some of the double interpretations used by the Pagan priests, (for this trick has been used wherever there has been an alleged book-revelation), gets off a happy sarcasm :—" As the traditions of pagan mythology were variously related, the sacred interpreters were at liberty to select the most convenient circumstances, and as they translated an arbitrary cipher, they could extract from any fable, any sense which was adapted to their favorite system of religion and philosophy. The lascivious form of a naked Venus was tortured into the discovery of some moral precept or physical truth ; and the castration of Atys explained the revolution of the sun between the tropics or the separation of the human soul from vice and error." In passages where no figurative interpretation will suffice, there it is seriously proposed to make the literal different from the apparent meaning. Professor Whewell, whose piety outruns his sense, gravely asks* :— " When should old interpretations [of Bible passages] be given up ; what is the proper measure for a religious and enlightened commentator to make a change in the current interpretation of sacred Scripture ? or, at what period ought the established exposition of a passage to be given up, and a new

---

* Philosophy of the Inductive Sciences—Chapter on the relation of History to Palæontology.

mode of understanding the passsage, such as is, or seems to be, required by new discoveries respecting the laws of nature, be accepted in its place? It is plain that to introduce such an alteration lightly and hastily would be a procedure fraugh with inconvenience; for if the change were made in such a manner, it might be afterwards discovered that it had been adopted without sufficient reason, and that it was necessary to reinstate the old exposition. And the minds of the readers of scripture, always to a certain extent, and for a time disturbed by the subversion of their long established notions, would be distressed without any need, and might be seriously unsettled. While, on the other hand, a too protracted and obstinate resistance to the innovation on the part of scriptural expositors, would tend to identify, at least in the minds of many, the authority of the scripture with the truth of the exposition, and therefore would bring discredit upon the revealed word, when the established interpretation was proved to be untenable."

The New Testament is exceedingly defective for the want of a clear and concise exposition of the doctrines of the early Christian Church. Every sect now writes its own "confession of faith" instead of repeating the words of Jesus. We do not know what the early Christian Church believed, and if we did, we would probably find reason to deny that their tenets were in accordance with the doctrines laid down by Christ, the apostles and the Evangelists. Nothing that is mysterious to the Pagan is less so to the Christian; and, in addition to the unexplained problems of nature, the believer in the Bible is burdened with numerous mysteries of his religion. "The temptation by a literal serpent in Paradise, the federal union of all mankind in Adam, the imputation of the actual guilt of Adam to ourselves, the various covenants enumerated as formally established between God and man, the Athanasian explanation of the Trinity, the eternal procession of the Son, the imputation of righteousness, unconditional election, the moral inability of man placed side by side with free agency on the one hand and his eternal condemnation on the other, and many more doctrines, which it is needless to mention—these, however stirring and awful in their nature, cannot certainly be regarded as forming a system peculiarly characterized by its simplicity."*

The Bible offers no new light upon the great problems of natural religion: it asserts that there is a personal and conscious deity: it asserts that the soul lives after the death of the body; it asserts that men are unhappy now because their forefathers sinned; but there is no appeal to the reason in connection with all these points; the appeal is made to faith alone; and if we say that we cannot believe without evidence, the only reply is—"he that believeth not shall be damned."

---

* Morell. Philosophy of Religion—Preface.

The claims of high literary merit for the Bible cannot be granted without increasing the importance of some of its defects.   The prophets and apostles have given to us no clear, compact, concise, comprehensive and evidently correct rules for our religious, moral and political conduct.   Jesus never expressly abrogated the Mosaic law or any important portion of it.   He never said expressly that slavery, polygamy or concubinage was wrong or right.   When asked about the authority of the emperors, he replied that it was necessary to render unto Cæsar the things that were Cæsar's, and that all governments derive their power from on high ; but it was left for the infidels of a much later age to give currency to—if not to discover—the truths, that people are not made for the benefit of kings and nobles, that sovereignty resides in the people, and that all men have an inalienable right to the possession and free enjoyment of life and liberty. The religious doctrines, in regard to which the Bible contradicts itself or is not explicit, are too numerous to be repeated here.   If the Bible be received as a patchwork, made from the writings of many ignorant and unwise men, many omissions, contradictions and errors may reasonably be expected and excused ; but if the book be represented as the composition of exceedingly able authors, we must at once say, they should have written a more harmonious and satisfactory work, even without any aid from Heaven.

Whatever the literary merit of the Bible may be, the book is not rated very highly by, nor is its influence very great with literary men in general.   Christianity is treated with respect and deference, and occasional praise, by authors, editors and statesmen, because it is the traditional faith of the European blood, and because it is deeply rooted in the prejudices of a respectable portion of the community, and because there is little zealous opposition to it ; but this respect, deference, and praise, are only such as are paid to all prevalent systems in all countries and in all times.   It has never been observed that any very powerful, social, political or religious institution has prevailed for any considerable length of time among men, without having been praised as superior to all rival systems.   It has been so with slavery, polygamy, polytheism and monarchy, and it is so with Braminism, Mahomedanism, Confucianism, and Christianity. But the general tone of our literature is hostile to the Bible.   The newspaper press generally ignore the plan of salvation and the theory of a future life, the delights of Heaven and the fears of Hell, or treat them with that patronizing air which betrays unbelief, with a desire to give no offense.   Bacon remarks : " Experience demonstrates how learned men have been arch heretics, and how learned times have been inclined to Atheism."   A great many authors have called attention to the unchristian tone of our general literature.   John Foster, a prominent man among the evangelical orthodox, wrote an Essay with the ominous title, " On the Aversion of Men of Taste to Evangelical Religion," wherein he says: "I fear it is incontrovertible, that what is termed polite · literature, the grand school in which taste acquires its laws and refined percep-tions, and in which are formed much more than in any higher austere discipline, the moral sentiment, is for the greater part hostile to the religion of Christ." Dr. Alexander, in his work on the Evidences of Christianity, says, "the scrip-tures, although they contain the highest excellence of composition, both in prose and poetry, of which a good taste cannot be insensible, are neglected by literary men, or rather studiously avoided." And again, "This common dislike of the Bible, even in men of refined taste and decent lives, furnishes a strong argument for its divine origin." Let due credit be given to Dr. Alexander for the discovery of a new rule ; *every doctrine rejected by men of refined tastes and decent lives is of divine origin*. This reasoning is more wonderful even than that of the bloody old Tertullian, who, in disputing with some heretics about the reality of Christ's human nature, wrote, "The son of God was crucified ; it is no shame to own it because it is a thing to be ashamed of. The son of God died ; it is wholly credible because it is absurd. When buried, he rose again to life ; it is certain because it is impossible." The North British Review (Feb., 1852,) confesses, "The genius of our literature is not only not consonant with that of the gospel, but often, though without any polemical purpose, quite hostile to it, so that every truly Christian mind must feel that the fascinations of literature are not without their danger." And on another occasion (Nov., 1853,) the same periodical says, "the vast majority of the works of imagination and fiction which come from the press in the present day, are as Pagan as works produced in the atmosphere of Christian influence can be." Strauss, in his Christliche Glaubenslehre, remarks, "the intellectual atmosphere of our time has become pregnant with anti-ecclesiastical ideas, and every theological institution which grants time to its pupils to breathe in this atmosphere, will produce few orthodox and sincere leaders for the Christian church."

LXII. The advocates of Christianity have argued that the spread of their faith among all the most civilized nations, unaided by the sword, and its permanence, furnish proof of its divine origin. It is not to be denied that the Bible has really attained a greater dominion than any other alleged revelation, and did at one time command the almost implicit belief of all the great and good men in Europe, but its success has surely not been so great as to prove its immediate divine origin. It is very doubtful whether any amount of success among men, even universal acceptation of a creed, would furnish reliable evidence of its truth. But universal acceptation the Bible never had. Christianity spread with comparative rapidity in the first three centuries after the death of Jesus, but its success can easily be accounted for by natural causes. It had its origin when the political power of the Roman empire, and the intellectual dominion of the Grecian mythology, were crumbling to pieces. The prevalent polytheism had ceased to command belief. The people were ignorant and superstitious, and little qualified to form a reasonable opinion of what we now call religious truth. The simple faith of the philosopher was beyond their intelligence and at variance with their prejudices, and they sought refuge in the reason-defying mysteries and in the pompous ceremonies of the Christian priests.

If the great success of Christianity, unassisted by the sword, may prove the truth of the Bible, surely the truth of Mormonism may be proved by the spread of that faith, which, during the first thirty years of its existence, has certainly gained as many converts as did the doctrines of Jesus within a like period. Jo. Smith began his ministry in the midst of the most intelligent people on earth, in the midst of a creed which, though dying, is far from dead, and in a rising civilization. Jesus began his ministry in the midst of a rude people, a dead creed—in Greece and Rome—and a rapidly decaying civilization. The Mormons number several hundred thousand; they have missionaries in all parts of the world, they are ready to die for their faith, and they are spoken of and treated by the "Gentiles" just as the early Christians were. Every argument from the spread of Christianity for the truth of the Bible can be used with far more force in favor of Mormonism. A similar argument might be adduced to show that the Koran is a divine revelation. It has long been asserted that Mohammedanism owed its great success to the sword, but this falsehood is completely refuted by Gibbon. The Mohammedans gave all their newly conquered subjects a free choice of the Koran, tribute or the sword; terms quite as liberal as those offered by Christian conquerors. Besides, where did Mohammed get his sword? Buddhism has as many believers as Christianity, and its teachers and propagators, unlike the followers of Jesus, have never resorted to the sword to convince unbelievers. But both Buddhism and Mohammedanism have a great advantage over Christianity, in that they have been preserved pure as when first taught. Gibbon, writing of Mohammed, says,* "It is not the propagation, but the permanency of his religion, that deserves our wonder; the same pure and perfect impression which he engraved at Mecca and Medina is preserved after the revolutions of twelve centuries, by the Indian, the African, and the Turkish proselytes of the Koran. If the Christian apostles, St. Peter and St. Paul, could return to the Vatican, they might possibly inquire the name of the Deity who is worshipped with such mysterious rites in that magnificent temple; at Oxford or Geneva they would experience less surprise, but it might still be incumbent on them to peruse the catechism of the church, and to study the orthodox commentators on their own writings and the words of their master." Jehovah then allows his own pure teachings to be corrupted with all manner of superstitions, and at the same time permits the fraudulent systems of heathen impostors to be preserved unadulterated through long ages! But if the Bible be the word of God, how is it that so many men, so many great and good men, still remain unconverted? "If He has spoken why is not the universe converted?" †

---

* Decline and Fall—Ch. L.   † System of Nature.

THE WITNESS OF THE SPIRIT.

LXIII. Believers in the Bible say that they have conclusive proof of the truth of their faith in the witness of the spirit—a peculiar exhiliration or confi dence which they feel at times in regard to their religion. That is to say, when thinking of Jehovah they are conscious of a superstitious awe, as children are scared when threatened by the nurse with the raw-head and bloody-bones; or they think of going to heaven with so much assurance that they enjoy part of the pleasure beforehand. Macaulay, in his review of Ranke's History of the Popes, speaking of the peculiar mental excitement or enthusiasm, known as "the witness of the spirit," says:—"It not unfrequently happens that a tinker or coal-heaver bears a sermon, or falls in with a tract, which alarms him about the state of his soul. If he be a man of excitable nerves and strong imagination, he thinks himself given over to the evil power. He doubts whether he has not committed the unpardonable sin. He imputes every wild fancy that springs up in his mind to the whisper of a fiend. His sleep is broken by dreams of the great judgment-seat, the open books, and the unquenchable fire. If, in order to escape from these vexing thoughts, he flies to amusement or to licentious indulgence, the delusive relief only makes his misery darker and more hopeless. At length a turn takes place. He is reconciled to his offended maker. To borrow the fine imagery of one who had himself been thus tried, he emerges from the Valley of the Shadow of Death, from the dark land of gins and snares, of quagmires and precipices, of evil spirits and ravenous beasts. The sunshine is on his path. He ascends the Delectable Mountains, and catches from their summit a distant view of the shining city which is the end of his pilgrimage," and he has the witness of the spirit. Such is the sum and substance of this weighty evidence, which is confidently appealed to in favor of all creeds wherein a heaven and hell contribute to raise the hopes and excite the fears of the superstitious and the ignorant. This witness of the spirit is supposed to be particularly strong with all martyrs; but if this testimony suffice for proof, all religious creeds, extensively received, must be true. All have martyrs, each equally convinced of the truth of his peculiar creed by the witness of his spirit. Locke says :—"A strong and firm persuasion of any proposition relating to religion, for which a man hath either no or not sufficient proofs from *reason*, but receives them as truths wrought in the mind by extraordinary influence coming immediately from God himself, seems to me to be enthusiasm which can be no evidence or ground of assurance at all, nor can by any means be taken for knowledge. If such groundless thoughts as these concerning ordinary matters and not religion, possess the mind strongly, we call it raving, and every one thinks it a degree of madness ; in religion, men accustomed to the thoughts of revelation make a greater allowance to it, though indeed it be a more dangerous madness ; but men are apt to think in religion they may, or ought to, quit their reason. I find that the Christians, Mohammedans, and Brahmans all pretend to this immediate inspiration ; but it is certain that contradictions and falsehoods cannot come from God ; nor can any one that is of the true religion be assured of anything by a way whereof those of a false religion may be and are equally confirmed in theirs. For the Turkish Dervishes pretend to revelations, ecstacies, visions, raptures, to be transported with the illumination of God, etc. The Jangis [Jaunas?] among the Hindoos talk of being illuminated and entirely united to God, as well as the most spiritualized Christians."

REVIEW.

LXIV.   We have thus examined the principal points of the evidence against the divine inspiration of the Bible.   Let us recall them to mind :

1. The Pentateuch was not written by Moses, nor by any one man, nor at the alleged date of its composition.

2. There is no satisfactory evidence that any of the books of the Bible were written by their alleged authors.

3. Many books said in the Bible to be of divine authority have been lost.

4. Those books, which we have, have not been preserved in purity.

5. The books, which we have, were selected from a number of other similar books, in a barbarous age, according to rules and for reasons unknown to us, by men known to have practiced numerous great frauds.

6. None of the prominent doctrines of the Bible were original with Moses, with Jesus, or with Paul. All the important doctrines of the Mosaic law— monotheism, worship by sacrifice, incense, singing and dancing, circumcision, observance of one day in seven as sacred, hereditary priesthood, use of sacred books, the divine nature, and the partiality of the Deity for their own nation —all were copied from the Egyptians. The important doctrines of the New Testament, the trinity, the incarnation, the logos, the redemption, the immortality of the soul, rewards and punishments in a future life, the necessity of belief to salvation, and the all-sufficiency of love—all these were common among, and learned from, heathen nations surrounding Judea.

7. Miracles are impossible.

8. If they were possible, man could never recognize them as violations of the laws of nature.

9. The miracles reported in the Bible never were done.

10. If they had been done they would not prove the Bible to be true.

11. If they were done, miracles ought to be common to this day.

12. The reported miracles are only appeals to vulgar superstitions.

13. There are no successful prophecies in the Bible.

14. The numerous appeals of the Evangelists to ancient Hebrew prophecies are all manifest errors.

15. The Hebrew priests had foretold the coming of a Christ, (Messiah, anointed person,) but he was to be a king, a political leader of the house of David, and not a religious teacher or Levite ; while Jesus was neither a political leader nor a descendant of David.

16. The Bible contains a vast number of false prophecies.

17. The miracles and prophecies reported in the Bible are not so well accredited as many others which are universally confessed to be the inventions of fraud and credulity.

18. The morality of the Old Testament is extremely coarse and defective.

19. The main precepts of morality of the New Testament are fit only for slaves.

20. The history of the creation of the universe, as given by Moses, is false from beginning to end.

21. The chronology of the Bible is false, and is confessed to be so by many of the greatest Christian authors.

22. The Mosaic story of the repeated revolts of the Jews during the time when Jehovah was leading the tribe from Egypt, with numerous and unexampled wonders, is contrary to all reason.

23. The Bible recognizes the miraculous powers of witches and sorcerers.

24. Jesus and the Evangelists believed that insane and epileptic persons were possessed by devils.

· 25. The Bible contains a vast number of contradictory statements.

26. It teaches a vast number of false doctrines—doctrines which cannot be proved to be true, and doctrines which can be proved to be untrue—such as the existence of a personal, anthropomorphic deity, the immortality of the soul, the moral accountability of man to the deity, and the immediate government of the universe by the deity without the intervention of general laws.

27. The scheme of redemption is absurd.

28. The Bible contradicts itself in regard to the immortality of the soul, the myth of Adam's sin, the oneness of God, the means of attaining divine favor, the existence of a devil, the general spirit of religious and moral law, and the permanence of Judaism.

29. Under the Mosaic law Jesus was a criminal and deserved to be executed.

30. The Bible has done no more good to man than has been done by many human institutions. The Hebrews, Jehovah's favorite people, did nothing for civilization. The heathen Greeks laid the foundation for all our arts, sciences, and philosophy.

31. The prophets and favorites of Jehovah were guilty of many great crimes.

32. The Bible is not written with any superhuman ability.

33. Christianity has not been as successful as it should have been if of immediate divine origin.

Nearly all these points strike at the very vitals of Christianity; on all of them the evidence is strong, if not conclusive; and nowhere in the whole course of the examination, with the purest desire to grant all that could reasonably be demanded for the Bible, have we found a solitary point of importance in its favor.

In the next section we shall endeavor to show that human reason can never be certain of having arrived at final, absolute, and perfect truth.

IS THERE ANY ABSOLUTE TRUTH ?

LXV. Is it possible for man to learn anything which he can prove to be absolutely true? If he cannot, Christianity will hardly deserve to be accepted as a certainty.

The only means we have to learn the reality of things, are the senses and reason. We learn premises by sensation, and we draw conclusions by reason.

Reason cannot discover original premises. The reliability then of our conclusions must depend upon the evidence of the senses. But it has been discovered that the senses are very liable to err. The eye says that grass is green, that the green color is in the grass, is part of it; and the idea seems to be finally confirmed by the knowledge that the green color may be boiled out of the grass and communicated to water. But philosophy or reason comes in and says the green color is not in the grass, it is only in the light; there is no color in the visible objects of nature; all the idea of color is a mere illusion—an apparent fact but not a real one—a cheat of the senses. The savage, taking his senses for a guide, supposes the stars to be small lights in the heavens; the philosopher knows them to be great planets. An uneducated man does not comprehend that sound is a mere movement of the air striking upon a delicate nerve of the ear; the noise, as generally conceived, is only in the idea. Men whose legs have been cut off while they were under the influence of chloroform, on returning to consciousness, but before learning of the amputation, have complained of pain or itching in different toes of the severed foot, and have insisted obstinately that they were not in error as to the locality of the pain. When told that the leg was cut off, they have obstinately refused to believe it, and could only be convinced by seeing. Physiology explains the error. All the senses are liable to error; not one of them can be implicitly relied on. If the senses are liable to error, then reason can draw no perfectly reliable conclusions from the premises founded on the evidence of the senses. The common belief in the absolute and unconditional existence of matter is founded only on the evidence of the senses, and is not accepted as truth by many—perhaps a majority—of the greatest philosophers. Diderot, D'Alembert, Mackintosh, Dugald Stewart, Brougham, and Carlyle, have agreed in saying that he who has never rejected the absolute existence of matter has no talent for metaphysics.

Man only knows by thinking, by an idea: he knows there is a sun only because he sees it, because he thinks he sees it. He cannot get beyond the idea; perhaps the idea agrees to the actual fact; perhaps it does not; perhaps there is nothing but the idea. There is no evidence—not the remotest particle of evidence—that anything exists independently of man's idea, or if there be any independent existence, that it is as the idea represents it to be.

For each individual man, there are two kinds of existence; himself, and all beyond himself—the "Me" and the "Not me." The "Not me" exists only in the idea of the "Me," is a purely ideal existence: but does the "Me" exist? You reply "I think, therefore I exist."* But in saying "*I* think" you take the existence of the "I" for granted—the very question at issue. It is true that the

* This was the argument of Descartes.

"I" is conscious of its existence; but consciousness is only a species of sensation. Without the aid of reason we could not know what consciousness is; nor could we comprehend its teachings, and therefore consciousness will not suffice to establish truth. Shakespeare* represents a certain Christopher Sly, a drunken vagabond, who had lived in misery and dirt all his life, as having been taken up while intoxicated and asleep, and placed in bed in the palace of a lord. When he had grown sober and awakened, he found a multitude of servants waiting upon him, and the principal ones asked anxiously how he was, expressed great joy at his recovery, and wished to know his commands. He replied that he was quite well, he was Christopher Sly, he dwelt in such a place. They told him that he was the hereditary lord of that castle, but had been crazy since childhood, and had supposed himself to be a certain Christopher Sly, vagabondizing, drinking bad liquor, keeping low company and lying in the gutters. Finally Christopher was persuaded that all his past life was a dream, and he began to act the lord. He soon got drunk, his fine clothes were taken off, his old rags put on and he was again placed in the gutter. When he came to himself, it was sometime before he could get back to the idea that he was only Christopher Sly, and then he came to the conclusion that the lordship was only a dream.

In this story Shakespeare has painted the nature of human knowledge truly. No man has any more secure knowledge of the past than Christopher Sly had, and he acted in accordance with the principles which ought to govern a philosophic mind. There is no man who, by skilful management, might not be brought to believe all past life to be only a dream, an unreality. Every man knows by experience that it is often very difficult to distinguish between things remembered and things dreamed of. Men in dreaming, often ask themselves whether they are not dreaming, and come to the conclusion that they are wide awake. All these things go to show the uncertainty of all human knowledge. There are certain things which we can safely assume that we will always believe, such as that two and two make four, but this is implied in the definition of the word "four;" and our continued belief in anything not a matter of definition is uncertain. The belief of men has often changed in regard to the nature and existence of the Deity. The Christians say that they have now the absolute knowledge that a Deity exists, and what his nature is; but all the other religious sects have said the same, and no two agree with their absolute knowledge. How can a Christian know but that to-morrow some development of science will compel him to change his creed in regard to the nature of Jehovah or the responsibility of man? There is no knowing. No man knows that he will believe to-morrow what he believes to-day. Man then can reach no positive knowledge to-day, and he can get no nearer to the final goal to-morrow.

* Prologue to " Taming the Shrew."

Matter cannot be proved to exist absolutely: and mind cannot exist without matter. Life is a dream—a dream of a dream. But though we know that the dreamer is only dreaming, yet we cannot wake him: he is the slave of his dream—of his idea. He is governed by certain laws, which must not be violated. The sword is only an idea, and yet to run a sword idea through a man-idea, is to violate a rule of the dreamer's existence, and a pain-idea, or a death-idea, is the consequence. There is no absolute truth capable of demonstation,* just as there is no human reason that is infallible. So long as reason is fallible, it can never demonstrate infallible truth.

CONCLUSION.

LXVI. The Christian Church must soon go down. She has long blockaded the pathways of science, of moral, political, social and religious philosophy. She has long persecuted and she continues to the extent of her power to persecute the disinterested friends of truth with a fiendish hate; but her time is past; they have now became too strong for her; they have turned upon her and with all tolerance for her followers, they are determined to exterminate herself. Her destruction is inevitable. It may be postponed for a few years and for a few only. "Like † other systems, Christianity has arisen and augmented, so like them it will decay and perish; as violence and deceit, not reasoning and persuasion have procured its admission among mankind, so when enthusiasm has subsided, and time, that infallible controverter of false opinions, has involved its pretended evidences in the darkness of antiquity, it will become obsolete."

The necessity of measuring every thing by the standard of the Bible, is a clog which must be cut off. No step forward in science or philosophy can be taken without the interference of the priests. When the propositions were advanced that the earth moved round the sun; that there were no ghosts; that devils did not enter the human body; that subjects had a right to resist tyrannical rulers; that the earth was millions of years old; that men were not all descended from one

---

* See Appendix—Note 13.   † Shelley.

pair, and had lived on this planet for tens of thousands of years; that there never was a universal deluge; that the mind was nothing more than a function of the brain—when these propositions were severally brought forward by learned men, the church at once interposed, said those doctrines were contrary to the Bible, and could not be true; and whoever should publicly advocate them, should be considered a child of the devil. The propositions having been established, the church admitted that they were true, and with many wry faces proceeded, amidst the jeerings of the infidels, to fit her interpretation of the scriptures to the teaching of science. Thus we have Scripture-Geologists, Scripture-Astronomers, Scripture-Chronologists, Scripture-Egyptologists and Scripture-Physiologists. Heretofore the advocates of Christianity have, to a certain extent, compensated by numbers and zeal for their inferiority in knowledge and talent; and they were forever reinforced from the standing army of black dragoons,* who are scattered all over the land, and find a profitable business in the miserable business of grinding over the empty ceremonies and the meaningless commonplaces of tradition to the church. But the church has lost her power to burn and exile and excommunicate her opponents. She has scarce the influence, though she lacks not the disposition, to excite her own sectaries to hate the skeptic. So long as the free-thinker could not express his opinions, without being persecuted by government or the mob, there was little probability of a free expression of thought. But the little odium which is still attached by a portion of the community to free inquiry and the expression of doubt about Christianity, will soon be swept away, and then it will be found that there are hundreds of sceptics where there are tens now. Let not sincere Christians grieve at these expressions. They are true. They are the expressions of the majority of the great men of the age. The tidings are not mournful. There is no danger that the morality of to-morrow will be worse than that of to-day. Morality is not founded on superstition, notwithstanding Robespierre's assertion that if there were no God it would be necessary to invent one, and the assertion of the Christian church that if there were no hell, it would be necessary to invent one—the fear of eternal fire being the only true conservator of morality.

"Morality† is usually said to depend upon religion; but this is said in that low sense, in which outward conduct is considered morality; [and it is not true even then]. In that higher sense in which morality denotes sentiment, it is more exactly true to say that religion depends on morality, and springs from it. Virtue is not the conformity of outward actions to a rule, nor is religion the fear of punishment, or the hope of reward. Virtue is the state of a just, prudent, benevolent, firm and temperate mind. Religion is the whole of these

---

* Carlyle's Life of Sterling.   † Sir James Mackintosh.

sentiments, which such a mind feels towards an infinitely good and perfect being. I am pleased with contemplations which trace piety to so pure and noble
a source—which show good men have not been able to differ so much from each
other as they imagined; that amidst all the deviations of the understanding,
the beneficent necessity of their nature keeps alive the same sacred feelings;
and that Turgot and Malesherbes,* so full of love for the good and fair had not
apostatized from the true God of Socrates and Jesus."

True religion† is in no danger, though old Christian dogmas must give way for
a human devotion to the just, the good, the true and the beautiful—a faith
without mysteries, and founded upon reason, free inquiry and thorough investigation and a morality comprehensible and practicable. "Celibacy,‡ fasting, penance, mortification, self-denial, humility, solitude and the whole train of
monkish virtues are every where rejected by men of sense, because they serve
no manner of purpose, neither advance a man's fortune in the world, nor render him a more valuable member of society, neither qualify him for the entertainment of company, nor increase his power of self enjoyment." Who will
lament for the banishment from this world of baptism and prayer, original sin
and redemption, predestination and grace, and last, but not least, of Hell and
damnation? Let them go; they never wrought any good; they always pre-
vented man from having his eye single to his duty toward his fellow. The
worship of Jehovah was never any thing but a ceremony, as though an all-
wise Deity was to be approached and propitiated by the same means used toward vain and foolish princes. The popular belief in Jehovah was almost
invariably the mere growth of ignorance and superstition. All that there was
ever adorable in a God was his good qualities. Those good qualities had their
origin in the nature of the human mind, and cannot be driven out of it. Atheism
cannot deprive us of them, and the practical worship of them without a personality by moral actions, will probably be no worse than an empty ceremonial
worship of a personality with them. "Human§ weakness has always confounded its representations of religion with religion itself, and predicted the fall
of religion if their own peculiar views were subjected to alteration. 'Religion
is in danger,' they cried at the time of the Waldenses, the Hussites, of Wick-
liffe, of Luther; but it was only that form of religion, which bore the name of
Catholic that was really in danger, not religion itself, which thus only gained a
new form, beneficial to itself and to its influence, and bloomed forth in a new
dress suitable to the times. Divine religion would indeed be a poor, paltry
thing, if it depended for its existence on any form of human representation,
which must always change as the time changes. Then long since would it
have perished."

---

* Two famous French Infidels.   † See Appendix, Note 14.
‡ Hume.   § Westminster Review, Dec. 1845.

" Let * not then the mind, which is compelled to renounce its belief in miraculous revelations, deem itself bound to throw aside at the same time all its
more cherished associations. Its generous emotions and high contemplations
may still find an occasion for exercise in the review of the interesting incidents
which have forever consecrated the plains of Palestine; but it may also find
pleasure in the thought that for this exercise, no single spot of earth and no
one page of its history, furnishes the exclusive theme. Whatever dimness may
gather from the lapse of time and the obscurity of tradition about the events of
a distant age, these capabilities of the mind itself remain, and always will remain, in full freshness and beauty. Other Jerusalems will excite the glow of
patriotism, other Bethanies exhibit the affections of home, and other minds of
benevolence and energy seek to hasten the approach of the kingdom of man's
perfections. Nor can scriptures ever be wanting—the scriptures of the physical and moral world—the book of the universe. Here the page is open and
the language intelligible to all men; no transcribers have been able to interpo-
late or erase its texts; it stands before us in the same genuineness as when
first written; the simplest understanding can enter with delight into criticism
upon it; the volume does not close, leaving us to thirst for more, but another
and another epistle still meets the inquisitive eye, each signed with the author's
own hand, and bearing undoubted characters of divine inspiration."

---

* Hennell's Origin of Christianity, concluding remarks.

APPENDIX.

References.

SECTION 1. NOTE 1.

I regret that I have neglected to take exact references in all cases where I have made quotations; but my purpose of making a book for the million, perhaps led me at first to attach too little importance to references. In most cases my quotations are taken from the original authors, but sometimes I have adopted quotations at second hand. Some quotations may not be literally exact, but in no case is any injustice done to the author, or any unfairness to the subject under consideration.

Where brackets are used thus [ ], they designate words inserted by the author among words quoted from another writer.

Penalties of Lifting the Veil from Truth.

SECTION 1. NOTE 2.

Goethe's Faust. Faust declares that those who have opened their hearts to the world have ever been crucified and burned.

Bacon laments that he cannot dismiss "all art and circumstance" in regard to the origin of existence, and exhibit the matter naked, so that every one might use his best judgment.

R. W. Mackay in his work "On the Progress of the Intellect," says: "The mind which has outgrown the idea of a partial God is expected to retract, and to submit to vulgar opinion, under pain of that reproach of atheism which, though never incurred by barbarians, is an objection commonly urged against philosophy by those intellectual barbarians, who cling like children to the god whom they suppose to feed them, speak to them, and flatter them."

"Reformers in all ages, whatever their object, have been unpitied martyrs; and the multitude have evinced a savage exultation in their sacrifice. Let in the light upon a nest of young owls, and they cry out against the injury you have done them. Men of mediocrity are young owls; when you present them with strong brilliant ideas, they exclaim against them as false, dangerous and deserving punishment."—*Adventures of a Younger Son.*

"An original thinker, a reformer in moral science, will thus often appear a hard and insensible character. He goes beyond the feelings and associations of the age; he leaves them behind him; he shocks our old prejudices; it is reserved for a subsequent generation to whom his views have been unfolded from infancy, and in whose minds all the interesting associations have collected round them, which formerly encircled the exploded opinions, to regard his discoveries with unmingled pleasure."—*Samuel Bailey, Essay on the formation of Opinions.*

"The artist, [The Philosopher,] it is true, is the son of his time; but pity for him, if he is its pupil, or even its favorite! Let some beneficent divinity snatch him when a suckling from the breast of his mother, and nurse him with the milk of a better time, that he may ripen to his full stature, beneath a distant Grecian sky. And having grown to manhood let him return like a foreign shape to his century: not, however, to delight it by his presence, but dreadful, like the son of Agamemnon, to purify it."—*Schiller—Translation by Carlyle.*

In 1624, at the request of the University of Paris, and especially of the Sorbonne, persons were forbidden by an *arret* of Parliament, on pain of death, to hold or to teach any maxim contrary to ancient and approved authors, or to enter into any debate, but such as should be approved by the doctors of the faculty of theology.

"Speedy end to superstition,—a gentle one if you can contrive it, but an end. What can it profit any mortal to adopt locutions and imaginations which do not correspond to fact; which no sane mortal can deliberately adopt in his soul as true; which the most orthodox of mortals can only, and this after infinite and essentially impious effort to put out the eyes of his mind, persuade himself to believe that he believes? Away with it; in the name of God come out of it, all true men!"—*Carlyle, Life of John Sterling.*

"The observer must be blind indeed, who does not perceive the vastness of the scale on which speculative principles, both right and wrong, have operated upon the present condition of mankind; or who does not now feel and acknowledge how deeply the morals and the happiness of private life, as well as the order of political society, are involved in the final issue of the contest between true and false philosophy."—*Dugald Stewart.*

The Dominion of Reason in Matters of Religion.

SECTION II. NOTE 3.

The Church Opposed to Reason.

It is a notorious fact that the Christian Church has always been bitterly opposed to the use of reason for the purpose of questioning or investigating the truth of the Bible.

The Apostles Denounced Reason.

"The carnal mind is enmity against God." Rom. VIII. 7.

"Avoid oppositions of science, falsely so called, which some professing have erred from the faith." 1 Tim. VI. 20.

"The things of the Spirit of God are foolishness unto the natural man." 1 Cor. II. 14.

"Beware, lest any man spoil you through philosophy." Col. II. 8.

The Fathers of the Church Denounced Reason.

The modern Catholic Church denounces the use of reason, and established bloody inquisitions to suppress the progress of free thought.

The leaders of the Reformation denounced the use of reason, if used for the purpose of going any further than they had gone; although, of course, it was all right if used to discover the fallibility and wickedness of the Catholic Church.

"Divine things, since they are beyond reason, appear contrary to reason."— *Luther*.

"There is nothing more hostile to faith than reason."—*Luther*.

"Reason is the bride of the devil."—*Luther*.

"Build not your faith in the Divine Word on the sand of human reason."— *Calvin*.

"It is folly to think of God according to the dictates of our mad, dazzled and corrupt reason."—*Luther*.

The same idea was also expressed by great men a century later, who sympathised with the Reformation.

"The principles of theology are above nature and reason."—*Pascal*.

"In theology we balance authorities, in philosophy we weigh reasons."— *Kepler*.

The leaders of the Protestant Church in our own day, as a body, are bitterly opposed to doubt or investigation of the truth of their doctrines. One citation must be sufficient in support of a fact already sufficiently notorious.

"It behoves us to make an entire and unconditional surrender of our minds to all the duty and to all the information which the Bible sets before us."— *Chalmers*.

Bayle, a sceptic, thus expresses the doctrine of the Church:—"The first thing Jesus Christ requires is faith and submission. This is commonly his first precept, and also of his apostles:—'Follow me, believe, and thou shalt be saved.' (Luke V. 27; IX. 59; Acts XVI. 31). Now that faith which was required was not obtained by a train of philosophical discussions and long reasoning, but was the gift of God, a pure grace of the Holy Ghost, which commonly fell on ignorant persons. (Mat. XI. 25). It was not even produced in the apostles by their reflecting on the holiness of the life of Jesus Christ, and the excellency of his doctrines and miracles. They stood in need of a revelation from God himself to know that he, whose disciples they were, was his eternal son." (Mat. XVI. 17).

Hobbes, another sceptic, says very wittily:—"When anything written in the Bible is too hard for examination, it is our duty to captivate our understandings to the words, and not to labor in sifting out a philosophical truth by logic, of such mysteries as are not comprehensible, nor fall under any rule of natural science, for it is with the mysteries of our religion as with the wholesome pills for the sick, which swallowed whole, have the virtue to cure, but chewed, are for the most part cast up again without effect."

Modern Churchmen in favor of Free Inquiry.

A few of the best modern Churchmen have been in favor of free inquiry; but the Church deserves little credit for, and certainly will derive little benefit rom, such opinions.

"We need not desire a better evidence that any man is in the wrong than to hear him declare against reason, and thereby acknowlege that reason is against him."—*Archbishop Tillotson.*

"What I most crave to see, and what still appears no impossible dream, is inquiry and belief going together."—*Dr. Arnold.*

"I shudder at the consequences of fixing the great proofs of religion upon any other basis than that of the widest investigation, and the most honest statement of facts."—*Rev. Sydney Smith.*

"With regard to Christianity itself, I creep toward the *light*, even though it *takes me away* from the more nourishing warmth. Yea, I should do so, even if the light made its way through a rent in the wall of the temple."—*S. T. Coleridge.*

"Let her [truth] and falsehood grapple! Who ever knew truth put to the worse in a free and open encounter?"—*Milton.*

"One who has an aversion to doubt, and is anxious to make up his mind, and to come to some conclusion on every question that is discussed, must be content to rest many of his opinions on very slight grounds."—*Archbishop Whately.*

"The love of truth, a deep thirst for it, a deliberate purpose to seek it, and hold it fast, may be considered as the very foundation of human culture and dignity."—*Wm. E. Channing.*

"There is a general obligation common to all Christians, of searching into the origin and evidences of our religion."—*Dr. Middleton.*

Philosophers on Reason in Religion.

"O, my dear Kepler, how I wish we could have one hearty laugh together! Here at Padua, is the principal professor of Philosophy, whom I have repeatedly and urgently requested to look at the moon and planets, through my glass, which he pertinaciously refuses to do. Why are you not here? What shouts of laughter we should have at this glorious folly."—*Galileo.*

"To steal into heaven, by the modern method of sticking, ostrich-like, your head into fallacies on earth, equally as by the ancient and by all conceivable methods, is forever forbidden."—*Carlyle's Life of Sterling.*

"Whenever obsequious reverence is substituted for *bold inquiry*, truth, if she is not already at hand, will never be attained."—*Hallam*

"He who dare not reason is a slave; he who will not is a bigot; he who cannot is a fool."—*Drummond.*

"True faith is a belief in things probable."—*Mackay.*

"The intellectual worth and dignity of man are measured, not by the truth which he possesses, or fancies that he possesses, but by the sincere and honest pains he has taken to discover truth. This it is that invigorates his mind; and by exercising the mental springs, preserves them in full activity. Possession makes us quiet, indolent, proud. If the Deity held in his right hand all truth, and in his left only the ever active impulse, the fond desire, and longing after truth, coupled with the condition of constantly erring, and should offer me the choice, I should humbly turn towards the left, and say 'Father, give me this'; pure truth is fit for thee alone.'"—*Lessing.—Translator unknown*.

"An opinion, though ever so true and certain to one man, cannot be trans-fused into another as true and certain, by any other way but by way of opening his understanding, and assisting him so to order his conceptions, that he may find the reasonableness of it within himself."—*Wollaston*.

"In entering upon any scientific pursuit, [or philosophic investigation,] one of the student's first endeavors ought to be to prepare his mind for the reception of truth, by dismissing, or at least loosening his hold on all such crude and hastily adopted notions respecting all the objects and relations, he is about to examine, as may tend to embarrass or mislead him: and to strengthen himself by something of an effort and a resolve for the unprejudiced admission of any conclusion which shall appear to be supported by careful observation and lo-gical argument, even should it prove adverse to notions he may have previously formed for himself, or taken up without examination on the credit of others. Such an effort is in fact, a commencement of that intellectual discipline which forms one of the most important ends of all science. It is the first movement of approach toward that state of mental purity, which alone can fit us for a full and steady perception of moral beauty as well as physical adaptation. It is the euphrasy and rue with which we must purge our sight before we can receive and contemplate, as they are, the lineaments of truth and nature."—*Herschel—Introduction to Astronomy*.

"It was not simply to arrive at a conclusion by a certain measure of plausi-ble premise—and then to proclaim it as an authoritative dogma, silencing or disparaging all objections—that Grecian speculation aspired. To unmask not only positive falsehood, but even affirmation without evidence, exaggerated con-fidence in what was only doubtful, and show of knowledge without the reality: to look at a problem on all sides and set forth all the difficulties attending its solution, to take account of deductions from the affirmative evidence, even in the case of conclusions accepted as true upon the balance—all this will be found pervading the march of their greatest thinkers. As a condition of all progres-sive philosophy it is not less essential that the grounds of negation should be fully exposed than the grounds of affirmation."—*George Grote.—History of Greece*.

"To ask for nothing but results, to decline the labor of verification, to be sa-tisfied with a ready-made stock of established positive arguments as proof, and to decry the doubter or negative reasoner, who starts new difficulties, as a com-mon enemy,—this is a proceeding sufficiently common in ancient as well as in modern times. But it is nevertheless an abnegation of the dignity and even of the functions of speculative philosophy."—*Grote.—History of Greece*.

"The strict rule of scientific, [and philosophic,] scrutiny exacts according to modern philosophers in matters of inductive, [and speculative,] reasoning an exclusive homage. It requires that we should close our eyes against all pre-sumptive and extrinsic evidence, and abstract our minds from all considera-tions, [such as traditional authority and prejudices of education,] not derived from the matters of fact which bear directly on the matter in question. The maxim we have to follow in such controversies is *fiat justitia, ruat cœlum*, [let us know the truth, even if it should send us to hell.] In fact what is actually true is always most desirable to know, whatever consequences may arise from its admission."—*Pritchard.—Natural History of Man, Section II*.

"No man is accountable for the opinion he may form, the conclusion at which he may arrive, provided that he has taken the pains to inform his mind and fix his judgment. But for the conduct of his understanding he certainly is responsible. He does more than err if he negligently proceeds in his inquiry; he does more than err if he allows any motive to sway his mind, save the constant and single desire of finding the truth; he does more than err, if he suffers the least influence of temper or of weak feeling to warp his judgment; he does more than err, if he listens rather to ridicule than to reason, unless it be that ridicule which springs from the contemplation of gross and manifest absurdity, and which is in truth argument and not ribaldry."—*Brougham—Life of Voltaire.*

"Divest yourself of all bias in favor of novelty and singularity of opinion. Indulge them in any other subject rather than that of religion. It is too important, and the consequences of error may be too serious. On the one hand, shake off all fears and servile prejudices, under which weak minds are servilely crouched. Fix reason firmly in her seat, and call to her tribunal every fact, every opinion. Question with boldness even the existence of a God; because if there be one, he must more approve of the homage of reason than that of blindfolded fear. You will naturally examine first the religion of your own country. Read the Bible then as you would read Livy or Tacitus. The facts which are within the ordinary course of nature, you will believe on the authority of the writer, as you would do those of the same kind in Livy and Tacitus. The testimony of the writer weighs in their favor, in one scale, and their not being against the laws of nature does not weigh against them in the other. But those facts of the Bible which contradict the laws of nature must be examined with more care, and under a variety of phases. Here you must recur to the pretensions of the writer to inspiration from God. Examine upon what evidence his pretensions are founded, and whether that evidence is so strong, that its falsehood would be more improbable than a change in the laws of nature, in the case he relates. For example in the books of Joshua we are told, the sun stood still several hours. Were we to read that fact in Livy or Tacitus, we should class it with their showers of blood, speaking of statues, beasts, &c. But it is said the writer of that book was inspired. Examine, therefore, candidly what evidence there is of his having been inspired. The pretension is entitled to your inquiry, because millions believe it. On the other hand you are astronomer enough to know how contrary it is to the law of nature, that a body revolving on its axis, as the earth does, should have stopped [suddenly], should not by that sudden stoppage have prostrated animals, trees, buildings, and should after a certain time have resumed its revolutions, and that also without a general prostration. Is this arrest of the earth's motion, or the evidence which affirms it, most within the law of probability? You will next read the New Testament. It is the history of a personage called Jesus. Keep in your eye the opposite pretensions; *first*, of those who say he was begotten by God, born of a virgin, suspended and reversed the laws of nature at will, and ascended bodily into heaven; and *secondly*, of those who say he was a man of illegitimate birth, of a benevolent heart, enthusiastic mind, who set out without pretensions, ended in believing them, and was punished capitally for sedition, by being gibbeted according to the Roman law. * * * Do not be frightened from this inquiry by any fear of its consequences. * * * In fine, I repeat, you must lay aside all prejudices on both sides, and neither believe nor reject anything, because any other persons or description of persons have rejected or believed it. Your own reason is the only oracle given you by heaven, and you are answer-

6

able, not for the rightness, but for the uprightness of your decisions."—*Thomas Jefferson.—Letter to Peter Carr, Aug.* 10, 1787.

The Origin of Hebrew and Christian Doctrines.

SECTION XXII. NOTE 4.

"The favor of the gods was believed to be obtained by means similar to those which are most efficacious with powerful mortals—homage and tribute, or in the language of religion, worship and sacrifice. * * * The image of earthly kings applied to the heavenly powers, suggested the persuasion that the efficacy of a sacrifice depended on its value, and that the feeling which prompted the offering was not merely to be expressed, but to be measured by it. This persuasion was cherished by two popular prejudices; by the notion that the gods were capable of envy and jealousy, which men might allay by costly profusion in their gifts, and by the view taken of the sacrifice as a banquet for the gods, the more agreeable in proportion as it was rich and splendid." *Thirlwall—History of Greece, chapter VI.*

"It is incontestible that the Bramins have formed their people to such a degree of gentleness, courtesy, temperance and chastity, or at least have so far confirmed them in these virtues, that Europeans frequently appear in comparison with them as beastly, drunken, or mad. Their air and language are unrestrainedly elegant, their behavior friendly, their persons clean, their way of life simple and harmless. Their children are educated without severity; yet they are not destitute of knowledge, and still less of quiet industry or nicely imitative art. * * * The leading idea the Bramins entertain of God is grand and beautiful; their morality is pure and elevated; and even their fables, when scanned by the eye of reason, are refined and charming."—*J. G. Herder—Philosophy of History.*

"Socrates, and Confucius, Plato, Cicero, and Zoroaster, agree unanimously in what constitutes clear understanding and just morals; in spite of their various differences, they have all labored to one point on wh'ch our whole species rests. As the wanderer enjoys no greater delight than when he everywhere discovers even unexpectedly, the traces of a thinking, feeling mind, like his own, so are we delighted, when in the history of our species, the echo of all ages and nations reverberates nothing but truth and benevolence towards man."—*J. G. Herder—Philosophy of History.*

"If a name were to be given to impartiality and firm resolve, to indefatigable activity in words and deeds and a determinate ardent pursuit of victory or honor—if to that cool courage, which peril cannot daunt, misfortune cannot bend and success cannot intoxicate—it must be that of Roman fortitude. Many persons, even of the lowest order in that state, displayed this virtue in so conspicuous a manner, that we, particularly in our youth, when we view the Romans chiefly on their brilliant side, honor such personages as great departed spirits. Their generals stride like giants from one quarter of the world to another and bear the fate of nations in their prompt and powerful hands."—*Herder.*

"The morality of the Zend-Avesta is entitled to praise: purity of word, action and thought is repeatedly inculcated. To multiply the human species, increase its happiness, and prevent evil are the general duties inculcated by Zoroaster to his disciples; agriculture and the multiplication of useful arts are particularly recommended to them. 'He,' says Zoroaster, 'who sows the ground with diligence, acquires a greater stock of religious merit, than he could gain by 10,000 prayers.' The disciple of Z roaster is enjoined to pardon injuries, to honor his parents and the king whose rights are derived from Ormuzd, to respect old age, to observe general gentleness of manners and to practice universal benevolence.—*Butler—Horæ Biblicæ.*

"Well-doing," said Socrates, "is the noblest pursuit of man. The best man and the most beloved by the Gods is he who as a husbandman, performs well the duties of husbandry; as a surgeon those of medical art; in political life, his duty toward the commonwealth. But the man who does nothing well, is neither useful nor agreeable to the Gods."

"The superior man looks at his situation and acts accordingly. He concerns not himself with what is beyond his station. If he possess riches, he acts as a rich man ought to do. If poor, he acts as a poor man ought to act. To a stranger he acts the part of a stranger. If a sufferer, he acts as a sufferer ought to do. The superior man enters into no situation where he is not himself. If he hold a superior situation, he does not treat with contempt those below him. If he occupy an inferior station, he does not court the favor of his superiors; he corrects himself and blames not others. He feels no dissatisfaction. He grumbles not with Heaven above; he feels no resentment with man below. Hence the superior man dwells at ease, calmly waiting the will of Heaven. But the mean man walks in dangerous paths, and covets what he has no right to obtain."—*Confucius.*

"Alas I have never seen one who loves virtue as we love beauty."—*Confucius.*

"To cultivate virtue with undeviating singleness of intention, without regard to a long or short life, is the way to fulfil the divine decree."—*Mencius, a Chinese Philosopher*, (500, *B. C.*)

"Let us vigorously exert ourselves to act toward others as we wish them to do to us."—*Mencius.*

"The genius of Plato, informed by his own moderation, or by the traditional knowledge of the priests of Egypt, had ventured to explore the mysterious nature of the Deity. When he had elevated his mind to the sublime contemplation of the first self-existent, necessary cause of the universe, the Athenian sage was incapable of conceiving how the simple unity of his essence could admit the infinite variety of distinct and successive ideas which compose the model of the intellectual world; how a Being purely incorporeal could execute that perfect model and mould with a plastic hand the rude and independent chaos. The vain hope of extricating himself from these difficulties, which must ever oppress the feeble powers of the human mind might induce Plato to consider the divine nature under the threefold modifications of the First caus, the reason or *Logos*, and the soul or spirit of the universe. His poetical imagination sometimes fixed and animated these metaphysical abstractions; the three archical or original principles were represented in the Platonic system as three Gods united with each other by a mysterious and ineffable generation; and the *Logos* was particularly considered under the more accessible character of the

Son of an eternal Father and the creator and Governor of the World. Such appear to have been the secret doctrines which were cautiously whispered in the gardens of the Academy, and which according to the more recent disciples of Plato could not be understood till after an assiduous study for thirty years."—*Gibbon, Chap. XXI.—Decline and Fall.*

In a note to this chapter Gibbon says, "The modern guides who lead me to the knowledge of the Platonic system are Cudworth, (Intellectual System, pp. 568—620,) Basnage, (Hist. of Jews, L. IV. C. 4, pp. 53—86.) Leclerc, (Epist. Crit. VII. pp. 194—209,) and Brucker, (Hist. Phil. V. I. pp. 675—706.)

In a note affixed to this chapter, Guizot says that according to the Zend-Avesta, it is by the word more ancient than the world that Ormuzd created the Universe. He also says that Philo personified the *Logos* as the ideal archetype of the world. Gibbon gives it as his opinion that Philo wrote before the time of Jesus.

"Tsze Kung asked if there was any one word which expresses the proper conduct of one's whole life. Confucius [500 B. C.] replied, will not the word *shoo* [love?] do it, i. e. do not to others what you do not wish them to do to you."—*The Four Books, XV.* 23.—*Translated by the Rev. David Collie.*

Confucius said, "I compile and transmit to posterity, but write not anything new. I believe and love the ancients, taking Laou Pang for my pattern."—*Ibid. VII.* 1.

Some one asked Diogenes the way to be revenged on an enemy? The cynic replied: "Become more virtuous."—*Plut. de aud. poet. Quoted by Barthelemy.*

Socrates said: It was not permitted to return evil for evil.—*Plato in Crit. Quoted by Barthelemy.*

"However much we may be resolved to charge their predictions with collusion and imposture, there are yet specimens of their [the Roman oracles] moral doctrines preserved which exhibit a purity and wisdom scarcely to be surpassed."—*Dr. Arnold. See Cicero de Officiis, III.* 28, 29.

A. W. Schlegel says we have express testimony that the division of time into weeks originated with the Egyptians.

"If we addressed a Mongol or a Thibetan this question, 'Who is Buddha?' he replied instantly, 'The Savior of men.' The marvellous birth of Buddha, his life and his instructions contain a great number of moral truths and dogmas professed in Christianity, and which we need not be surprised to find also among other nations, since these truths are traditional and have always belonged to the heritage of humanity. There must be among a Pagan people more or less of Christian truth, in proportion as they have been more or less faithful in preserving the deposit of primitive traditions. From the concordant testimony of Indian, Chinese, Thibetan, Mongol and Cingalese books, we may place the birth of Buddha about the year 960 before Christ."—*Huc's Journey through the Chinese Empire. Chap. V.*

"The Boodhists of the west, accepting Christianity on its first announcement, at once introduced the rites and observances which for centuries had already existed in India. From that country Christianity derived its monarchical institutions, its form of ritual and church service, its councils or convocations to settle schisms on points of faith; its worship of relics, and working of miracles through them; and much of the discipline and dress of the clergy, even to the shaved heads of the monks and friars."—*Prinsep—Quoted in Pococke's India in Greece.*

"Piety, obedience to superiors, resignation in misfortune, charity, hospitality, filial, parental and conjugal affection, are among the distinguishing characteristics of the Hindoos."—*Forbes—Oriental Memoirs.*

"The philosophic observers in Greece boasted of the sense of personal dignity as the characteristic of the Greeks as distinguished from Barbarians.—*Grote.*

"Where is to be found theology more orthodox, or philosophy more profound, than in the introduction to the Shasta? 'God is one creator of one universal sphere, without beginning, without end. God governs all the creation by a general providence, resulting from his eternal designs. Search not the essence and the nature of the eternal, who is one; your research will be vain and presumptuous. It is enough that day and night you adore his power, his wisdom and his goodness, in his works. The eternal willed in the fullness of time to communicate of his essence and of his splendor to beings capable of perceiving it. They as yet existed not. The eternal willed and they were. He created Birma, Vistnou, and Siv.' These doctrines—sublime if ever there were any sublime—Pythagoras learned in India and taught them to Zaleucus and his other disciples."—*John Adams—Letter to Thomas Jefferson, Dec. 25, 1813.*

"A spirit of sublime devotion, of benevolence to mankind, and of amiable tenderness to all sentient creatures pervades the whole work [The Institutes of Menu]; the style of it has a certain austere majesty, that sounds like the language of legislation and extorts a respectful awe: the sentiments of independence on all beings but God, and the harsh admonitions even to kings, are truly noble; and the many panegyrics on the Gayatu, the mother, as it is called, of the Veda, prove the author to have adored (not the visible, material sun, but) that divine and incomparably greater light, to use the words of the most venerable text in the Indian Scripture, which illumines all, delights all, from which all proceed, to which all must return, and which alone can irradiate (not our visual organs merely, but our souls and) our intellects."—*Sir Wm. Jones.*

"The Samaritans in Aram were Buddhists, (see Johann von Mueller's Welt-Geschichte,) as were likewise the Essenes in Palestine; at least they were so in their esoteric doctrines, though subsequently they conformed externally to the Mosaic and afterwards to the Christian system. The Essenes subsequently joined the Gnostics. * * * * * * * * *
The Gnostics were divided into two chief sects—the Asiatic and the Egyptian [Theræpeutæ?]. The former were properly Buddhists, who for the most part adopted the outward forms of Christianity, because, in accordance with their own tenets, they considered Jesus to be a Buddha, who had appeared on earth. * * * * * * * * * * * *
The Druids, too, in ancient Britain were Buddhists: they admitted the metempsychosis, the pre-existence of souls, and their return to the realms of universal space. They had a triad of gods, consisting, like that of the Buddhists, of a creator, a sustainer, and a destroyer. The Druids constituted a sacerdotal order, which reserved to itself the exclusive privilege of expounding the mysteries of religion. Their wisdom was so renowned that Lucan says in his epic poem, 'If ever the knowledge of the gods has come down to earth, it is to the

Druids of Britain.' They afterwards, in Cæsar's time, propagated their doctrines in Gaul, whence they spread among the Celtic tribes in Spain, Germany and in the Cimbrian Peninsula. The ban of the Druids was as terrible as that of the Bramins ; even the king, whom it smote, fell like grass before the scythe. The Druids must have obtained their doctrine through traffic of the Phœnicians with Britain, the latter people having been of the Buddhist creed. Nav, even in the far North did Buddhism make its way; for it cannot be denied that the doctrine of Odin is an echo of that of Buddha. The Scandinavians had their divine trinity of the creator, sustainer, and destroyer."—*Count Bjornsterna.* —*Quoted in the Foreign Quarterly Review, Jan.* 1844.

Miracles not Recorded in the Bible.

Section XXIV. Note. 5.

Miraculous Cure by Vespasian.

"Of all the miraculous cures on record, the best attested are those of the blind man and the paralytic man, whom Vespasian cured of their ailments. These miracles were done in Alexandria, before a multitude of people, Romans, Greeks, and Egyptians, and the Emperor was at the time on his throne. He did not seek popularity, of which the emperor of Rome, firmly established on his seat, had no need. The two unfortunate men threw themselves in his way, and begged to be cured. He blushed for them and ridiculed their prayer. He said that such a cure was beyond the power of man : but the two unfortunates insisted, and asserted that the god Serapis had appeared to them and assured them that they should be cured by the miraculous power of Vespasian. Finally he consented to utter the words, but he did so without any expectation of success, and on the instant the blind man was restored to see, and the lame man to walk without imperfection. Alexandria, Egypt, and the whole empire were filled with the fame of the event ; and the record of the miracle was placed in the archives of State, and preserved in all the contemporary histories. Nevertheless this miracle is now believed by nobody, because nobody has any interest in maintaining it."—*Voltaire.—Essai sur les Miracles.*

Miracle at Tipasa.

"Tipasa, a maritime colony of Mauritania, was purely orthodox, and had braved the fury of the Donatists and the tyranny of the Arians. Their disobedience exasperated the cruelty of Hunneric ; a military count was dispatched from Carthage to Tipasa ; he collected the Catholics in the forum, and in the presence of the whole province, deprived the guilty of their right hands and of their tongues. But the holy Confessors continued to speak without tongues ; and this miracle is attested by Victor, an African bishop, who published a history of the persecution within two years after the event. 'If any one' says Victor ' should doubt the truth, let him repair to Constantinople, and listen to the clear and perfect language of Restitutus, the sub-deacon, one of these glorious sufferers, who is now lodged in the palace of the Emperor Zeno, and is respected by the devout Empress.' At Constantinople, we are astonished to find a cool, learned, and unexceptionable witness, without interest and without passion. Æneas of Gaza, a Platonic Philosopher, has accurately described his own observations on these African sufferers :—'I saw them myself, I heard them speak, I diligently inquired by what means such an articulate voice could be formed without any organ of speech ; I used my eyes to examine the report of my ear; I opened their mouths, and saw that their whole tongues had been completely torn away by the roots—an operation which the physicians generally suppose to be mortal.' The testimony of Æneas of Gaza might be confirmed by the superfluous evidence of the Emperor Justinian, in a perpetual edict; of Count Marcellinus in his chronicle of the times; and of Pope Gregory the First, who had resided at Constantinople, as the minister of the Roman Pontiff. They all lived within the compass of a century; and they all appeal to their personal knowledge, or to the public notoriety for the truth of the miracle, which was repeated in several instances, displayed on the greatest theatre of the world, and submitted during a series of years to the calm examination of the senses."—*Gibbon—Decline and Fall, chap. XXXVII.*

Miracles at the Tomb of Abbe Paris.

The miracles reported to have been done about 1650. A. D., at the tomb of Abbe Paris, the Jansenist, in the city of Paris, are famous in history. The Rev. Dr. Middleton gives the following account of them:

"Within six years after his [Abbe Paris'] death, the confident report of miracles wrought at his tomb, began to alarm not only the city of Paris, but the whole nation; while infinite crowds were continually pressing to the place and proclaiming the benefits received from the saint, nor could all the power of the government give a check to the rapidity of this superstition, till by closing the tomb within a wall, they effectually obstructed all access to it."

"This expedient though it put an end to the external worship of the saint, could not shake the credit of his miracles; distinct accounts of which were carefully drawn up, and dispersed among the people, with an attestation of them, much more strong and authentic, than what has ever been alleged for the miracles of any other age since the days of the apostles. Mons. de Montgeron, a person of eminent rank in Paris, (Counsellor to the Parliament), published a select number of them, in a pompous volume in quarto, which he dedicated to the king, and presented to him in person, being induced to the publication of them, as he declares,, by the incontestible evidence of the facts; by which he himself, a libertine and professed deist, became a sincere convert to the Christian faith. But, besides the collection of M. de Montgeron, several other collections were made, containing in the whole above a hundred miracles, which are all published together in three volumes, with their original vouchers, certificates, affidavits and letters annexed to each of them at full length.

"The greatest part of these miracles were employed in the cure of desperate diseases in their last and deplored state, and after all human remedies had for many years been tried upon them in vain; but the patients no sooner addressed themselves to the tomb of this saint, than the most inveterate cases, and complications of palsies, apoplexies, and dropsies, and even blindness and lameness, &c., were either instantly cured or greatly relieved, and within a short time after, wholly removed. All which cures were performed in the church yard of St. Medard, in the open view of the people, and with so general a belief of the finger of God in them that many infidels, debauchees, schismatics, and heretics are said to have been converted by them to the Catholic faith.' And the reality of them is attested by some of the principal physicians and surgeons in France, as well as the clergy of the first dignity, several of whom were eye-witnesses of them, who presented a *verbal process (proces-verbal)* to each of the archbishops, with a petition signed by above twenty *cures* or rectors of the parishes of Paris, desiring that they might be authentically registered, and solemnly published to the people as true miracles."

On the wall erected about the tomb to keep away the crowd and stop the miracles, some scoffer stuck up a notice,

"De par le roi, il est defendu a Dieu
De faire de miracles dans ce lieu."

.(The king has ordered that God shall perform no more miracles in this place.)

"Miracles, most doubtful on the spot and at the moment, will be received with implicit faith at a convenient distance of time and space."—*Gibbon.—Decline and Fall, Chap. LVII. See an example there cited.*

Cicero says of the Pythian oracle, "When men began to be less credulous, its power vanished."

"Were miracles really indispensable for religious improvement and consolation, heaven forbid there should be any limits to our credulity."—*Mackay—Progress of the Intellect.*

Miraculous Cure of Pascal's Niece.

"Mademoiselle Perrier was the niece of Blaize Pascal. She was a child in her eleventh year, and a scholar residing in the monastery of Port Royal. For three years and a half she had been afflicted with a *fistula lachrymalis.* The adjacent bones had become carious, and the most loathsome ulcers disfigured her countenance. All remedies had been tried in vain; the medical faculty had exhausted their resources. * * * Now it came to pass that M. de la Potherie, a Parisian ecclesiastic, and an assiduous collector of relics, had possessed himself of one of the thorns from the crown worn by Christ just previous to the crucifixion. Great had been the curiosity of the various convents to see it, and the ladies of Port Royal had earnestly solicited the privilege. Accordingly on the 24th of March, in the year 1656, a solemn procession of nuns, novices and scholars moved along the aisles of the monastic church, chanting appropriate hymns, and each one in her turn kissing the holy relic. When the turn of Mademoiselle Perrier arrived, she, by the advice of the school mistress, touched her diseased eye with the thorn, not doubting but that it would effect a cure. She regained her room and her malady was gone. The cure was instantaneous and complete. * * * All Paris rang with the story. It reached the ear of the Queen Mother. By her command M. Felix, the principal surgeon to the king, investigated and confirmed the narrative. * * * The greatest genius, the most profound scholar, and the most eminent advocate of that age, all possessing the most ample means of knowledge, all carefully investigated, all admitted, and all defended with their pens, the miracle of the Holy Thorn. Europe at that time produced no three men more profoundly conversant with the laws of the material world, with the laws of the human mind, and with the municipal law, than Pascal, Arnauld and Le Maitre; and they were all sincere and earnest believers. Yet our Protestant incredulity utterly rejects both the tale itself and the inferences drawn from it, and but for such mighty names might yield to the temptation of regarding it as too contemptible for serious notice."—*Edinburgh Review, July* 1841.

"An historian ought not to dissemble the difficulty of defining with precision the limits of that happy period, exempt from error and from deceit, to which we might be disposed to extend the gift of supernatural powers. From the first of the fathers to the last of the Popes, a succession of bishops, of saints, of martyrs, and of miracles is continued without interruption; and the progress of superstition was so gradual and almost imperceptible, that we know not in what particular link we should break the chain of tradition.—*Gibbon.*

See Forbes Oriental Memoirs, vol II. ch. IV. for an account ot the success of several wonderful Hindoo prophecies.

Prophecy of Josephine's Greatness.

Memes, in his biography of the Empress Josephine, thus records the famous prophecy of Josephine's royal destiny: "On one of these occasions, an inc'dent occurred, the only one recorded of her early years, which exercised an influence, at least over her imagination, almost to the latest hour of her existence. The following is the narrative, in her own words, as she long afterward related the circumstances to the ladies of her court:—

"One day some time before my first marriage, while taking my usual walk, I observed a number of negro girls assembled round an old woman, engaged in telling their fortunes. I drew near to observe their proceedings. The old Sibyl, on beholding me, uttered a loud exclamation, and almost by force seized my hand. She appeared to be under the greatest agitation. Amused at these absurdities, as I thought them, I allowed her to proceed, saying, 'So you discover something extraordinary in my destiny?' 'Yes.' 'Is happiness or misfortune to be my lot?' 'Misfortune. Ah, stop! and happiness too.' 'You take care not to commit yourself, my dame; your oracles are not the most intelligible.' 'I am not permitted to render them more clear,' said the woman, raising her eyes with a mysterious expression towards heaven. 'But to the point,' replied I, for my curiosity began to be excited; 'what read you concerning me in futurity?' 'What do I see in the future? You will not believe me if I speak.' 'Yes, indeed, I assure you. Come my good mother what am I to fear and hope?' 'On your own head be it then; listen! You will be married soon; that union will not be happy; you will become a widow, and then—then you will be Queen of France! Some happy years will be yours; but you will die in a hospital, amid civil commotion.'"

How the Stories of Miracles were Forged.

"The passage concerning Jesus Christ, which was inserted into the text of Josephus, between the time of Origen and that of Eusebius, may furnish an example of no vulgar forgery. The accomplishment of the prophecies, the virtues, miracles and resurrection of Jesus are distinctly related."—*Gibbon— Decline and Fall, Chap. XVI. No. 36. Not contradicted by Milman or Guizot.*

"The monks of succeeding [the dark] ages, who in their peaceful solitudes, entertained themselves with diversifying the deaths and sufferings of the primitive martyrs, have frequently invented torments of a very refined and ingenious nature. In particular it has pleased them to suppose that the zeal of the Roman magistrates, disdaining every consideration of moral virtue or public decency, endeavored to seduce those whom they could not vanquish, and that by their orders the most brutal violence was offered to those whom they found it impossible to seduce. It is related that pious females who were prepared to despise death, were sometimes condemned to a more severe trial, and called upon to determine whether they set a higher value on their religion or on their chastity. The youths to whose licentious embraces they were abandoned, received a solemn exhortation from the judge, to exert their most strenuous efforts to maintain the honor of Venus against the impious Virgin who refused to burn incense on her altars. Their violence however was commonly disappointed, and the seasonable interposition of some miraculous power preserved the chaste spouses of Christ from the dishonor even of an involuntary defeat."
—*Gibbon.*

"How shall we know that the alleged revelation is of divine authority? By the miracles and prophecies which accompanied it. And how shall we know that the alleged miracles and prophecies were true? From the testimony of the Scriptures. And how do we know that the testimony of the Scriptures is reliable? Because they were inspired by God. And how do we know they were inspired by God? By the testimony of the Holy Ghost, which when we read the Scriptures recognises his own work. But how do we know that this internal evidence is the testimony of the Holy Ghost and not of some evil spirit? Here the string breaks."—*Strauss—Christliche Glaubenslehre.*

"A prophetical pamphlet, published in 1651, by the famous astrologer Lilly, was thought to be so signally verified by the great fire of London, that the author was summoned before the House of Commons, and publicly requested there to favor them with his advice respecting the prospects of the nation."— *Edinburgh Review, July,* 1844.

Opinions of Great Free-Thinkers on the Character of Jesus.

SECTION XXXII. NOTE 6.

"Whatever be the spirit with which the four Gospels be approached, it is impossible to rise from the attentive perusal of them without a strong reverence for Jesus Christ. Even the disposition to cavil and ridicule is forced to retire before the majestic simplicity of the Prophet of Nazareth. Unlike Moses or Mahomet he owes no part of the lustre which surrounds him to his acquisition of temporal power; his is the ascendancy which mankind, in proportion to their mental advancement, are least disposed to resist—that of moral and intellectual greatness. The virtue, wisdom and sufferings of Jesus, will secure to him a powerful influence over men so long as they continue to be moral, intellectual and sympathising beings. And as the tendancy of human improvements is towards the progressive increase of these qualities, it may be presumed that the empire of Christianity, considered simply as the influence of the life, character and doctrine of Christ over the human mind, will never cease."—*Hennell— Origin of Christianity.*

Goethe says The Spirit of God is nowhere more beautifully revealed than in the New Testament.

The celebrated Hindoo Free-Thinker and reformer, Rammohun Roy, wrote: "After long and uninterrupted researches into religious truth, I have found the doctrines of Christ more conducive to moral principles and better adapted for the use of rational beings, than any others which have come to my knowledge."

Carlyle styles Jesus a divine man.

"Abstracting what is really his, from the rubbish in which it is buried, easily distinguished by its lustre from the dross of his biographers, and as separable from that as the diamond from the dunghill, we have the outlines of a system of the most sublime morality, which has ever fallen from the lips of man."— *Thomas Jefferson—Letter to Mr. Short, Oct.* 31, 1819.

"I think Christ's system of morals and his religion as he left them to us, the best the world ever saw or is likely to see; but I apprehend that they have received various corrupting changes."—*Benjamin Franklin.—Sparks' Biography,* p. 515.

" The Christian religion raises the dim perception of divine existence, which is apparently born with, and natural to all men, to the simplest and most enlightened ideas of the Deity—to ideas the most worthy of the Godhood and the most elevating to mankind; purifies the mind from all superstitions of the agency of demons and wizards, and creates in every human soul, wherein it prevails, an overflowing fountain of unbounded confidence in God, of love for all good, of all-embracing humanity, of exhaustless fortitude in adversity, ot temperance and humility in prosperity, of patience in suffering, of peace of heart, of content with the present, and of never-dying hope for a better future. The faith of Jesus was a pure theosophy in the simplest sense of the word."— *Wieland— Ueber den freien Gebrauch der Vernunft in Glaubenssachen. Section XXVII.*

From Rousseau's Confession of a Savoyard Vicar.

" I confess to you that the holiness of the gospel is an argument which speaks to my heart, and to which I should regret to find a refutation. Look at the books of the philosophers, with all their pomp, how small are they in comparison. Can it be that a book, at once so simple and so sublime, can be the work of man? Can it be that he, whose history is there written, was but a man? Are these the words of a fanatic or of an ambitious partizan? What sweetness, what purity of manners! What touching grace in his discourses! What nobleness in his maxims! What profound wisdom in his words! What presence of mind, perspicacity and justice in his replies! What command over his passions! Where is the man, the sage who can live, suffer and die without weakness and without ostentation? When Plato described his imaginary just man, covered with all the disgrace of crime, and worthy of all the rewards of virtue, he painted Jesus Christ, feature for feature; the likeness is so striking that all the fathers of the Church perceived it, and it was impossible to mistake it. How prejudiced, how blind must not he be, who would dare to compare the son of Sophroniscus to the Son of Mary. How little resemblance between them! Socrates, dying without pain, without ignominy, easily supported his character to the last; and if this easy death had not honored his life, we should doubt whether Socrates, with all his genius, was more than a sophist. He invented, it is said, moral law; but others before him had practiced morality; he said no more than others had done; he only reduced to precepts previous examples. Aristides had been just before Socrates defined justice; Leonidas died for his country before Socrates taught the duty of love of country; Spartans were self-denying before Socrates inculcated sobriety; before he defined virtue, Greece had abounded in virtuous men. But whence from among the Jews did Jesus derive that elevated pure morality, of which he alone gave the example and the precept? In the midst of the most furious fanaticism, was heard the sublimest wisdom, and the simplicity of the most heroic virtues honored the vilest of all people. The death of Socrates, philophising among his friends, was the mildest possible; that of Jesus, by a horrible torture, abused, derided, cursed by the whole people, was the most fearful that could be imagined. Socrates taking the prisoner's cup from the weeping officer, pardons him; in the midst of his frightful sufferings Christ blesses his executioner. Yes, the life and death of Socrates were those of a sage; but the life and death of Jesus were those of a God."

Paine styles Jesus a virtuous reformer.

Voltaire says, "He must have been a sage since he declaimed against priestly impostors and superstitions; but the sayings and doings imputed to him, were not always those of a wise man."

Mendelsohn said the Jews in his days considered Jesus as a generous enthusiast.

"Religion and morality, as they now stand, compose a practical code of misery and servitude; the genius of human happiness must tear every leaf from th accursed book of God, ere man can read the inscription on his heart."— *Shelley.*

Antiquity of the Egyptian Empire.

Section XXXV. Note 8.

"The Egyptian empire first presents itself to view about 4000 years before Christ, as that of a mighty nation, in full tide of civilization, and surrounded by other realms and races already emerging from the barbarous stage.—*Types of Mankind, page* 57.

"The Egyptian monuments and records carry us to the beginning of the third millenium, [2000 years,] before the birth of Christ; and the earliest glimpse we gain of the condition of mankind in this country, exhibits them as already far advanced in civilization, and bearing no marks of so recent an origin from the single family as even the Septuaguint Chronology supposes." * * * * *
"The consequence of the method which has been commonly adopted of making the Jewish Chronology the bed of Procrustes, to which every other must conform its length, has been, that credence has been refused to histories, such as that of Egypt resting upon unquestionable documents; and we have voluntarily deprived ourselves of at least a thousand years, which have been edeemed for us from the darkness of ante-historic times."—*Rev. John Kenrick.*

Kenrick says :—"The negro with all his peculiarities of form, color, and hair, appears just the same in the paintings of the age of Thothnies III, fifteen centuries before the Christian era, as he is now seen in the interior of Africa."

"Without going beyond the history itself, it must appear incredible that a little more than four hundred years after the world was dispeopled by the flood Abraham should have found a Pharaoh reigning over the monarchy of Egypt, and that the East as far as its condition is disclosed to us, should present no, trace of recent desolation, but is already occupied and divided into communities."—*Kendrick.*

Dr. Usher, one of the authors of the "Types of Mankind," asserts that the plain on which the city of New Orleans is situated, is at least one hundred and fifty thousand years old. In digging down into the earth there has been found to be a considerable depth of alluvial deposits; and the remains of ten distinct cypress forests have been discovered one above the other. Each of these forests must have required many hundreds of years to grow, and then to sink to become the foundation for another growth. In the remains of the fourth forest from the top, and seven feet below the level of the Gulf of Mexico, were found a human skull and some burned wood, which, according to Usher's estimate, were deposited there 40,000 years ago.

The North China *Herald*, published at Shanghae, of Oct. 29, 1853, contained an able article on Chinese Chronology, by Dr. Macgowan, a high authority. He says in substance that the literature of China reaches back to the reign of Yaou, who lived 4000 years ago, or 2200 years before Jesus. The strongest evidences of the approximate correctness of their Chinese Chronology are drawn from the Chinese astronomy. The group or Star Maou, one of the 28 constellations known to us under the name of Pleiades, is said in the first chapter of the Shoo-King to have been a criterion for the time of the winter Solstice. This means that the Star would appear in the South at sunset at that time of the year. The Pleiades are now distant a little more than a sign from the summer Solstice, or nearly 150 degrees from the winter Solstice. In order to account for the removal of 90 degrees from this latter point, an interval of 4000 years must be allowed, for the equinoctial points do not move more than a degree in 71 years.

While the pole of the ecliptic remains unmoved, the north pole, by the slow displacement of the earth's position, revolves round it on a circle whose radius is $23\frac{1}{2}$ degrees. It happens that on this circle, about 60 degrees in advance of the present pole star, are two stars named respectively T'een-yih, and T'ae-yih, the former being the more distant. These names mean the Heavenly One, and the Great One; and the names, being very ancient, suggests the idea that these stars were the successive pole stars of early observers.

The Chinese calendar Hia-Sia-ouching, said by the Chinese writers to be a relic of the time of Yu, (B. C. 2200,) says, that among the stars of the Fourth Month, (one day of which corresponded to our 21st May,) "Maou, (Pleiades,) is seen at the beginning of evening twilight; Nau-mun, (Southern door,) is on the meridian." This last star is at the foot of the Centaur and is a very bright one, as those who have seen it in the southern latitudes are aware. It had through the precession of the equinoxes long retreated beneath the horizon of Chinese astronomers, and was restored to their maps by the Jesuits.

Existence and Nature of God.
SECTION XLII.   NOTE 7.

The System of Nature says:

"In rising from cause to cause men have ended by seeing nothing; and in this obscurity they placed their God: in this dark abyss their restless imaginations toil to manufacture chimeras which will oppress them, until an acquaintance with nature shall have stripped the phantoms which they have in all ages so vainly adored.

"If we wish to render an account to ourselves of the nature of our belief in the Deity, we must confess that, by the word God, men have never been able to designate more than the most hidden cause, the most unknown and distant of effects. The word is not used until natural and known causes cease to be visible; not until they lose the thread of causes, or being unable to follow it and cut through the difficulty by styling God the first cause: that is, he is the last cause of which they knew anything. Thus they only give a vague title to an unknown force, before which their ignorance or idleness force them to stop. Whenever any one says that God is the author of such phenomenon, it is as much as to say that he does not know how that phenomenon could be produced by natural causes known to us."

Atkinson, in "Man's Nature and Development," says that the application of the word Design to "nature's doings, and the fitness and form of things," is absurd. "Man designs, Nature is."

Pantheism.

Webster defines Pantheism to be the belief that the universe is God. Pantheism—at least as generally understood now by men acknowledging themselves pantheists—is a belief that the only cause—be it styled Deity, Divinity, God, or any other name—of the present order of things, is a principle of order inherent in matter, inseparable from it, and all-pervading; and this principle is unconscious, and has existed with matter from all eternity. A belief similar to this is now adopted by a large portion if not by a majority of the great philosophers and the scientific men of the age. The most of the so-called atheists are or were pantheists. The majority of the Greek philosophers were Pantheists.

Goethe has a few famous lines beginning—
> "Was waer ein Gott der nur von aussen stiesse," &c.

For this passage I can find no translation to suit me, and must reduce it to prose as follows: "Alas for the creed whose God lives outside of the universe and lets it spin round his finger. The universal spirit dwells within and not without. He includes Nature and Nature includes Him."

Faust, in talking to Margaret, speaks as though the name of the universal spirit were a matter of no consequence—Good, Heart, Love, God, either being sufficient.

A French author says: "To say what God is, it would be necessary to be himself."

"You are fit [says the supreme Krishna of Braminism to a sage] to apprehend that you are not distinct from me: that which I am, thou art, and that also is the world with its gods, and heroes, and mankind. Men contemplate distinctions because they are stupefied with ignorance."—*Emerson on Plato.*

Strauss says, the idea of God is his existence. Hegel says, God arrives at consciousness only in man.

Emerson is a Pantheist; and Carlyle appears to be, though the shade of the latter's belief is not seizable from his works. In the life of Sterling he relates a conversation between Sterling and another person (probably Carlyle). Sterling declared the faith of the other to be "flat Pantheism! It is mere Pantheism, that!" "And suppose it were Pot-theism," cried the other, "if it is true?"

Bacon appears to have been a Pantheist. He says in his *De Cupidine* (on the Source of Existence), "Almost all the ancients—Empedocles, Anaxagoras, Anaximenes, Heraclitus, Democritus—though disagreeing in other respects upon the prime matter, joined in this—that they held an active matter with a form, both arranging its own form, and having within itself a principle of motion. Nor can any one think otherwise without leaving experience altogether. All these, then, submitted their minds to Nature." Again, he says of this same Pantheism of Democritus: "But while the dicta of Aristotle and Plato are celebrated with applauses and professional ostentation in the schools, the philosophy of Democritus was in great repute among the wiser sort and those who more closely gave themselves to the depth and silence of contemplation." Again he says, "The prime matter is to be laid down, joined with the primitive form as also with the first principle of motion as it is found. For the abstraction of motion has also given rise to innumerable devices, concerning spirits—life and the like—as if there were not laid a sufficient ground for them through matter and form, but they depended on their own elements. But here three (matter, form and life) are not to be separated, but only distinguished; and matter is to be treated (whatever it be) in regard to its adornment, appendages and form, as that all kind of influence, essence, action, and natural motion may appear to be its emanation and consequence."

Bacon was long supposed to be no enemy of Christianity, because he did not vio'ently oppose it. But he was not disposed to be a martyr to Christian fanaticism. He laments that he cannot "dismiss all art and circumstance, and exhibit the matter naked to us,·that we might be enabled to use our judgment. Thinkest thou," he says, "that when all the accesses and motions of all minds are besieged and obstructed by the obscurest idols, deeply rooted and branded in, the sincere and polished areas present themselves in the true and native rays of things; but as the delirium of phrenetics (frenzy) is subdued by art and ingenuity, not by force and contention, raised to fury; so in this universal insanity, we must use moderation "—*Quoted by Atkinson.*

About forty years ago De Maistre, a French author, published a large book to prove Bacon an Atheist. De Maistre could not distinguish between Atheism and Pantheism.

On this subject, see "Man's Nature and Development," by Henry Atkinson and Harriet Martineau.

Shelley was a Pantheist.

Fichte says, "You give personality and consciousness to your God. What do you mean by 'personality' and 'consciousness?' The slightest attention to the meaning which you attach to these words, would convince you that they presuppose limitation and finite condition in their possessor. In representing God as conscious and personal, you make him finite, and reduce him to your own level: when you think Him, you do not think a God but a man. We feel and know ourselves to be persons only by our separation from other similar persons outside of us, from whom we are separated; and consequently we are finite. In and for this domain of finitude only, an idea of personality exists; beyond it the word loses its meaning. To speak of a personal divinity, or a divine personality appears from this point of view as a connection of ideas which exclude and annihilate each other. Personality is a self-hood fenced in against outsiders; absoluteness, on the contrary, is the comprehensive, unlimited, infinite which excludes all personality."

"That none of the ancient philosophers conceived God, for instance, as a being distinct from the world, or a pure metaphysical monad, but all adhered to the idea of a soul of the world was perfectly consonant to the childhood of human philosophy, and perhaps will forever remain consonant to it."—*Herder. Philosophy of History.*

The Moral Government of the Universe.

The attempts to account for the moral government of the world, the sufferings of the good and the prosperity of the wicked have been very numerous, but the solution of the problem is beyond the reach of the human mind. The stoics and the optimists say there is no evil; all is good.

Hume says: "Are there any marks of a distributive justice in the world? If you answer in the affirmative I conclude that, since justice here exerts itself, it is satisfied. If you reply in the negative, I conclude that you have then no reason to ascribe justice in our sense of it to the Gods. If you hold a medium between affirmation and negation, by saying that the justice of the Gods at present exerts itself in part, but not in its full extent, I answer that you have no reason to give it any particular extent, but only so far as you see it at present exert itself."

Leibnitz remarks: "That is a queer kind of justice which has for object, neither the reform of the offender, nor the warning of others, nor the reparation of evil done by the offender."

Gibbon speaks of Zoroastrianism as "a bold and injudicious attempt of Eastern philosophy to reconcile the existence of a Beneficent Creator and Governor of the Universe with the prevalence of physical and moral evil."

An ancient author thought there would be no difficulty in accounting **for the** moral government of the world, if we would suppose the sufferings **of the** righteous to be trials and those of the wicked to be punishments. Voltaire, speaking of the drowning of a boat load of people, among whom was a great criminal, said, "God has punished that rogue, the devil has drowned the rest." Diderot in recording the different fate of two rascals, said, "Providence has chastised one, but has granted some moments of respite to the other." Bayle, in the course of some observations upon the Mosaic myth of Adam in Paradise, and the fall, compares Jehovah to "A mother, who knowing certainly that her daughter would lose her virginity at a certain place and time, if solicited by a certain person, should manage the interview and leave her daughter there unguarded."

"The man who first pronounced the barbarous word Dieu, [God,] ought to have been immediately destroyed," says Diderot.

Robespierre declared that if there was no God, it would be necessary to invent one. He lectured so much about his Deity, that one of his companions at last exclaimed, *Avec votre Etre-Supreme vous commencez m'embeter*—(You are beginning to bore me with your Supreme Being.)

"Either God would prevent evil and cannot, or he can and would not, **or he** cannot and would not, or he will and can. If he would prevent evil and cannot, he is not omnipotent; if he can and would not, he is not all good; if he cannot and would not desire to do so, he is limited in both power and goodness; and if he has the power and the desire to prevent evil, why does he not do so?"— *Epicurus.*

"If experience and observation and analogy be indeed the only guides which we can reasonably follow in inferences of this nature, both the effect and causes must bear a similarity and resemblance to other effects and causes which we know and which we have found in many instances to be conjoined with each other. * * * * If you saw, for instance, a half-finished building surrounded with heaps of brick, and stone, and mortar and all the instruments of masonry, could you not infer from the effect that it was a work of design and contrivance? and could you not return again from this inferred cause to infer new additions to the effect, and conclude that the building would soon be finished and receive all the further improvements which art could bestow upon it? If you saw upon the sea shore the print of one human foot, you would conclude that a man had passed that way, and that he had also left the traces of the other foot, though effaced by the rolling of the sands or the inundations of the waters. Why do you refuse to admit the same method of reasoning with regard to the order of nature? Consider the world and the present life only as an imperfect building from which you can infer a superior intelligence; and **arguing** from that superior intelligence, which can leave nothing imperfect, why may you not infer a more finished scheme or plan, which will receive its completion in some distant point of space or time? Are not these methods of reasoning exactly similar? And under what pretence can you embrace the one while you reject the other? * * * * But what is the foundation of this method of reasoning? Plainly this, that man is a being whom we know by experience, whose motives and design we are acquainted with, and whose projects and inclinations have a certain coherence according to the laws which nature has established for the government of such a creature."—*David Hume.*

"To say that God is the author of all good, and man the author of all evil, is to say that one man made a straight line and a crooked one, and another man made the incongruity."—*Shelley.*

The Mind is the Function of the Brain.

SECTION XLIV. NOTE 8.

All the statements which I now make are well established principles of the science of physiology, and I give below some extracts from 'Carpenter's Elements of Physiology,' a work of the highest authority. The extracts which I present, prove that the cerebellum, or lower and back part of the brain, is the seat of the power of the harmonious movement of the muscular system; that the cerebrum, or upper and fore part of the brain, is the seat of intelligence; and that the brain is worn away by the activity of its function, the mind.

The extracts from Carpenter are as follows:

Functions of the Cerebellum.

Much discussion has taken place, of late years, respecting the uses of the Cerebellum; and many experiments have been made to determine them. That it is in some way connected with the powers of *motion*, might be inferred from its connection with the anteriolateral columns of the Spinal Cord, as well as with the posterior; and the comparative size of the organ, in different orders of Vertebrated animals, gives us some indication of what the nature of its functions may be. For we find its degree of development corresponding pretty closely with the variety and energy of the muscular movements which are habitually executed by the species; the organ being the largest in those animals which require the *combined* effort of a great variety of muscles to maintain their usual position, or to execute their ordinary movements; whilst it is the smallest in those which require no muscular exertion for the one purpose, and little combination of different actions for the other. Thus in animals that habitually rest and move upon four legs, there is comparatively little occasion for any organ to combine and organize the actions of their several muscles; and in these the Cerebellum is usually small. But among the more active of the predaceous fishes, (as the shark,)—birds of the most powerful and varied flight, (as the swallow,)—and such Mammals as can maintain the erect position, and can use their extremities for other purposes than support and motion—we find the Cerebellum of much greater size, relatively to the remainder of the Encephalou. There is a marked advance in this respect, as we ascend through the series of Quadrumanous animals; from the baboons, which usually walk on all-fours, to the semi-erect apes, which often stand and move on their hind-legs only. The greatest development of the Cerebellum is found in Man, who surpasses all other animals in the number and variety of the combinations of muscular movement, which his ordinary actions involve, as well as of those which he is capable, by practice, of learning to execute.

From experiments upon all classes of Vertebrated animals, it has been found that, when the Cerehellum is removed, the power of walking, springing, flying, standing, or maintaining the equilibrium of the body, is destroyed. It does not seem that the animal has in any degree lost the *voluntary* power over its individual muscles; but it cannot *combine* their actions for any general movement of the body. The *reflex* movements, such as those of respiration, remain unimpaired. When an animal thus mutilated, is laid on its back, it cannot recover its former posture; but it moves its limbs, or flutters its wings, and evidently not in a state of stupor. When placed in the erect position, it staggers and falls like a drunken man—not, however, without making efforts to maintain its balance.

When the Cerebellum is affected with chronic disease, the motor function is seldom destroyed; but the same kind of want of combining power shows itself, as when the organ has been purposely mutilated. Some kind of lesion of the motor function is invariably to be observed; whilst the mental powers may or may not be affected—probably according to the influence of the disease in the Cerebellum upon other parts. The same absence of any direct connection with the Psychical powers, is shown in the fact, that inflammation of the membranes covering it, if confined to the Cerebellum, does not produce delirium. Sudden effusions of blood into its substance may produce apoplexy or paralysis; but this may occur as a consequence of effusions into *any* part of the Encephalon, and does not indicate, that the Cerebellum has anything to do with the mental functions, or with the power of the will over the muscles.

Functions of the Cerebrum.

The results of the removal of the Cerebral Hemispheres, in animals to which the shock of the operation does not prove immediately fatal, must appear extraordinary to those who have been accustomed to regard these organs as the centre of all energy. Not only Reptiles, but Birds and Mammalia, if their physical wants be supplied, may survive the removal of the whole Cerebrum for weeks, or even months. If the entire mass be taken away at once, the operation is usually fatal; but it it be removed by successive slices, the shock is less severe, and the depression it produces in the organic functions is soon recovered from. It is difficult to substantiate the existence of actual sensation, in animals thus circumstanced; but their movements appear to be of a higher kind than those resulting from mere reflex action. Thus they will eat fruit when it is put into their mouths: although they do not go to seek it. One of the most remarkable phenomena of such beings, is their power of maintaining their equilibrium; which could scarcely exist without consciousness. If a rabbit, thus mutilated, be laid upon its back, it rises again; if pushed, it walks; if a bird be thrown into the air, it flies; if a frog be touched it leaps. If violently aroused, the animal has all the manner of one waking from sleep; and it manifests about the same degree of consciousness as a sleeping man, whose torpor is not too profound to prevent his suffering from an uneasy position, and who moves himself to amend it. In both cases, the movements are *consensual* only, and do not indicate any voluntary power; and we may well believe that, in the former case as in the latter, though *felt*, hey are not *remembered*; an active state of the Cerebrum being essential to *memory*, though not to sensations, which simply excite certain actions.

The relative amount of *intelligence* in different animals bears so close a correspondence with the relative size and development of the Cerebral Hemispheres, that it can scarcely be questioned that these constitute the organ of the Reasoning faculties, and issue the mandates by which the Will calls the muscles into action. It must be borne in mind, however, that *size* is not by any means the only indication of their comparative development.

In the condition of dreaming, it would seem as if the Cerebrum were *partially* active; a train of thought being suggested, frequently by sensations from without; which is carried on without any controlling or directing power on the part of the Mind, and which is not corrected, or is only modified in a limited degree, by the knowledge acquired by experience. This condition is still more remarkable in somnambulism, or (as it has been better termed) sleep-waking; on which the dreams are not only *acted*, but may be often *acted on* with the utmost facility—a suggestion conveyed through any of the senses excepting sight, (which is usually in abeyance,) being apprehended and followed up with the utmost readiness, and, in like manner, with little or no correction from experience. Between this condition, and that of ordinary dreaming, on the one hand, and that of complete insensibility on the other, there is every shade of variety; which is presented by different individuals, or by the same individuals at different times. The Cerebellum, in the sleep-waking state, seems to be frequently in a condition of peculiar activity; remarkable power of balancing and combining the movements of the body being often exhibited.

The faculty of *memory* appears to be the exclusive attribute of the Cerebral Hemispheres; no impressions made upon the Organs of Sense being ever remembered, unless they are at once registered, (as it were,) in this part of the nervous centres. This faculty is one of those first awakened in the opening mind of the infant; and it is one of which we find traces in animals, that seem to be otherwise governed by pure instinct. It obviously affords the first step towards the exercise of the reasoning powers; since no *experience* can be obtained without it; and the foundation of all intelligent adaptation of means to ends, lies in the application of the knowledge which has been acquired and stored up in the mind. There is strong reason to believe that no impression of this kind, once made upon the Brain, is ever entirely lost—except through disease or accident, which will frequently destroy the memory altogether, or will annihilate the recollection of some particular class of objects or words.

Wear of Brain.

Like all other tissues actively concerned in the vital operations, Nervous matter is subject to *waste* or *disintegration*, which bears an exact proportion to the activity of its operations;—or, in other words, that every act of the Nervous system involves the death and decay of a certain amount of Nervous matter, the replacement of which will be requisite in order to maintain the system in a state fit for action. We shall hereafter see, that there are certain parts of the Nervous system, particularly those which put in action the respiratory muscles which are in a state of unceasing, though moderate, activity; and in these, the constant nutrition is sufficient to repair the effects of the constant decay. But those parts, which operate in a more powerful and energetic manner, and which therefore waste more rapidly when in action, need a season of rest for their reparation. Thus a sense of fatigue is experienced, when the mind has been long acting through its instrument—the brain; indicating the necessity of rest and reparation. And when *sleep*, or cessation of the cerebral functions, comes on, the process of nutrition takes place with unchecked energy, counterbalances the results of the previous waste, and prepares the organ for a renewal of its activity. In the healthy state of the body, when the exertion of the nervous system by day does not exceed that, which the repose of the night may compensate, it is maintained in a condition which fits it for constant moderate exercise; but unusual demands upon its powers—whether by the long continued and severe exercise of the intellect, by excitement of the emotions, or by combination of both in that state of *anxiety* which the circumstances of man's condition so frequently induce—produce an unusual waste, which requires, for a complete restoration of its powers, a prolonged repose.

There can be no doubt that (from causes which are not known,) the amount of sleep required by different persons, for the maintenance of a healthy condition of the nervous system, varies considerably; some being able to dispense with it, to a degree which would be exceedingly injurious to others of no greater mental activity. Where a prolonged exertion of the mind has been made, and the natural tendency to sleep has been habitually resisted by a strong effort of the will, injurious results are sure to follow. The bodily health breaks down, and too frequently the mind itself is permanently enfeebled. It is obvious that the nutrition of the nervous system becomes completely deranged; and that the tissue is no longer formed, in the manner requisite for the discharge of its healthy functions.

As the amount of muscular tissue that has undergone disintegration is represented, (other things being equal,) by the quantity of urea in the urine, so do we find that an unusual waste of the *nervous* matter is indicated by an increase in the amount of *phosphatic* deposits. No others of the soft tissues contain any large proportion of phosphorus; and the marked increase in these deposits, which has been continually observed to accompany long-continued *wear* of mind, whether by intellectual exertion or by anxiety, can scarcely be set down to any other cause. The most satisfactory proof is to be found in cases in which there is a periodical demand upon the mental powers; as, for example, among clergymen, in the preparation for, and discharge of, their Sunday duties. This is found to be almost invariably followed by the appearance of a large quantity of the phosphates in the urine. And in cases in which constant and severe intellectual exertion has impaired the nutrition of the brain, and has constantly weakened the mental power, it is found that any premature attempt to renew the activity of its exercise, causes the reappearance of the excessive phosphatic discharge, which indicates an undue waste of nervous matter.

Thus far Carpenter.

From Vogt's Physiology.

"But it was always principally theology that wished to speak a word to hem the progress of the natural sciences, which planted these [orthodox, anti-scientific] representations in the theory of human development, and sought to keep them there. The soul was indeed given to the priest as his domain; he was to care for it, not only while it was in the body, but also after it should have left its earthly dwelling; and to prevent their subject from escaping, the priests asserted, in the face of all evidence, the existence of an immaterial mind which would live after death independently of the body.

"It is not necessary to go into a lengthy essay to show the manner in which sound philosophy views this question. There are only two points of observation. Either the function of every organ of an animated body is an immaterial being which only makes use of the organ; or the function is a property of the matter. In the latter case the intellectual faculties are only functions of the brain, develop themselves with it, and expire with it. The soul, therefore, does not take possession of the fœtus, as the evil spirit was represented to enter lunatics, but is a product of the development of the brain, as the muscular power is a product of the development of the muscles."—*Vogt's Physiologische Briefe fuer Gebildete aller Staende.*

The same author says elsewhere:

"Physiology breaks the support of the views of theologians in regard to the soul, by declaring that there are no active powers in man except the material organs and their functions, and that the latter must die with the former. We have seen that we can destroy the intellectual faculties by injuring the brain. By the observation of the development of the embryo, we can easily convince ourselves that the mental powers grow as the brain is gradually developed. The fœtus makes no manifestations of thought or consciousness, but its movements evince the capability of reflex action and the susceptibility to nervous influence. Only after birth does the child begin to think, and only after birth does its brain acquire the material development of which it is capable. With the course of life, the mind changes, and it ceases to exist with the death of the organ.

"Physiology declares itself positively and clearly against any individual immortality, and against all those representations which connect themselves with the special existence of a soul. She is not only entitled to speak a word on this subject, but it is her duty, and physiologists are justly liable to reproach for not having sooner raised their voices to point out the only true method of solving the problem of the soul."

Free Agency.

SECTION XLV. NOTE 9.

Charles Lamb, in his "Confessions of a Drunkard," says:

"I have known one in that state, when he has tried to abstain but for one evening—though the poisonous potion had long ceased to bring back its first enchantments—though he was sure it would rather deepen his gloom than brighten it—in the violence of the struggle and in the necessity he has felt of getting rid of the present sensation at any rate, I have known him to scream out, to cry aloud, for the anguish and pain of the strife within him. Why should I hesitate to declare that the man of whom I speak is myself?"

"Free will in man is nothing more than a vicisitude of the supremacy of the faculties."—*Vestiges of Creation.*

Immediate Divine Government.

SECTION XLVI. NOTE 10.

Bacon says, in his Advancement of Learning, "It is certain that God worketh nothing in nature except by second causes."

The Rev. Sydney Smith on Special Providences.

"It is obvious that the Methodists entertain very erroneous and dangerous notions of the present judgments of God. A belief that Providence interferes in all the little actions of our lives, refers all merit and demerit to bad and good fortune, and c uses the successful man to be always considered as a good man, and the unhappy man as an object of divine vengeance. It furnishes ignorant and designing men with a power which is sure to be abused,—the cry of a *judgment*, a *judgment*, is always easy to make, but not easy to resist. It encourages the grossest superstitions; for if the Deity rewards and punishes on every slight occasion, it is quite impossible but that such a helpless being as man will set himself at work to discover the will of heaven in the appearances of outward nature, to apply all the phenomena of thunder, lightning, wind, and every striking appearance, as the regulation of his conduct; as the poor Methodist, when he rode into Piccadilly in a thunder storm, imagined that all the uproar of the elements was a mere hint to him not to preach at Mr. Romaine's chapel. Hence a great deal of error and a great deal of secret misery. This doctrine of a theocracy, must necessarily place an excessive power in the hands of the clergy; it applies so instantly and so tremendously to men's hopes and fears, that it must make the priest omnipotent over his people, as it always has done where it has been established. It has a great tendency to check human exertions, and to prevent the employment of those secondary means of effecting an object which Providence has placed in our power. The doctrine of the immediate and perpetual interference of divine providence is not true. If two men travel on the same road, the one to rob, the other to relieve a fellow-creature who is starving, will any but the most fanatic contend that they do not both run the same chance of falling over a stone and breaking their legs? and is it not often matter of fact that the robber returns safe and the just man sustains the injury?"—*Article on Methodism.*

" The Homeric Greek looked for wonders and unusual combinations in the past; he expected to hear of gods, heroes, and men, moving and operating together upon earth; he pictured to himself the foretime as a theatre in which the gods interfered directly, obviously, and frequently, for the protection of their favorites and the punishment of their foes. The rational conception, then only dawning in his mind, of a systematic course of nature, was absorbed by this fervent and lively faith. And if he could have been supplied with as perfect and philosophical a history of his own real past time, as we are now enabled to furnish with regard to the last century of England or France, faithfully recording all the successive events, and accounting for them by known positive laws, but introducing no special interventions of Zeus or Apollo—such a history would have appeared to him not merely unholy and unimpressive, but destitute of all plausibility or title to credence."—*Grote—History of Greece.*

Sleeman on Hindoo Credulity.

" The popular Hindoo poem of Ramaen describes the abduction of the heroine by the monster king of Ceylon, Rawan, and her recovery by means of the monkey general Hunnooman. Every word of this poem, the people assured us, was written, if not by the hand of the deity himself, at least by his inspiration. Ninety-nine out of a hundred among the Hindoos implicitly believe not only every word of the poem, but every word of every poem that has ever been written in Sanscrit, [the sacred language of Hisdostan]. If you ask a man whether he really believes any very egregious absurdity, quoted from these books, he replies, with the greatest *nuivete* [simplicity] in the world, 'Is it not written in the book? and how shall it be there written, if not true?' The Hindoo religion reposes on an entire prostration of mind—that continual and habitual surrender of the reasoning faculties which we are accustomed to make occasionally while we are at the theatre or in the perusal of works of fiction. * * * With the Hindoos the greater the improbability, the more monstrous and preposterous the fiction—the greater is the charm it has over their minds; and the greater their learning in the Sanscrit—the more they are under the influence of this charm. Believing all to be written by the deity or under his inspiration, and the men and things of former days to have been different from the men and things of the present day, and the heroes of these fables to have been demi-gods or people endowed with powers far superior to those of the ordinary men of their own day, the analogies of nature are never for a moment considered; nor do questions of probability or possibility according to those analogies ever obtrude to dispel the charm with which they are so pleasingly bound. They go on through life, reading and talking of their monstrous fictions, which shock the taste and understanding of other nations, without ever questioning the truth of one single incident or having it questioned."

"History for this people [the Hindoos] is all a fairy tale."—*Rambles and Recollections of an Indian Official, by Col. Sleeman.*

Pausanias, a heathen, who wrote in the first half of the second century, said: -

"The men of those ancient days, on account of their righteousness and piety, were on terms of hospitality with the gods and their companions at the board, and when they acted uprightly they openly received honor from the gods, just as they were also visited with anger if they committed any iniquity. And then also they who are still honored in this manner, become gods instead of men. Thus also we can believe that a Lycaon was transformed into a beast, and Niobe, the daughter of Tantalus, into a stone. But in my time when vice has reached its loftiest summit, and has spread itself abroad over the whole country and in all cities, no one has passed from man to god, except only in name and out of flattery to power, and the anger of the gods arises at evil more tardily, and is not executed on men till after they have left this world. And much which used in former times to take place, and which happens even now, those persons who have mixed falsehood with truth, have rendered incredible to the multitude."

Dionysius Halicarnassus says:—"The atheistic philosophers, if those persons deserve the name of philosophers, who scoff at all the appearances of the gods, which have taken place among the Greeks and the barbarians, would deduce all these histories from the trickery of man, and turn them into ridicule, as if none of the gods ever cared for any man; but he who does not deny the gods a providential care over men, but believes that the gods are benevolent to the good, and angry against evil men, will not judge these appearances to be incredible."

"This injury, they [the Amazons] avenged by invading Attica—an undertaking neither ' trifling nor feminine.' They penetrated even into Athens itself, where the final battle, hard fought and at one time doubtful, by which Theseus crushed them, was fought in the very heart of the city. Attic antiquaries confidently pointed out the exact position of the two contending armies; the left wing of the Amazons rested upon the spot occupied by the commemorative monument of the Amazoneion; the right wing touched the Pnyx, the place in which the public assemblages of the Athenian democracy were held. The details and fluctuations of the combat, as well as the final triumph and consequent truce, were recounted by these authors, with as complete faith and as much circumstantiality as those of the battle of Platea by Herodotus. No portion of the ante-historical epic appears to have been more deeply worked into the national mind of Greece than this invasion and defeat of the Amazons. It was not only a constant theme of the logographers, but was also constantly appealed to by the popular orators along with Marathon and Salamis, among those antique exploits of which their fellow citizens might justly be proud. It formed a part of the retrospective faith of Herodotus, Lysias, Plato, and Isokrates, and the exact date of the event was settled by the Chronologists."— *Grote's Greece.*

"These myths or current stories, [tales of the interference of the gods, &c.] the spontaneous and earliest growth of the Grecian mind, constituted at the same time the entire intellectual stock of the age to which they belonged. They are the common root of all those different ramifications into which the mental activity of the Greeks subsequently diverged, containing as it were the preface and germ of the positive history and philosophy, the dogmatic theology and the professed romance * * * * They furnished aliment and solution to the vague doubts and aspirations of the age; they explained the origin of those customs and standing peculiarities with which men were familiar; they impressed moral lessons, awakened patriotic sympathies, and exhibited in detail the shadowy but anxious presentiments of the vulgar, as to the agency of the gods; moreover they satisfied that craving for adventure and appetite for the marvellous, which has in modern times become the province of fiction proper. It is difficult, we may say it is impossible, for a man of mature age to carry back his mind to his conceptions, such as they stood when he was a child, growing naturally out of his imagination and feelings, working upon a scanty stock of materials, and borrowing from authorities whom he blindly followed but imperfectly apprehended. A similar difficulty occurs when we attempt to place ourselves in the historical and *quasi* philosophical point of view which the ancient myths present to us. We can follow perfectly the imagination and feeling which dictated these tales, and we can admire and sympathise with them as animated, sublime, and affecting poetry; but we are too much accustomed to matter of fact and philosophy of a positive kind, to be able to conceive a time when these beautiful fancies were construed literally, and accepted as serious reality."—*Grote's Greece.*

"The great religious movement of the Reformation, and the gradual formation of critical and philosophical habits in the modern mind, have caused these legends of the saints, once the charmed and cherished creed of a numerous public, to pass altogether out of credit, without even being regarded among the Protestants, at least, as worthy of a formal scrutiny into the evidence—a proof of the transitory value of public belief, however sincere and fervent, as a certificate of historical truth, if it be blended with religious predispositions."— *Grote.*

The Condemnation and Redemption.

Section XLVII. Note 11.

Shelley's Paraphase of some Prominent Points of Christian Doctrine.

> "From an eternity of idleness
> I, God, awoke: in seven days toil made earth
> From nothing; rested, and created man:
> I placed him in a paradise, and there
> Planted the tree of evil, so that he
> Might eat and perish, and my soul procure
> Wherewith to sate its malice, and to turn,
> Even like a heartless conqueror of the earth,
> All misery to my fame. The race of men
> Chosen to my honor, with impunity
> May sate the lusts I planted in their hearts."

"I will beget a son, and he shall bear
The sins of all the world: he shall arise
In an unnoticed corner of the earth,
And there shall die upon a cross, and purge
The universal crime; so that the few
On whom my grace descends, those who are marked
As vessels to the honor of their God,
May credit this strange sacrifice, and save
Their souls alive: millions shall live and die,
Who ne'er shall call upon their Saviour's name,
But, unredeemed, go to the gaping grave.
Thousands shall deem it an old woman's tale, .
Such as the nurses frighten babes withal:
There in a gulf of anguish and of flame
Shall curse their reprobation endlessly,
Yet tenfold pangs shall force them to avow,
Even on their beds of torment where they howl,
My honor and the justice of their doom."
— *Queen Mab.*

"Slaves, I desire your welfare! My goodness proposes to enrich you, and to render you all happy. Do you see these treasures? Well, they are for you. Every one of you must cast these dice. He who throws a six shall be master of the treasure; but he who throws a smaller number shall be imprisoned forever in a narrow dungeon, and roasted on a slow fire, according to the demands of my justice."—*Abbe Meslier.*

"Augustus having learned that Herod, King of Judea, had slain his own son, exclaimed, 'It were better to be his hog than his son.' The philosopher may say as much of Jehovah and Adam. The favorite of the Creator is subject to far more risks and sorrow than the brutes. He lives in suffering on earth, and then is in danger of going to hell after death."—*Abbe Meslier.*

"If you do not burn any paper in honor of Fo, and if you do not deposit any offerings on his altar, he will be displeased you think, and send his judgments on your head. What a miserable creature must your god Fo be then! Let us take the example of the magistrate of your district; should you never go to compliment him, and pay your court to him, if you are honest people, attentive to your duty, he will not the less be well disposed toward you; but if you transgress the law, commit violence, and encroach on the rights of others, he will always be dissatisfied with you, though you should find a thousand ways of flattering him."—*Chinese Philosopher, quoted in Huc's Journey Chap. V.*

"A poor man in our day has many gods foisted on him, and big voices bid him—'worship or be damned.'"—*Carlyle.*

"Weakness of faith is partly constitutional and partly the result of education and other circumstances, and this may go intellectually almost as far as skepticism: that is to say a man may be perfectly unable to acquire a firm and undoubting belief of the great truths of religion, whether natural or revealed. He may be perplexed with doubts all his days: nay his fears lest the gospel should not be true may be stronger than his hopes that it will, and this is a state of great pain and of most severe trial—to be pitied heartily, but not to be condemned."—*Dr. Arnold.*

The preceding paragraph may show how a great man may be enslaved to the Church.

"If believing too little or too much is so fatal to mankind, what will become of us all?"—*John Adams.*

Sydney Smith makes the following quotation from the journal of a Methodist ; "1794, Jan. 26, Lord's day. Found much pleasure in reading Edward's sermon on the Justice of God in the damnation of sinners."

Gibbon says: "The condemnation of the wisest and most virtuous of the Pagans, on account of their ignorance or disbelief of the divine truth, seems to offend the reason and humanity of the present age. But the primitive Church whose faith was of a much firmer consistence, delivered over without hesitation, to eternal torture, the far greater part of the human species. A charitable hope might perhaps be indulged in favor of Socrates or some other sages of antiquity, who had consulted the light of reason before that of the gospel had risen. But it was unanimously affirmed, that those who since the birth or death of Christ had obstinately persisted in the worship of the demons, neither deserved nor could expect a pardon from the irritated justice of the deity. These rigid sentiments, which had been unknown to the ancient world, appear to have infused a spirit of bitterness into a system of love and harmony. The ties of blood and friendship were frequently torn asunder by the difference of religious faith ; and the Christians who in this world found themselves oppressed by the power of the Pagans, were sometimes induced by resentment and spiritual pride, to delight in the prospect of their future triumph. 'You are fond of spectacles' exclaimed the stern Tertullian, 'expect the greatest of all spectacles, the last and eternal judgment of the universe. How shall I admire, how laugh, how rejoice, how exult, when I behold so many proud monarchs, so many fancied gods groaning in the lowest abyss of darkness : so many magistrates who persecuted the name of the Lord, liquefying in fiercer fires than they ever kindled against the Christians ; so many sage philosophers blushing in red hot flames with their deluded scholars ; so many celebrated poets trembling before the tribunal, not of Minos, but of Christ ; so many tragedians, more tuneful in the expression of their own sufferings : so many dancers.' "
Tertullian was "the doctor and guide" of all the Church of western Europe in his day.

"Hell is paved with good intentions."

Burns, in "Holy Willie's Prayer" apostrophises the deity of the New Testament thus :—

> "O thou, wha in the heavens dost dwell,
> Wha, as it pleases best thysel',
> Sends ane to heaven and ten to hell,,
>   A' for thy glory,
> And no for ony gude or ill
>   They've done afore thee."

"Whence could arise the solitary and strange conceit that the Almighty, who has millions of worlds equally dependent on his protection, should quit the care of all the rest, and come to die in our world, because they say one man and one woman had eaten an apple. And on the other hand are we to suppose that every world in the boundless creation had an Eve, an apple, a serpent and a redeemer? In this case, the person who is irreverently called the son of God, and sometimes God himself, would have nothing else to do, than to travel from world to world in an endless succession of death with scarcely a momentary interval of life."—*Thomas Paine—Age of Reason.*

Gibbon says; "One of the most subtle disputants of the Manichean school, has pressed the danger and indecency of supposing that the God of the Christian, in the state of a human fœtus, emerged at the end of nine months from a female womb. The pious horror of his antagonists provoked them to disclaim all sensual circumstances of conception and delivery; to maintain that the divinity passed through Mary like a sunbeam through a plate of glass; and to assert that the seal of her virginity remained unbroken even at the moment when she became the mother of Christ."

Christianity not Taught by Christ.

Section LX. Note 12.

Morell says, that the apostles did not understand the teachings of Christ until long after his death. It was not "immediately after the resurrection of the savior, that Christianity as a moral phenomena in human life, was completed. So far from that, much darkness, much doubt, and many dim perceptions of christian truth were long observable in the minds of the apostles themselves, as well as their followers. Often did they meet together; often did they deliberate over great and essential points; often did they correct each other, as one saw his brother lingering too much amongst Jewish prejudices; often did they pray for divine light and guidance: and it was not until years of fellowship had been enjoyed—until the common consciousness had become awakened—until the spirit of truth had moulded their hearts and minds into some appreciable unity of thought and feeling, that Christianity as an entire religious system appeared."

Idealistic Philosophy.

Section LXV. Note 13.

The idealistic philosophy is very old. It was prevalent in India in the time of Alexander: it was common in Greece, and is very common in our own age. The great effort of German transcendentalism was to prove that man could possess some positive knowledge; that his own existence is an absolute truth. Kant styles man's consciousness of his existence a teaching of pure reason, of a faculty higher in authority than the judgment by which we draw ordinary conclusions from given premises.

Bacon said:—"All that which is past is a dream; and he that hopes or depends on time coming, dreams waking."

Socrates said:—"All that we know is that we know nothing."

"For anything I know, this world may be the Bedlam of the universe."—*John Adams.*

The Eleatic Philosophers said:—"Thought and its object are one."

Protagoras said:—"Man is the measure of all things."

"I imagine a man must have a good deal of vanity who believes, and a good deal of boldness, who affirms, that all the doctrines he holds are true, and all he rejects are false."—*B. Franklin—Letter to Josiah Franklin, 13th April,* 1738.

Religion.

SECTION LXVI.   NOTE 14.

Religion is man's idea of the nature of his existence. the existence, of the external universe and of its relations to him.   In a common acceptation of the word, it means man's belief in regard to the existence of a deity, man's duties toward that deity, if any, and toward his fellow men and himself.

Shelley defines religion to be "man's perception of his relation to the principle of the universe."

Coleridge defines religion to be the union of the "subjective and the objective."   The subject is the *Me,* the object is the *Not-me.* God is part of the *Not-me,* and according to Coleridge's definition, subjective and objective knowledge must be placed upon the same level, before a man can possess religion.·

Palfrey defines Natural Religion to be "the Science of the being and attributes of God, of the relations which man sustains to him, and of the duty of man as they are discovered or discoverable by the human understanding, exerted without supernatural aid."

The growing skepticism of our time had its almost exact counterpart in Greece four hundred and fifty years before Christ. Æschylus, the great tragedian, lamented greatly the advance of unbelief. He presaged every evil from it, and truly enough the mythology and glory of Greece went down together, and neither has ever risen.

"Let us with caution indulge the supposition that morality can be maintained without religion."— *Washington's Farewell Address, written by Alexander Hamilton. See Hamilton's Works.*

"The Church as it now stands no power can save."—*Arnold.*

Stray Notes.

Description of a Fashionable Priest.

"A bishop among us is generally supposed to be a stately and pompous person, clothed in purple and fine linen, and faring sumptuously every day; somewhat obsequious to persons in power, and somewhat haughty and imperative to those who are beneath him: with more authority in his tone and manner, than solidity in his learning: and yet with much more learning than charity or humility; very fond of being called my lord, and driving about in a coach with mitres in the panels, but little addicted to visiting the sick and fatherless, or earning for himself the blessing of those who are ready to perish,

—————' Familiar with a round
Of ladyships—a stranger to the poor'————

decorous in his manners, but no foe to luxurious indulgences: rigid in maintaining discipline among his immediate dependents, and in exacting the homage due to his dignity from the undignified mob of his brethren, but perfectly willing to leave to them the undivided privileges of comforting and of teaching their people, and of soothing the sins and sorrows of their erring flocks; scornful, if not openly hostile, upon all occasions, to the claims of the people, from whom he is generally sprung, and presuming everything in favor of the royal will and prerogative, by which he has been exalted; setting indeed, in all cases, a much higher value on the privileges of the few, than the rights that are common to all, and exerting himself strenuously that the former may ever prevail; caring more accordingly for the interests of his order, than the general good of the church, and far more for the church than the religion it was established to teach; hating dissenters still more bitterly than infidels; but combating both rather with obloquy and invocation of civil penalties, than with the artillery of a powerful reason, or the reconciling influences of an humble and holy life; uttering now and then haughty professions of humility, and regularly bewailing at fit seasons, the severity of those Episcopal labors, which sadden and even threaten to abridge life, which to all other eyes appear to flow on in almost unbroken leisure and continuous indulgences."—*Edinburgh Review*, *Dec.* 1828.

"The French clergy does not live now [1823] as in times past, but shows a regularity of conduct worthy of the apostles. Happy effect of poverty!— Happy fruit of the persecution suffered in the grand epoch when God visited his church. It is not one of the least blessings of the revolutio ., that not only the cures, always respectable, but even the bishops are moral men."—*Courier.* —*Quoted in the Edinburgh Review, March,* 1829.

"Instead of the four gospels adopted by the church, the heretics produced a multitude of histories in which the actions and discourses of Christ and of his apostles were adapted to their respective tenets."—*Gibbon, Ch. XV.*

"It is customary [among the Chinese] to ask to 'what sublime religion' you belong. One perhaps will call himself a Confucionist, another a Buddhist, a third a disciple of Lao-tze, a fourth a follower of Mohammed, of whom there are many in China, and then every one begins to pronounce a panegyric on the religion to which he does *not* belong, as politeness requires; after which they all repeat in chorus, '*Pou-toun-kiao, toun-ly.*' 'Religions are many; reason is one; we are all brothers.' This phrase is on the lips of every Chinese, and they handy it from one to the other with the most exquisite urbanity."— *Huc's Journey through the Chinese Empire. Chap. V.*

"For if enlightening the people with regard to those things in which they are most concerned, ought to be the object of a political establishment, Athens was unquestionably the most enlightened city throughout the whole world. Neither Paris nor London, neither Rome nor Babylon, aud still less Memphis, Jerusalem, Pekin or Benares can enter into competition with it."—*Herder.* —*Philosophy of History.*

The more mysteries there are in a religion, and the more absurdities it contains, the more it attracts the imagination of ignorant people. The more obscure a creed is the more divine it appears, and the more likely to be the teaching of an unknown and incomprehensible being. It is the nature of ignorance to prefer the unknown, the hidd n, the fabulous, the wonderful, the incredible and even the terrible [in religion] to the clear and simple. ✻ * * The inhabitants of a village are never more pleased with their curate than when he mixes an abundance of Latin in his sermons. They always imagine that he who speaks to them of things which they do not understand, is an able man."— *Abbe Meslier.*

Acknowledgments.

I am indebted to the "Critical Introduction to the Old Testament" by W. M. L. De Wette, translated by Theodore Parker, for most of my information in regard to the authenticity of the books of the Old Testament, and to Hennell's "Origin of Christianity," for information as to the miracles recorded, and the prophecies referred to, by the Evangelists. Strauss' "Life of Jesus," and his "Christliche Glaubenslehre" have furnished me with many ideas which are scattered throughout this book. I am also indebted to "Hume's Essays on Miracles," and "On a Providence and a Future State," two of the most deeply philosophical works in existence: to chapters XV and XVI of Gibbon's "Decline and Fall of the Roman Empire;" to Voltaire's works, and to the "Vestiges of Creation." Paine's "Age of Reason" has had a great influence in breaking the bonds of superstition, but this influence has been owing not to any deep philosophy or extensive information contained in the book, but to its forcible style and the contagious boldness of the author's thoughts. He who wishes to read what may be said in defense of the Bible, will find Paley's "Evidences of [for] Christianity", "Butler's Analogy of Religion," Palfrey's "Evidences of Christianity," and Morell's "Philosophy of Religion" to be excellent works.

Typographical Errors.

Page.	Line from top.	Is.	Should be.
108	last,	Note 7,	Note 8.
108	last,	Note 8,	Note 9.
109	fourth,	above,	to.
111	last,	Note 9,	Note 11.
129	twenty-eighth,	natural,	national.
136	twenty-third,	rewarded.	reward.

There are a great many other minor errors, but they do not violate the meaning of the sentences.

The author erred in stating, on page 153, that the Church had admitted that the mind was only a function of the brain, and that all men were not descended from one pair of ancestors.

THE END.

CPSIA information can be obtained
at www.ICGtesting.com
Printed in the USA
BVHW08*1521041018
529297BV00008B/294/P